A LIVE GATHERING: PERFORMANCE AND POLITICS IN CONTEMPORARY EUROPE

EDITED BY ANA VUJANOVIĆ WITH LIVIA ANDREA PIAZZA

ACKNOWLEDGEMENTS

This book project started with an invitation to reflect on the (art) audience and the (social) community. The invitation came from the European network of theatre venues, festivals and the organisations of Create to Connect. After several performance productions, festivals, publications and seminars, the partner organisations wanted to complete the project with a more extensive publication and in 2016 invited me, Ana Vujanović, to edit it. The invitation was generous and I gladly accepted it, as, apart from the fact that I have been concerned with its focus, the invitation gave me freedom to define and refine the topic and choose collaborators and writers. Since at that time I was engaged with a programme fostering critical thinking on contemporary dance and performance – with the somewhat humorous title *Critical practice (Made in Yugoslavia)* – where I mentored several younger writers, critics and choreographers, I invited Livia Andrea Piazza to join me in editing the book and Stina Nyberg to contribute artist's pages. My long-term collaborators Jelena Knežević from Walking Theory [TkH] and Marta Popivoda of TkH and Theory at Work [TnD] then joined us as producer and executive producer.

After sketching the concept, Jelena, Livia and I created this book together – but not alone. This book came into existence thanks to the enthusiasm, patience and productive dialogues with the contributors, and thanks to the support of Alma R. Selimović, development manager of Bunker and leader of the Create to Connect network. Her respect for the opaqueness and slow pace of the process of developing a theoretical discourse has been precious. A special thanks goes out to Stephan Geene and b_books, for a supportive and caring publishing process and for providing a publishing context that sharpens our book, politically and theoretically.

8 – ANA VUJANOVIĆ AND LIVIA ANDREA PIAZZA –
INTRODUCTION: PEOPLE ARE MISSING…

 ANA VUJANOVIĆ AND LIVIA ANDREA PIAZZA

ANA VUJANOVIĆ AND LIVIA ANDREA PIAZZA

To think of the audience and the community together in the performing arts, especially in the critical and socio-politically concerned segments thereof, usually presupposes a direct interaction between the artists and the audience. It happens in the in-between spaces of copresence and togetherness in public where the artists and the audience create both the sense of themselves and the performance that connects them and project or disrupt the sense of wider social community. This implies a great investment of hope when it comes to the political dimension of theatre, dance and performance as live and performing arts. That hope is additionally ignited by a recognised proximity between artistic performance and democratic politics, a similarity revolving around the live gathering of people in public. However, while attending numerous 'political performances'[1] in the contemporary performing arts scenes across Europe and reading and writing on topics such as performance and politics, the artist-citizen, community theatre or participatory performance, we have realised that often there is a somewhat neglected difference between performance and politics today, which obscures our understanding of their relations. In order to comprehend how exactly the performance, with its liveness, being-with and togetherness, is located in its social context and how its imaginaries can radiate through society, we must attend to that point and scrutinise it analytically and meticulously.

1 | Performances characterised by clear social concerns and political aspirations and ambitions.

Apart from the long history of the metaphor of *theatrum mundi* – from Ancient Greece, via the Christian Middle Ages, the Baroque, Shakespeare and 18th-century European bourgeois society, up to the present – which embeds theatre in its social environment as a sort of metaphysical *mise en abyme*, a number of 20th-century directors, choreographers and theatre and performance theorists explored the proximity of performance and politics in a more concrete and analytical manner. We refer, for instance, to Blue Blouse, Bertolt Brecht, Workers Dance League, Augusto Boal, Milan Knížák, Valie Export, Sanja Iveković, Christof Schlingensief, or Richard Schechner, Peggy Phelan, Janelle Reinelt, Alan Read, Hans-Thies Lehmann, Randy Martin and many others. These voices however come not only from the field of performing arts but also from the field of social-political investigations; let us mention here at least Hannah Arendt, Richard Sennett, Judith Butler, Jacques Rancière, Giorgio Agamben, Paolo Virno and newer voices such as Margot Morgan and Shirin Rai.[2] Hannah Arendt is especially important in this regard, owing to her explicit and famous insistence on the performative character of political practice and on the political dimension of artistic performance alike. In *Between Past and Future*, she explains this proximity in the following way:

> *In the performing arts (as distinguished from the creative art of making), the accomplishment lies in the performance itself and not in an end product which outlasts the activity that brought it into existence. … The performing arts have indeed a strong affinity with politics. Performing artists – dancers, play-actors, musicians and the like – need an audience to show their virtuosity, just as acting men need the presence of others before whom they can appear; both need a publicly organised space for their work, and both depend upon others for the performance itself.[3]*

However, although this oft-cited explanation has been largely used to emphasise the political relevance of the performing arts and we find some of its aspects still valid, the problem with this juxtaposition is that it is actually ahistorical. It is ahistorical in terms of 'the grammar of politics and performance', as Joe Kelleher assumed and Janelle Reinelt and Shirin Rai explicitly named it,[4] referring to the notions of liveness and sociality, involvement of actors and spectators, 'nowness' and the gathering of strangers around certain issues. In these terms, Arendt's explanation neglects, at the site of performance of her time and to an extent of our time as well,[5] the grammatical and procedural differences between the political

---

2 | Margot Morgan, *Politics and Theatre in Twentieth-Century Europe* (New York: Palgrave Macmillan 2013); Janelle Reinelt and Shirin Rai, *The Grammar of Politics and Performance* (London and New York: Routledge 2015).
3 | Hannah Arendt, *The Human Condition* (Chicago: University of Chicago Press 1961), 153–154.
4 | Joe Kelleher, *Theatre and Politics* (Basingstoke: Palgrave 2013); Reinelt and Rai, *The Grammar*.
5 | Although the artistic performance in European society is still predominantly a public practice, which gathers people, depends on others and reaches its political momentum in the performance itself, its ephemerality and a lack of 'an end product which outlasts the activity that brought it into existence' has been largely disputed. Among the main criticisms, we would single out Rebecca Schneider's work on the performance 'remains', its

practice of Athenian democracy (the direct participation of citizens) and the official political practice of modern Western society (a representative system). That is to say, in her explanation the notion of politics tacitly refers to the Athenian model of direct democracy, while in a representative democracy, contemporary to the 20th-century's performing arts, public space is not the main site of politics nor do professional politicians gather 'others' to discuss and consult about their decisions, coalitions and votes. In a specific and paradoxical way, it is a *democracy* wherein people (*demos*) are commonly absent from ruling (*kratos*) their society, resulting in the situation where artistic performance and politics start to diverge from some previously or supposedly common grammatical elements, and above all from public space and the public sphere, liveness, people's gathering and involvement.

While politics started relinquishing these elements, performance did not. In this way, counting on grammatical and further procedural overlaps between performance and democratic politics in general – and thus on political openness to subjects, images, voices and social relations that derive from artistic performance – becomes a pitfall for a number of performance makers and theorists. That especially addresses an alternative and critical segment of the performing arts in the 20th and early 21st centuries, which opposes the theatrical paradigm of mimetic representation and frontal presentation and sees the political power of performance in the direct interaction and live copresence of people in public. Richard Schechner was among many who, in the 1960s and 1970s, claimed that representational theatre is a capitalist construction, which should be replaced with 'environmental theatre' that involves a live and flexible interaction between the audience and performers.[6] In the 1990s, Peggy Phelan considered liveness, next to ephemerality and immateriality, as grounding performance's political potential within capitalism.[7] There it operates at a symbolic level as 'a representation without reproduction' that by virtue of its immateriality and non-mediation remains 'unmarked', thus escaping absorption into the system.[8] Speaking of today's art scenes, explicit examples of the idea that the political power of performance lies in its live social situation in public can be found in *artivism*. It is a hybrid practice which intertwines art and political activism thereby reopening Benjamin's conclusion on the aestheticisation of politics as typical of Fascism and the politicisation of art as a Communist response to it.[9] Artivist performances and actions are

archival potential, and the role of re-enactments (2011) and Italian post-Operaist thinkers, like Maurizio Lazzarato and Paolo Virno, who wrote about the role of performance and self-performance – including expressivity, communicability, virtuosity etc. – in immaterial labour and post-Fordist production.

6 | Richard Schechner, *Environmental Theatre* (New York: Applause Books (1973) 1994).

7 | Peggy Phelan, *Unmarked: The Politics of Performance* (London and New York: Routledge (1993) 2005).

8 | Ibid, 146.

9 | Aldo Milohnić, "Artivism", in *republicart: real public spaces*, 2005.

in principle based on a spontaneous and direct method of political acting: one steps out onto the public stage as a responsible citizen, spotlights a particular social problem by (usually minimal) aesthetic means and calls for public debate, around which people gather. However, as we already indicated, the problem here, in all of these otherwise diverse examples, is that this basic mode of political practice doesn't correspond to the social paradigm of (democratic) politics today, which is representative. At the same time it disturbingly corresponds to the economic paradigm of politics that revolves around immaterial value, cultural contents and 'production of subjectivity' by means of a virtuosic performance.[10]

Furthermore, speaking from the present day European perspective – marked with thirty years of protracted and troubled 'democratisation and capitalisation' of former socialist societies; the evolving of the European Union, characterised with the 'proceduralism' of formal democracy; and the protests of the precarious and outraged during the 2010s caused by a massive discontent with representation in political institutions – we would proffer that the representative democratic system in Europe of today is mediated, professionalised and bureaucratised to such a degree that it almost mutes singular citizens' voices in the process of making decisions. In that context, the political power of performing arts drawing on radical democratic experience decreases dramatically and the efficacy argument of artistic performance becomes undefendable. It is so especially if we accept Baz Kershaw's elaboration of Schechner's idea of performance efficacy as 'the potential that theatre may have to make the immediate effects of performance influence, however minutely, the general historical evolution of wider social and political realities'.[11]

The main question we raise with this book is how to understand and what to do – artistically as well as politically – with this kind of historical asynchrony between performing arts and democratic politics, which is focused on the live gathering of people in public. That question does not diminish the value of the political and artistic practices that appear in those exceptional social moments, 'social dramas' to use Victor Turner's term, which cause a standstill or disruption in the social order. Such practices are recently well described in the book *Performing Antagonism: Theatre, Performance & Radical Democracy*, whose point of departure is Chantal Mouffe's antagonistic view of democracy and recent protests, from Occupy to the Arab Spring, where theatre joined a wave of radical democracy

---

10 | Maurizio Lazzarato, "Immaterial Labour", 1996, http://www.generation-online.org/c/fcimmateriallabour3.htm (last accessed February 22, 2019).
11 | Baz Kershaw, *The politics of performance: Radical theatre as cultural intervention* (London and New York: Routledge 1992), 1.

practised on the street.[12] In our view, these moments are valuable but exceptional, and thus do not resolve our central issues: how to be political by means of performance in the context of representative democracy as the ruling political system in Europe today.

While unfolding a rich overview of the segments of current European performing arts scenes, which address these questions with numerous artistic examples, the contributions in this volume come to the point where Deleuze's thoughts about the missing people from *Cinema 2* further sharpen editors' initial reflections:

> *Art [...] must take part in this task: not that of addressing a people, which is presupposed already there, but of contributing to the invention of a people. The moment the master, or the colonizer, proclaims 'There have never been people here', the missing people are a becoming, they invent themselves, in shanty towns and camps, or in ghettos, in new conditions of struggle to which a necessarily political art must contribute.[13]*

These thoughts may provide a wider, metaphorical framing of this volume, especially since it seems that the missing people in our democratic society today are not only the colonised, marginalised or excluded ones; it is citizenry at large that is paralysed. As a response to these conditions, in the aftermaths of the protests of the precarious and outraged in the 2010s, new social and civil initiatives which explore different democratic processes have emerged, such as the Solidarity movement in Greece or Municipal Confluences, like Ahora Madrid, Barcelona en Comú and Cádiz Sí Se Puede in Spain. They pave the way to reinvent ordinary people as political agents of their society, which is alternative to both neo-liberal proceduralism and the professionalisation of politics, from which ordinary people are excluded, and right-wing populism, where individuals become fused into an abstract category of people. They also offer long-term, although still relatively small-scale, practical alternatives to the official European democracy, in the form of citizen-run infrastructures such as schools and hospitals, cooperative cryptocurrencies such as FairCoin, bottom-up municipalist discourse located outside Spanish political binary 'nationalism – separatism', or citizens' platforms for communal engagement in finding fast solutions for various urgent social issues.[14] This book analyses precisely those artistic practices that have emerged alongside, simultaneously with or in relation to these social movements, investigating how theatre, dance and performance respond to the new

12 | Tony Fisher and Eve Katsouraki (Eds.), *Performing Antagonism: Theatre, Performance & Radical Democracy* (Basingstoke: Palgrave 2017).

13 | Gilles Deleuze, *Cinema 2: The Time-Image* (Minneapolis: University of Minnesota Press 1989), 217.

14 | Greece Solidarity Campaign; Vicente Rubio-Pueyo, *Municipalism in Spain From Barcelona to Madrid, and Beyond* (New York: Rosa Luxemburg Stiftung 2017).

political insights, experiments and climate in Europe. As the contributions in this book manifest, it is a context wherein the previously well-known tactics and tools, such as participation, identity politics or spontaneous usage of public space don't suffice and wherein we must build and learn a new vocabulary of politicality of performance, which focuses on (re) inventing people and which includes such opaque and strange words as 'innervation', 'preenactment', 'prefiguration', 'recreation', etc.

The fact that today's mainstream democratic politics in Europe diminishes the relevance of the physical copresence of living people discussing their society in public is in this volume considered not only a failure on the part of the performing arts. Going back to Reinelt and Shirin's concept of the grammar of performance and politics, this fact is thought self-reflectively throughout the book in a wider social realm, and thereby becomes also an invitation to rethink politics itself. In other words, it seems that what performance as a type of cultural-artistic practice does politically today is to mark that empty place of democracy and publicly perform proposals of different socio-political praxis. This makes performance as a live, public event a real place on the public scene that confronts images of society as it presently is with those of a different, possible and virtual one. As most of the contributions in this book indicate, in the current European – and even wider – context, characterised by both neoliberal capitalism and representative democracy, performance may not owe its political relevance to being 'unmarked', as Phelan claimed in the 1990s, but rather its political potential might lie in the gesture of marking. In a political register, it marks a space of democracy that is empty, inviting the public to engage in inventing the people who populate it and create the social imaginary. In a theoretical register, it could also mark a space of cohabitation where differences are cultivated and produced.

What are the theoretical underpinnings and the concrete dynamics that emerge as performance and politics coinhabit society? How does performance have consequences on the world as we know it, not only in spite of but also by virtue of its differences from today's politics? These assumptions bring our book to the proximity of Kelleher's insistence on writing about theatre *and* politics rather than on political theatre and Reinelt and Shirin's ambition to 'bring practical political processes back into theatre and performance studies'.[15] Where the contributions in this volume differ from these two positions is that they, through their versatile discourses and various tactics and rhetoric of analysis, consider artistic performance itself a repository of critical and resistant knowledge to the extent that the book eventually examines how to be politically active through and by the means of performance today. By taking the difference separating performance and politics as a point of departure, the book thus analyses how performance can be a political part of its social context today and at same time asks: What is relevant for a democracy in which the live gathering of people in public is irrelevant?

* * *

The content of our book is edited dramaturgically. We have organised it as a speculative and imaginary journey through the concept of live gathering from the political public sphere to the artistic performance. There are two main movements along the journey. One is a linear progression which goes from one part of the book to the next. The other comprises lateral steps and movements that take place within each part: they are transversal and multilayered and hence render the book's parts into networks through which readers can wander and drift. Let us briefly present the three parts of the book before we move to each individual chapter.

In Part I, 'What is people's gathering to democracy?' the authors discuss the live gathering as a political practice by looking at today's democratic public sphere with its challenges and paradoxes. Isabell Lorey, Bojana Cvejić and Bojana Kunst offer thorough analyses of recent protest movements and other gatherings in public space from the perspective of revolutionary, performative and prefigurative political tendencies. The social context they discuss – European societies of today, including the specificities of former Eastern Europe – outline the geopolitical framework of the whole book and launch important questions into the sphere of the performative. In Part II, 'The New Politicality of Performance: The Time of Gathering, (Re) creative Labour and the Domestic', the performative responds with a new and unexpected approach to the political dimension of the performing arts by opting for certain political detours. The contributions of Stina Nyberg, Ana Vujanović, Giulia Palladini, Livia Andrea Piazza and Valeria Graziano explore creative labour and recreation, the private and domestic, the experience of gatherings, and liveness as a temporal category. They speak about the politics of performing arts as a politics that disperses and enters the sphere of production, private life and an overall sense of the world. This opening of the performance also implies a new understanding of people's gathering in the political public sphere, whereby Part II becomes a terrain where these two spaces – performing arts and politics – meet and intersect, on a new ground. From that in-between terrain, the book moves to the sphere of the performing arts in PART III, 'Radiation Patterns of Performance'. Here Florian Malzacher, Goran Sergej Pristaš and Silvia Bottiroli discuss concrete artworks, unfolding the problematics of live gathering in theatre and performance as a political challenge. Their texts focus on contemporary European performances and then try to articulate some tactics by which the performance radiates in society: preenactment, refraction and undecidability, which operate in the the domain of the radical imaginary and real-life experience.

Part I opens with the essay 'The Power of the Presentist-Performative: On Current Democracy Movements' by Isabell Lorey, who starts from the refusal of representation and the engagement with democracy that has defined the most recent social movements, not disregarding them as apolitical but meeting them with the desire to articulate the 'presentist-performative' and breaking the dichotomy of presence and representation that characterises both aesthetics and politics. Lorey's critique of representation is paired with a critique of the metaphysics of presence in order to ground political action in the bodies that constitute live gatherings. The dichotomy between the public and the private is left behind to open up to assemblies of bodies that occupy space and time, suspending representation and yet not simply settling for their visibility and presence in public space. Looking at practices that measure themselves with the possibility of creating new democracies grounded in mutual affecting and connectedness, she proposes a shift from the 'in-between' to the 'being with', an alliance of precarious bodies that don't belong to self-contained individuals but rather to singularities who are always de-instituting and instituting, becoming common in the present time as a creative midpoint of current and future democracies.

The performative aspect present in these assemblies emerges as a tool of analysis and affirms itself as a voice in 'The Procedural, the Prescriptive and the Prefigurative Performance: Some Reflections on the Question of Time of Political Action'. In this article, Bojana Cvejić addresses the temporality of political action through these three models listed in her title. A critique of the procedural as an alignment with a present that is given, opens up the way for the two alternative models. Prescription operates by rupture and looks at the future as a rehearsal of revolution. As such it stands in contrast to prefiguration, which removes the gap between present struggles and future political goals to find political relevance in the performativity of a collective experimentation grounded in a present that is not given but under construction. Yet, at the end of the article, performance shifts from being a tool of analysis to being a fourth voice in the debate. Through the example of *Time Bombs* by BADco (2017), Cvejić explores the specific capacity of art to re-narrate the present. In contrast to the other models that keep us in a present closed off from other temporalities or set political goals in an indefinite future, artistic practice emerges as a voice bestowed with the chance of engaging with temporal displacements able to open a different way for re-imagining the present and the future.

The live gathering that constitutes the background of these texts becomes the focus of inquiry in 'Performance, Institutions and Gatherings: Between Democratic and Technocratic European Cultural Space' by Bojana Kunst, who investigates it across both performance and politics. Here we enter the context of Eastern Europe through a reflection on right-wing populism and fascism in their different and yet equivalent ways of reducing the relevance of the public sphere as a multiplicity of cultural and political gatherings. Bojana Kunst reads attacks on the arts and its institutions as part of a broader context, where the political aim is to reduce space for the public to come together and where the rejection of different kinds of gatherings as embodiments of the audience and its political expression becomes explicit and politically sustained as such. These populist attacks are matched by the economic dynamics of neoliberal capitalism, which marks art institutions with professionalisation rather than democratisation. As a bitter consequence, live gatherings sustained by art institutions are becoming more and more of the same. However, the current situation is also a chance for institutions to act differently: in resonance with Lorey's being-with, art institutions might act as support structures for gatherings, embracing the deep ambivalence they entail.

While these essays punctuate the meaning of live gatherings within democratic practices in today's European geopolitical context, Part II takes an unexpected escape route through Stina Nyberg's 'A Live Gathering Dictionary' that brings the discussion elsewhere. The shift regards not only the content but also the perspective, because here it is an artist who takes the floor. Her contribution to this book springs from her inhabiting, and building together with others, Stockholm's dance and performance scene, where in recent years artists' self-organised gatherings have become a prominent force and have given voice to their political concerns. The dictionary unpacks the notion of live gatherings from the micropolitical scale of the kindergarten as a first ground on which to experiment with forms of collective action, to live gatherings on a bigger scale. At no level is there room for the apolitical, the word opening the dictionary. In this spirit, the dictionary explores the words and practices that recur and inform our ways of getting together: it embraces dysfunctionality and celebration; it challenges the assumption of mutual understanding as well as the traps we fall into while practicing critique; and it looks for unexpected alliances not by fetishising the idea of collaboration but rather by reappropriating it. Nyberg's dictionary accomplishes this by continuously jumping from the individual to the collective level and, most importantly, by challenging this distinction.

The chance of performance as a live gathering that calls into question the dichotomy between the individual and the common emerges also in Ana Vujanović's essay 'Performances that Matter: From Public Sphere to Creative Labour', which tackles the current political dimension of performance by shifting attention from the public sphere to the realm of creative labour. In such a current context, performance emerges not so much as a model of political practice but rather as a model of production, along the lines of two social macro-processes: the economisation of politics and the politicisation of production. The first exposes the base for the second: today politics is latently present in production, and since the performing arts in neoliberal capitalism belong to the tertiary sector of production, their politics functions in the form of Jamenson's 'political unconscious'. As such, a performance's politicality is not only weakened, but also by definition complicit with the dominant mode of production. And yet this context allows the argumentation to be turned upside down: in a negation of negation, performance operates like a litmus test for democracy. Through the examples given by different stage performances as well as by European performance initiatives, the chances of the performing arts to address not only their politicality but also politics at large emerge in what Vujanović defines as propositions for 'walking through ourselves populated with others'. Such gestures understand the political as seizing democracy from the representative political system and rethinking it within the relationships of our being and working together.

The book offers another entry point into the debate on the politics of performance with a text by Giulia Palladini, who proposes dropping 'politics' in favour of 'domestics'. 'On Coexisting, Mending and Imagining: Notes on the Domestics of Performance' looks at the domestic not as a pre-given domain, but rather as a field of struggle and imagination like the *polis*: the domestic is political. On this premise, the investigation of the domestics of performance sets out from a non-domesticated notion of the domestic, to be freed from the set of naturalised dichotomies to which it is still attached. Using different examples from politics and performance, the text unfolds the notion of the domestic as a domain opening to an idea of home grounded in the proximity of bodies; and a feeling at home that emerges in the direct experimentation of a coexistence that cannot be only represented. In separating the idea of home from that of the private, the article suggests using performance as a field of invention and experimentation of coexistences where the proximity of bodies offers a home to the homelessness affecting subjectivities within neoliberal capitalism. Through the investigation of Fourier's choice of domestics as a field of invention and Barthes' notion of the marvellous real, domestics discloses also a particular temporality that re-proposes the present as a privileged shelter for action in the form of a persistent doing.

The dimension of time is interspersed throughout the pages of this book only to take the floor in 'Performance and Liveness: A Politics of the Meantime' by Livia Andrea Piazza, which investigates performance as an instrument of time-building. The reflection starts from Virno's metaphor describing people's relation to time as spectators watching themselves live: today's present appears as if it were already lived, past and thus unchangeable. Focusing on performance as a specific field of work and as a live gathering, the article proposes to dismiss the question 'how to use time?' to ask instead how to build it; and proposes *the meantime* as a fruitful dimension to to think about the politicality of performance today. The meantime is explored in its double meaning: a time simultaneous to the present and a time separating us from the future. It appears as a gap within the general rhythms, where performance can challenge the conditions of its own production and experiment with different ones. Dispensing with the notions of ephemerality and duration usually attached to the time of performance as a live gathering, the meantime emerges as an ordinary temporality able to question the notion of 'normal time' and the separation between the collective and the individual. In the meantime, performance unfolds as a collective instrument to build time and opens up the present as a time porous to the time of others.

The possibility of building time and the tools for different collectivities to intervene in the current political and economic situation appears in Valeria Graziano's 'Recreation at Stake'. The article stems from her previous work on prefigurative practices and belongs to a larger inquiry into the speculative notion of recreative industries. Recreation is unpacked in its multiple meanings following the potential that it discloses for challenging the dichotomy between the intimate and the public and for tackling the conditions of creative labour. It becomes the ground to envision organisational practices that can counter the dominant managerial culture and reappropriate creativity, calling for a creative reproduction. Through examples from the past and the present, such as the Danish 'junk playground' of the 1940s and the recent experience of the Italian cultural centre MACAO, the framework of recreative industries exposes an alternative, minoritarian history of organisational forms that looked at cultural production as intertwined with social reproduction. In this history, the live gathering appears as a key practice of cultural production and, while exemplifying its traditional intersection with politics, it is also reframed through the recreative industries. In this shift, performance as a live gathering becomes part of a framework that can intervene politically in the present and enable a specific kind of social collaboration based on experiencing the presence of others, and of our differences, as a source of pleasure.

The desire to experiment directly with the politics of organisational forms is matched by the willingness to overcome the metaphors of audience as a community, and deal directly with the politics of spectatorship. Part III starts with 'Theatre as Assembly: Spheres of Radical Imagination and Pragmatic Utopias', in which Florian Malzacher pleads for a theatre that not only mirrors society but can directly challenge the way it functions. Through the work of artists such as Milo Rau, Jonas Staal, Public Movement, Philippe Quesne and others, who recently used the assembly as an artistic format, the article opens up a reflection on the nexus between consensus and participation, and especially on the possibilities emerging from breaking it: from a theatre in public space to a theatre as public space. Here preenactment is set in contrast to immersive theatre, which exemplifies a form of 'fake participation' – bound to remain on the level of representation – leaving no room for a true emancipation of the spectators. Preenactments, as artistic anticipations of a political event, relate differently to the representation. They are the rehearsal of the political as event, rather than the rehearsal of a determinate political event. As such, preenactments shift from showing possible alternatives to being possible alternatives. Yet, according to the author, the possibilities of breaking those limits correspond to the end of theatre and to the beginning of reality, since the fine line marking the borders of theatre and politics can be played with, but certainly not ignored.

The idea of theatre as a mirror of society is completely dismissed by Goran Sergej Pristaš, who in 'The View from Matter', claims that theatre has a character that is refractive rather than reflective. Through the works by Slaven Tolj and Oleg Kulik, this article enters the deep darkness of the black box, which sheds light on how the very manifestation of theatre always already contains multiple gazes rather than two poles reflecting each other. The duality of theatre is different and composed of the relationship between artist and the audience, and the theatre as a whole poetic gathering of animate and inanimate spectators and actors: here is where the refraction occurs, springing out from innervation. The process constituting the base of imagination for Benjamin becomes, in the encounter with theatre, a potential for a different kind of watching: the view from matter. An example of this encounter is the performance *Noordung Prayer Machine* by Dragan Živadinov. From matter, no spectator is confined in the activity of watching one image and theatre's apparatus becomes a density of gazes. Refraction exposes its political potential: the world sees itself in and through theatre, and the latter becomes a ground of reflection on social objects, without losing its self-reflective character. In this possibility, of watching neither as a subject nor as an object but rather from the side, appears the chance to provoke a radical rearrangement of that which exists, in theatre and outside of it.

A similar density of gazes opens Silvia Bottiroli's 'An Undecidable Object Heading Elsewhere'. The article starts from the work *Yes Sir I can Boogie* by the Zapruder filmmakers' group and explores undecidability as an artistic feature able to create political spaces by challenging the concept of representation in its figures of visibility and readability. Undecidability is in Calvino 'the paradox of an infinite whole containing other infinite wholes' linking the realms of imagination, reality and art. In this text an alliance with darkness also appears to be quickly overcome by the idea of opacity: undecidable performances challenge reality on the same level of visibility and complexity that characterises it. In performance situations, undecidability grows out of the coexistence of real and fictional worlds that, rather than cancelling each other out, establish a logic of addition and excess, making representation crumble under the layers. The tension of the artwork *Yes Sir I can Boogie* travels unvaried to the level of performance as a live gathering, where a radical collectivity becomes aware of the world among itself, the world it lives with in its being continuously done and undone by the bodies that constitute it. In the live gathering, a new 'whole of the wholes' is created where individual identities are challenged by being continuously redefined as entity in transformation across the individual and the collective: a condition of life is produced that appears inherently and utterly political exactly as it is, with no territory or perimeter in which to settle.

In between the lines of these texts appears the second movement we envisaged for this book, as they interweave a network that can be navigated in different directions. The ongoing dialogue between performance and politics does not only present the insistent detours these two spheres make into each other; it also reveals the persistent challenges the texts in this book pose to the dichotomies that often mark the way we think and act in these spheres. The book is opened by a breaking of the dichotomy between representation and presence, and the same breakage recurs throughout it, investigating the difference between performance and politics and opening up different ways of representing, watching and being in the live presence of others. The politicality of performance emerges in this break as well as in the break of the dichotomy between production and reproduction. A parallel challenge is made to approaches that separate the private and the public, and the individual and the common. In addition to deconstructive analyses, there is also a constructive force emerging in the lines of this book that regards the practice of instituting. It appears in unexpected, optimistic turns in thorough analyses of the bleak situation that characterises both performance and politics today. That optimistic force concerns institutions, those of the arts as much as those of politics, but it exceeds them in a chance to institute time and space. It travels through this entire book as a fight for reclaiming and reappropriating imagination and production in lieu of cynicism and deconstruction, which have previously countered attempts at the direct politicality of performance; it is an instituing at large that might start small, in sharing the gaze in performance, in the ways we work together and in the micropolitics that act as if things could always be imagined and done differently; and finally, that optimistic force overflows into the potentiality of instituting more egalitarian and more just conditions of our being alive together.

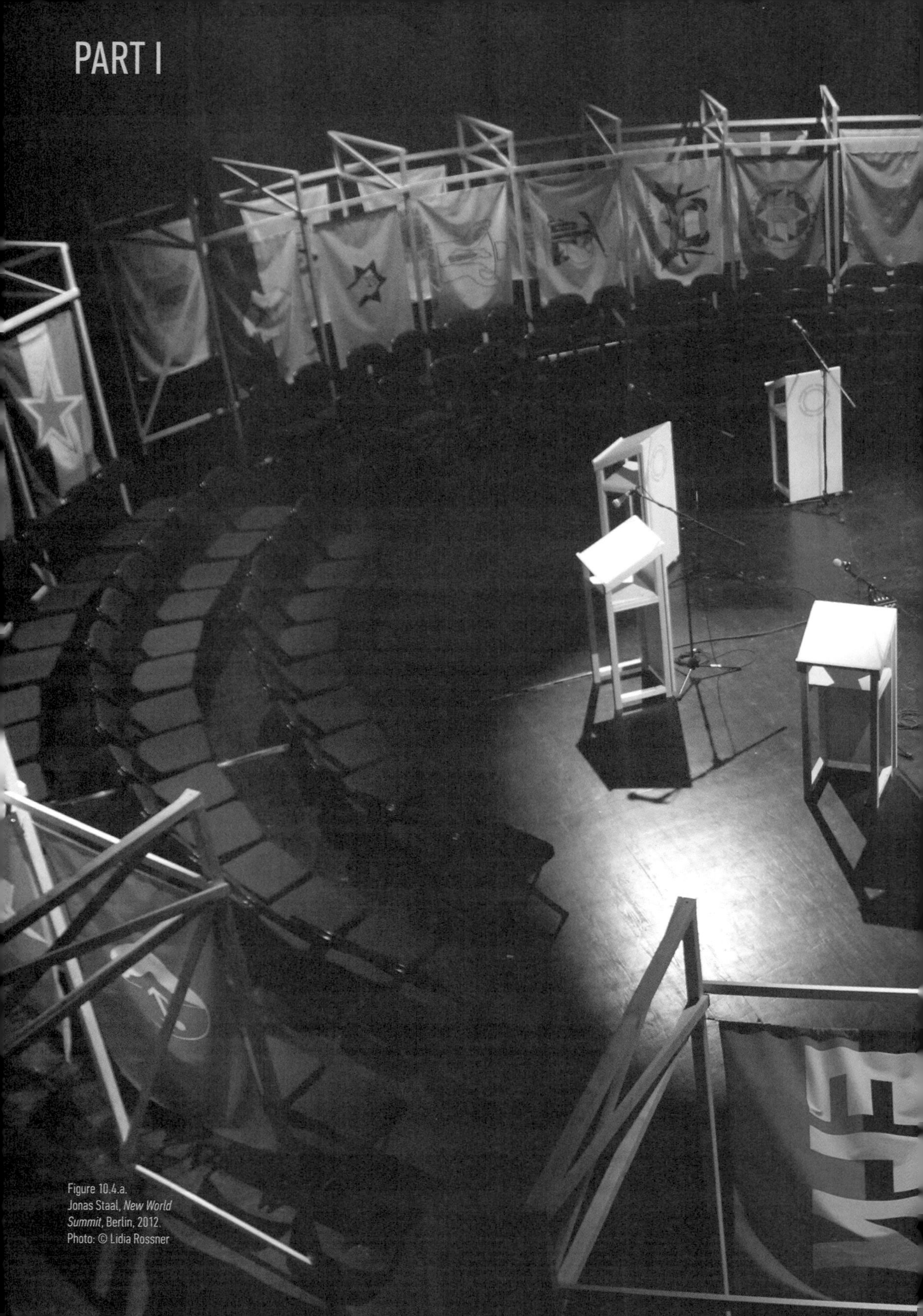

PART I

Figure 10.4.a.
Jonas Staal, *New World Summit*, Berlin, 2012.
Photo: © Lidia Rossner

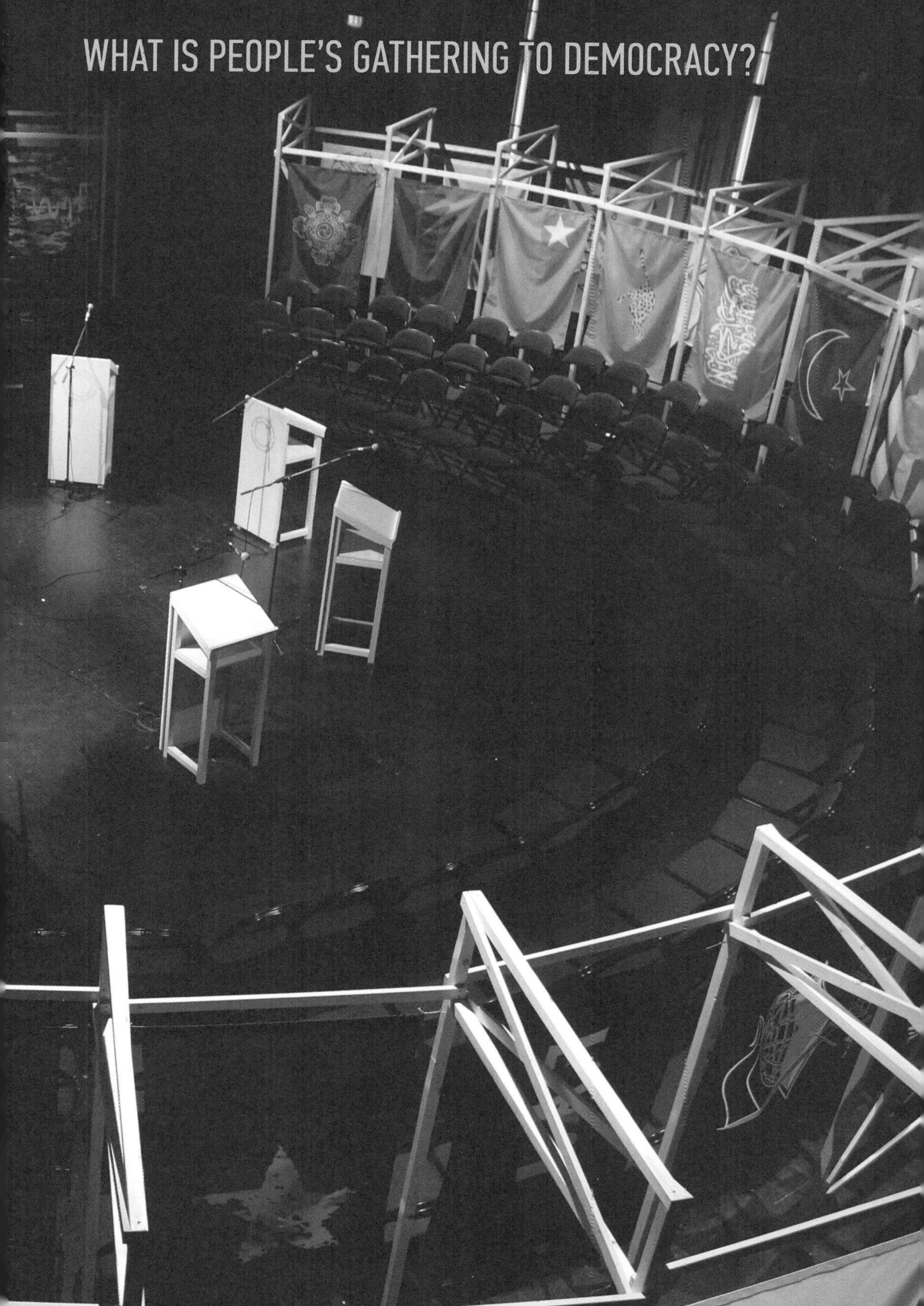

WHAT IS PEOPLE'S GATHERING TO DEMOCRACY?

PERFORMATIVE: ON CURRENT DEMOCRACY MOVEMENTS

The social movements that have grown from the occupations of squares since 2011 refuse representation and relate positively to democracy. They assemble and exchange amongst themselves. They make no demands on political representatives, wanting instead to find common ways to make possible another, better life. Against this backdrop, considerations from aesthetic theory can be brought together with political philosophy in order to understand how the performative practices of these new movements exceed existing democratic forms. To not disregard these as apolitical and ineffective requires a break with the aesthetic and political dichotomy of presence and representation and the invention of the present-st-performative.

ISABELL LOREY — THE POWER OF THE PRESENTIST-

SUSPENDING THE STAGE

The rejection of representation both revives practices from various social and political movements of the past decades and reasserts classic interventions in aesthetic practice. Paradigmatic places for collective gatherings include not only the streets or central squares of a city, but also the theatre, which stands for a certain form of 'community'. The theatre of the 'emancipated spectator', writes Jacques Rancière, 'emerged as a form of aesthetic constitution – sensible constitution – of the community'.[1] This common constitution is not one that unites and unifies all those involved. It can be better grasped, and this is how I would like to understand Rancière, in the sense of the Latin word *constituo*. This assembling is not a state, but a process. The common that emerges through such a process means 'a way of occupying a place and a time, as *a body in action* as opposed to a mere apparatus of laws; a set of perceptions, gestures and attitudes that precede and pre-form laws and institutions'.[2] The acting bodies are that through which the common emerges. The many occupy time and place, and in composing they suspend it; their bodily practices are not individual but singular, in their difference always already connected with and affected by others. They are in movement, without identitarian constitution, not immediate because never undivided, but 'before the law' and thus before representation.

In the Rancièrian imaginary of aesthetic revolution the theatre breaks the dynamics of the state and the law. To achieve such force means from my perspective, however, to break with the logic of representation, to allow the spectators to assemble. This kind of mutual exchange does not emerge through representation, with its distancing assumptions and effects, but from the presence of others, through assembly and talk. The active composing of anyone and everyone can simultaneously unfold destituent and instituent actions, which suspend classical models of not only aesthetic but also of political representation, and 'precede' it. Without experts acting as teachers on stage, without interceding and mediating parties, without representatives, the assembled moved singularities[3] exchange ideas and in

---

1 | Jacques Rancière, *The Emancipated Spectator*, trans. Gregory Elliot (London and Brooklyn: Verso 2009), 1-24, cf. 6, emphasis IL. I personally would not rely on the concept of community, on this see Isabell Lorey, *Figuren des Immunen. Elemente einer politischen Theorie* (Zurich: diaphanes 2011), 199-228; Isabell Lorey, "Constituent Immunisation. Paths Towards the Common," *Open! Platform for Art, Culture and the Public Domain*, January 24, 2015, series Communist Aesthetics, http://www.onlineopen.org/essays/constituent-immunisation-paths-towards-the-common/ (last accessed May 24, 2019).
2 | Rancière, *The Emancipated Spectator*, 6.
3 | A singularity can never exist alone and independently, it always refers to a multiplicity of singularities that refer to one another and in this sense it is a social, a relational category. Singularity is, however, not only connected with other singularities, but is itself constituted by manifoldness. Not identity, but rather the dynamics of a unique manifoldness characterise a singularity. In the multifarious multitudes the singularity relentlessly finds itself in a process of change, in a process of becoming, in a process of constituting.

the words of Rancière create an 'equality of intelligence'.[4] This empowerment unfolds less through role play and the building of a new stage, less by the many participating theatrically or as functional parts in a staging, and more, rather, as they take part in mutual exchange with other anyones and are affected by it.[5] When the audience occupies the stage in this way, it suspends it, breaking with the theatrical staging. This is how new spaces of the common potentially emerge, in which another way of living together is not only negotiated and invented, but can already be practiced on the spot. I understand this practicing as a presentist-performative power.

To see here the logic of a 'metaphysics of presence' at work would be a misunderstanding. It was Jacques Derrida who in his *Grammatology* criticised Jean-Jacques Rousseau for the latter's longing for metaphysical presence. According to Derrida Rousseau prefers – particularly with respect to politics – the presence of assembly and talk: small communities in which the immediate living-together of the citizens and the 'unanimity of "assembled peoples"'[6] would be possible. Here, presence means a 'completely self-present'[7] being, complete self-identity, selfness and sentience. In his deconstruction Derrida not only cuts through representation-critical, even anarchistic references to Rousseau; to a certain extent he repeats Hegel's disregard for the present.[8] And precisely when he wants to exhibit Rousseau and his gendered ideas, he simultaneously reproduces gender-specific dichotomous ascriptions that grasp sentience, feeling, immediacy and presence as feminine and ratio, reflexion, deferral and representation as masculine.

Yet when the audience is no longer watching and instead becoming common, appearing as common and passively/actively determining what happens, it becomes less about erasing 'the difference between the actor and the spectator, the represented and the representer, the object seen and the seeing subject'.[9] That would be nothing but authenticity or – as Derrida formulates – 'auto-affecting', 'intimacy of a self-presence', 'the sentiment of self-proximity, of self-sameness'.[10] The classical forms of theatre would be dissolved, the public festival would take place, imagined as presence of

---

4 | Rancière, *The Emancipated Spectator*, 10.

5 | For a critique of the fetish of participation and activated spectators in the cultural field, see Bojana Kunst, *Artist at Work. Proximity of Art and Capitalism* (Winchester and Washington: Zero Books 2015).

6 | Jacques Derrida, *Of Grammatology*, Corrected Edition, trans. Gayatri Chakravorty Spivak (Baltimore and London: Johns Hopkins 1997), 137.

7 | Ibid.

8 | Cf. G.W.F. Hegel, *Phänomenologie des Geistes, Werke in zwanzig Bänden*, Bd. 3 (Frankfurt am M.: Suhrkamp 1970). Drawing negative associations between terms such as 'presence' or 'presentist' and 'immediate', 'authentic', and 'bodily' continue today to reveal traces into the Hegelian philosophy of history.

9 | Derrida, *Of Grammatology*, 306.

10 | Ibid and 165.

the identical. And this festival would be but nothing but the community of the proper, it would be consonant with the political forms absent of 'representative difference'[11] that Rousseau prefers in the *Social Contract*: with respect to the political committees as well as to the assembled, free, legislating 'people'.[12] But what happens when Rousseau introduces the assembly of the 'people' in order to let the audience suspend the stage by withdrawing from its role in the plot of representation, by becoming many who move, dance, mutually affect one another? In his "Letter to d'Alembert" Rousseau writes: '... gather the people together there, and you will have a festival. Do better yet; let the spectators become an entertainment to themselves; make them actors themselves; do it so that each sees and loves himself in the others so that all will be better united'.[13] Surely, Rousseau wants the united people, which is only sovereign when assembled. His ideas should not be adopted uncritically, but they do go beyond that which can be deconstructed simply as a metaphysics of presence.

When the public becomes common, when any many compose themselves, they not only leave the private, the dark space of spectatorship, and come into the light of the public realm. They compose themselves beyond subjectivistic self-affecting and authentistic corporeality – and maybe they have a festival. To break through the opposition of immediate presence and mediating representation, political action must be newly determined with respect to practices that allow new forms of democracy to emerge on the basis of mutual affecting and connectedness with others – a presentist democracy, which is more than present, visible, bodily presence.

THE 'PEOPLE' OF JURIDICAL DEMOCRACY AND THE ANY MANY

At the institutionalised level we in the 'Western' context are accustomed to distinguishing between two complementary forms of 'the rule of the people': between representative and direct democracy. These are considered the two forms of realisation of so-called popular sovereignty. Political representation alone appears to be insufficient, the citizens must also be directly involved in legislative decisions. There is debate over the extent of participation, direct democracy is certainly the less widespread form of political decision-making in the 'West', but 'under good conditions' it complements the representative model. In the case of representation, there must be free elections, in the case of direct democracy there must be free referenda. In accordance with the logic of sovereignty, free decision plays

11 | Ibid.

12 | Cf. Jean-Jacques Rousseau, *On the Social Contract* [1762], trans. and ed. Donald A. Cress (Indianapolis: Hackett 1988), III 12 and 15; IV 4.

13 | Jean-Jacques Rousseau, "Letter to d'Alembert", quoted in Derrida, *Of Grammatology*, 307.

an essential role at the moment votes are cast: in the former case, for a party or a political representative, in the latter with reference to an objective question generally posed between two alternatives, which can usually be answered with yes or no. This is not about the assembly and speech of the anyhow equal, but the sovereign decision by vote of the legally equal.

Sovereignty is the force (*Gewalt*) of decision to make laws for oneself. As popular sovereignty it is the decision of those who are the citizens of a state within whose borders the self-legislated laws should apply. This understanding of democracy, at the political level, is always juridical. The 'people' assembles and speaks on the political stage in an enduring way only through its representatives in parliament – evidently, Rousseau's ideas did become hegemonic. In addition to political representation and direct voting there is a third political practice: that of protest, of demonstration in the street. Such collective forms of manifestation, in which individuals raise their voices and submit their votes, tend to be counted as a political act when they refer to these first two forms of democracy and formulate an aim in this sense: when concrete demands are directed to political representatives or when there is a demand for a greater degree of participation in their decisions. Moreover, according to this understanding of processes of social negotiation, movements should be organised such that within the movements themselves representatives are determined who can function as contact persons for politicians and media, and with whom a process of negotiation can occur in this sense.

However, in a democracy the 'people' must not necessarily be embodied, that is, united, in a specific place or in a specific manner. Neither the constitution or individual laws, nor representation or an institutional site are capable of encompassing the democratic process. All these forms of the embodiment of the 'people' reduce and mince the practicing of democracy. From this perspective the 'people' is nothing but an effect of representation; representative democracy is not possible without the construction of *one* 'people'.[14] A performative power, however, cannot emerge from a unitary people, but only through the any many, the affected singularities. The democratic will of the many is not representable, it cannot be embodied in a juridically institutionalised power – neither as legislative constituent force nor as constituted force of the law or representation. The practicing of democracy constantly overshoots the juridical logic of law and state and evades it. The any many must be distinguished from a represented *demos*; when they assemble and exchange amongst themselves, they introduce a

14 | Cf. Isabell Lorey, "On Democracy and Occupation. Horizontality and the Need for New Forms of Verticality", trans. Aileen Derieg, in Pascal Gielen (Ed.), *Institutional Attitudes. Instituting Art in a Flat World* (Amsterdam: Valiz 2013), 77–99; Isabell Lorey, "Presentist Democracy. Reconceptualizing the Present", trans. Aileen Derieg, in Quinn Latimer, Adam Szymczyk (Eds.), *documenta 14 – Reader* (München: Prestel 2017), 169–202.

suspension, a secession, which unfixes democracy from its juridical clutch and separates it from the idea of the sovereignty of the *demos*.[15]

FROM IN-BETWEEN TO _WITH_

Hannah Arendt is the political theorist who most closely associated the political and the performative. She speaks of the public sphere as a space of appearance and of political action as exposing oneself to the eyes of others.[16] Arendt defines the political with recourse to theatre:

> *'Exactly as music, the ballet and theatre have need of an audience before which to unfold their virtuosity, [political] action, too, requires the presence of others in a politically organised sphere...'*[17]

The theatre audience corresponds for Arendt to the composition of a space that emerges from the presence of others and from presence with others: the political stage is here transformed into a performative praxis. The 'space of appearance' is characterised by mutual negotiation. Only when the assembled speak with one another and exchange their different perspectives does 'that which is common to many, lies *between* them, separates and connects them'[18] emerge. For Arendt, this *between* links the performative with the political; it is based on the presence of others, who are not conceived as mere observers; rather, according to Arendt, a space emerges *between* those who actively engage – a space that allows sociality and the political to appear. It is not possible to enter the space of appearance of the political as if it were already given. Rather, it first constitutes itself through action between those who participate, and it is not bound to a fixed place. Interaction allows the place of the political to emerge. Acting and speaking establish 'a space between',[19] which can find its place anywhere and at any time. This place is there, where people appear before one another.[20]

---

15 | See also Jacques Rancière, "Political Impurity", trans. Mary Foster, in Jacques Rancière, *Moments politiques: Interventions 1977-2009* (New York: Seven Stories 2014); Isabell Lorey, "The 2011 Occupy Movements: Rancière and the Crisis of Democracy", trans. Aileen Derieg, *Theory, Culture & Society*, Special Issue on Jacques Rancière, 31, no. 7-8 (2014): 43-65.

16 | Cf. Hannah Arendt, *The Human Condition: Second Edition* (Chicago: University of Chicago Press 2013), 198.

17 | Hannah Arendt, "Freedom and Politics" in Albert Hunold (Ed.), *Freedom and Serfdom* (Dordrecht, NL: D. Reidel, 197. See also "its [the polis'] true space lies between people living together for this purpose, no matter where they happen to be" in Arendt, *The Human Condition*, 198.

18 | Hannah Arendt, *Was ist Politik? Fragmente aus dem Nachlass*, ed. Ursula Ludz (Munich and Zurich: Piper 2003), 52 (all translations of this text IL).

19 | Arendt, *The Human Condition*, 198.

20 | Ibid.

Arendt primarily has the free men of the Greek polis in mind, who step out of their daily life, in particular out of the private household, and first make their appearance explicit in the sphere of the public. These are discrete individuals who act together, which is the precondition for conceiving of a space 'between' them that connects and separates them. Interestingly, against the bourgeois conception of the Enlightenment, these citizens do not act as sovereign. Arendt stresses that her conceptions of political action and political freedom have nothing to do with sovereignty. To act together with others can only take place 'under the condition of non-sovereignty'.[21] The limits of Arendt's thoughts on the political-performative lie in a double sense in the conception of those who act politically. They are discrete individuals, and it is a bourgeois and masculine-defined political action. Arendt separates the political-performative space of appearance from a non-political private and female-connoted sphere. She reproduces the ancient distinction between the household, in which free women, children and slaves can exert themselves, the place of reproduction, and the public, in which only free men can appear in the political sense. Through this distinction Arendt separates body and action and assigns them to the two spheres. And further: she divides the body itself into one which takes care of one's life in the private sphere, and another which shows itself in public and assembles and exchanges there with others.[22] But who can appear under what conditions, whose voice is heard, whose vote is asked for, and who can hold a speech? The possibilities to create resonance for oneself in the public sphere and to create a political space, in which struggle can be undertaken with others for certain goals, are not equal for all. The possibilities of performative power are based on social hierarchies, discriminations and relations of inequality. Not every exchange with others in which a political space emerges allows for multiplication and sustainability. And coming together with others, talking and assembling in the street, is always again threatened by police repression. Yet Arendt alludes to this when she writes that political action in the public sphere is always bound up with risk. When the head of the household steps across the threshold of his house, he not only leaves the private 'place in which men were ruled by necessity and force', she writes, but at the same time the place 'where the life of everyone was secured [...]. Thus, only one who was ready to risk his life could be free'.[23] In this understanding, political freedom is not to be distinguished from insecurity and risking life. 'The same holds for linking the political to danger and risk at all'.[24]

21 | Arendt, "What is freedom", 165.

22 | Cf. Arendt, "Freedom and Politics," 191–92. See also Linda Zerilli, "The Arendtian Body" in Bonnie Honig, (Ed.), *Feminist Perspectives on Hannah Arendt* (University Park: Pennsylvania State University Press 1995), 167–94.

23 | Arendt, *Was ist Politik?*, 44.

24 | Ibid, 45.

From the perspective of various dimensions of the precarious, social insecurity and precarisation emerge not through the action of individuals in the public sphere after leaving the sphere of reproduction behind.[25] Rather, it is about politically, economically, legally, and socially induced insecurities that are historically specific (precarity) and which are maintained through modes of government, relations to the self and social positionings (governmental precarisation). A further dimension of the precarious is socio-ontological precariousness, which refers to the dependence of every creature on the care of and reproduction by others, to a connectedness with others that cannot be shaken off. Yet within the scope of a gender-specific division of labour, care and reproduction are structurally fenced into the private, devalued and connoted as female. This devaluation not only influences the occidental-modern understanding of an autonomous individual who is independent of others and capable of acting on one's own authority. The devaluation of precariousness and thus of care and reproduction itself structures a conception of collective political action as Arendt proposes it. Thus, it requires more than a performative *between* as space of appearance to reconceptualise common action, such that basic dependency on others and mutual connectedness with others must not first be left behind in the private sphere in order to make an encounter between autonomous individuals in the public sphere thinkable.

This means dispensing with the idea of a closed-off individual who is separated from others, and instead referring to connectedness and relationality with others. When Arendt writes that theatre like the public sphere is exposing oneself to the eyes of others, that political action must take place in the presence of others, she places political action under the paradigm of visibility and the physical presence of the agents. As it were, Arendt should not be accused of dealing in a metaphysics of presence in the classic sense, as the public-political space is an effect of a performative interaction of many; yet she restricts presence and the present to physical presence and visibility, to bodily appearance. If, however, rather than the between, we stress the _with_, which means a mode of existence conceived in ceaseless becoming, then this _with_ takes the connections and not the separations as the starting point.[26] The _with_ underscores the mutual affecting of and with living beings, environments and things. When the _with_ is understood as a condition of existence, it does not emerge

---

25 | For my differentiation between three dimensions of the precarious (precariousness, precarity and governmental precarisation) see Isabell Lorey, *State of Insecurity. Government of the Precarious*, trans. Aileen Derieg, with Introduction by Judith Butler (New York: Verso 2015); Judith Butler, "Autonomy and Precarization. (Neo)Liberal Entanglements of Labour and Care in the Former West", trans. Aileen Derieg and Kelly Mulvaney, in Maria Hlavajova and Simon Sheikh, (Eds.), *FORMER WEST: Art and the Contemporary after 1989* (Cambridge: MIT Press 2016), 427–39.

26 | See also Gerald Raunig, *Dividuum. Machinic Capitalism and Molecular Revolution* (New York: Semiotext(e) 2016).

from the public presence of others. Thus, others do not first connect in the public sphere with an individual otherwise separated from them. Rather, each singularity is always already manifold. The concept of presence also no longer necessarily has to do with physical presence or visibility. The present is much more, in the Benjaminian sense, graspable as the untimely now-time (*Jetztzeit*).[27] In this sense it is precisely not a temporality that sticks with itself in a self-identical way, as immediate presence, as authenticity of body and affect. Instead, it breaks through any connotation of a metaphysical restriction of presence and overshoots any reduction to physical presence. Now-time is constellational, constructive, performative temporality, in which the slivers of history are composed anew, in which history unceasingly emerges. Now-time is the creative midpoint, not a bridge or a transit from the past into the future.[28]

SUPPORTED ACTION

In her recent writings on the democracy movements that grew largely from the occupation of squares since 2011, Judith Butler stresses that at Tahrir Square in Cairo, in Zuccotti Park with Occupy Wall Street, or in Istanbul's Gezi Park, the materiality of public space was configured.[29] As it were, these locations offer material conditions that make it possible for many to assemble in various ways; the architecture itself regulates to a large degree the conditions of convergence and has its own political dimension. And yet the many assembled refigured the material environment of these places in a new way, for example in camps lasting for weeks. In the organisation of camps there was already a practice of social reproduction according to the needs of demonstrating bodies and of forms of commonality that emerge when not simply more democracy is demanded, but aspects of another democracy in the now-time are probed.[30] These practices make evident that political action is not autonomous action, but always 'supported action', as Judith Butler rightly emphasizes. However, support as attentiveness and care does not come only from connections with other people, but also from and with things and environments. These act, even passively, when they support political actions, such as tanks onto which demonstrators climb in order to speak to the crowd.[31]

---

27 | Cf. Walter Benjamin "On the Concept of History" [1974], trans. Dennis Redmond, https://www.marxists.org/reference/archive/benjamin/1940/history.htm (last accessed May 24, 2019). Trans. note: We have opted for the translation of *Jetztzeit* as 'now-time', rather than the 'here-and-now' in the Redmond translation.

28 | Cf. Isabell Lorey, "Presentist Democracy. The Now-Time of Struggles" in Andreas Oberprantacher and Andrei Siclodi (Ed.), *Subjectivation in Political Theory and Contemporary Practices* (London, South Yarra and Sydney: Palgrave Macmillan 2016), 149–64; or Isabell Lorey, "Presentist Democracy. Reconceptualizing the Present".

29 | Judith Butler, *Notes Toward a Performative Theory of Assembly* (London: Harvard University Press 2015), 71.

30 | Cf. Lorey, "On Democracy and Occupation".

31 | Cf. Butler, *Notes Toward a Performative Theory*, 71. See also Henri Lefebvre, *The Production of Space*, trans. Donald Nicholson-Smith (Oxford: Basil Blackwell [1974] 1991).

The dissolution of the squares occupations and the spreading out of any many into various neighbourhoods does not mark the end of a movement. In Spain it became clear that a common space of manifold singularities would not simply vanish in dispersion, as if the alleged restoration of the architecture of the square that is empty or not being used for protest would indicate that the movement no longer exists. Such logic would follow the metaphysics of presence. When the presence of the many is no longer immediately visible, presentist democracy movements are by no means gone. Distributed, living on in neighbourhoods and behind walls, they rather demonstrate that politically affected subjectivations, embodied politics, also determine the so-called private.[32] A division between public and private domains, which is the basis of not only Arendt's theorisation, is therefore inadequate. To disregard politicisation beyond traditional forms of organisation leaves precisely revolutionary events like the occupation of Tahrir Square uncomprehended and appearing to rise from nothing, since the 'private' according to this perspective counts in the best case only as pre-political.[33]

Not only political action is always supported action. The current struggles for another form of democracy and economy are struggles of the heterogeneous precarious for new modes of social reproduction. They are the protests of those who are increasingly subjected to social insecurity with respect to housing, health, education and nutrition; they are struggles against governing through precarisation, which also encompasses the middle social strata. Sharp critiques of neoliberal political and economic developments run through these struggles. The demands for another democracy are neither merely about the return to the Fordist social states, nor do they aim for increased national security. Rather, they are about new organizational processes of social reproduction.[34] This probing does not end with the occupations of squares, but continues to be practiced at the municipal level in and by the representation-critical takeover of the political system, as is the case in many Spanish cities.[35]

Even those parts of the movement that decided against the march through the existing institutions are exemplary of presentist-performative practices. The Spanish platform for those affected by mortgage debts, the PAH,[36] fights with success against governmental precarisation. People unable to

---

32 | Cf. Butler, *Notes Toward a Performative Theory*, 71.
33 | Cf. Asef Bayat, "Revolution in Bad Times", *New Left Review* 80, March/April 2013, 47–60.
34 | Cf. Lorey, "Presentist Democracy".
35 | On Spain, see Raul Zelik, *Mit PODEMOS zur demokratischen Revolution? Krise und Aufstand in Spanien* (Berlin: Bertz+Fischer 2015).
36 | PAH is the acronym for the Plataforma de Afectados por la Hipoteca, www.http://afectadosporlahipoteca.com/.

pay back their mortgages due to unemployment, who are often hundreds of thousands of euros in debt, are organised in the PAH. In assemblies and local grassroots groups, those affected by mortgage debt not only find support to fight to continue living in their homes or to occupy empty residential units that belong to banks. One of the central interests of the PAH is to empower people through support practices and opportunities for exchange, so as to break through the hegemonic governmental precarisation in which people are made responsible as individuals for their social insecurity. Instead of this, collective action allows singularity to be experienced and new social spaces and other modes of living together to emerge. From alliance with others, as Butler writes, emerges 'performative power to lay claim to the public in a way that is not yet codified into law, and that can never be fully codified into law'.[37] This performative power 'before the law' overshoots the juridical. Presentist practices, because they are performative and processual, are neither representable in the traditional sense nor reducible to a metaphysics of presence.

PRESENTIST DEMOCRACY

The activists of the various democracy movements do not formulate concrete catalogues of demands on those governing, they do not organise in traditional ways, and they reject again and again cooperation with state institutions, or they transform these with the help of representation-critical decision-making structures. The Spanish 15M movement, which first assembled on May 15, 2011 at the Puerta del Sol in Madrid, used the term 'real democracy' from the very beginning – a term most prominently expressed in the slogan *¡Democracia real ya!*. This democracy is real, less in the sense of the one true, correct democracy; in conjunction with the Spanish word *ya* it actually and materially already exists in this moment, especially in the practices of assembly and the political practices that set out from an assumed mutual connectedness. It is not about a direct democracy in which citizens participate in political decision-making by responding yes or no, but a performative practice of _with_, as was successfully tried out in Barcelona. There, the citizen platform Barcelona en comú, which put forward the city's current mayor, Ada Colau, in the municipal election of May 2015, emerged from the 15M movement and is developing the 're-appropriation of democracy from below'[38] in *municipalismo*, a new city-level politics. The programme of Barcelona en comú was created during the summer of 2014 at well-attended public assemblies for another kind of

37 | Judith Butler, "Bodies in Alliance and the Politics of the Street", *transversal »#Occupy and Assemble ∞«*, October 2011, http://transversal.at/transversal/1011/butler/en (last accessed May 24, 2019).
38 | Zelik, *Mit PODEMOS*, 111.

municipal politics. In addition, city administration employees were asked before the election in a kind of militant investigation what they would change and what they would preserve.[39] Their knowledge and experience were incorporated into the process of a *municipalismo*, which emerges in and through those who want a better life in the city, and not beyond it.

These practices, initiatives and convergences are elements of a presentist democracy. This understanding of the presentist breaks through the linearity of time and breaks it open, it is practiced in the present and not postponed into the future in a programme that must first be implemented. Presentist means the simultaneity of break, as suspension of that which has been up to now, and breach, as opening of a space of possibility. Presentist refers to an actual becoming, to a stretched out and intensive present. It is not the event of a great, one-off break, but an enduring unfolding of affective connections, an 'affect virus'[40] through which new socialities emerge.

When, in governing through precarisation, the future can no longer be planned, democratisation cannot remain a future promise. In presentist democracy, other democratic practices, other forms of protection and mutual support, other economies that break through dominant power relations, are not postponed to the future but rather at once practiced and extended. This present becoming of presentist democracy demands that singular people enter into the process of becoming in the experience of singularity, into the actual constituting, and with this, out from their past and future. The becoming-common emerges from current compositions that suspend time and place and produce new socialities and economies in an untimely now-time. These are assemblies based on the _with_, in the process of constituting, which is always dual: a destituting and an instituting, 'before the law', before representation, and before the institution, but not independent of these. In the exchange of singularities, no new stage of political action is built, instead a field of immanence of self-changing social spaces of the _with_ is dynamised. It is not structured by dialectical distinctions between public and private or by visibility and invisibility. The field of immanence of the presentist-performative overshoots bodily presence, identity and filiation, because it unfolds itself from the _with_ as expanded present.

39 | On the history of militant investigation, see Käthe Knittler, "Wissensarbeit und militante Untersuchung: Zwischen Produktion und Rebellion. Über Möglichkeiten widerständiger Wissensproduktion" *Kurswechsel. Zeitschrift für gesellschafts-, wirtschafts- und umweltpolitische Alternativen* 2014 (1), 74–83.
40 | Raúl Sánchez Cedillo, "15M: Something Constituent This Way Comes", *South Atlantic Quarterly* 111, no. 3 (2012): 573-84; see also Raúl Sánchez Cedillo, "15M als Aufstand der Körper-Maschine", trans. Dominic Widmer, in Isabell Lorey, Roberto Nigro, Gerald Raunig (Eds.), Inventionen 2: *Exodus. Reale Demokratie. Territorium. Immanenz. Maßlose Differenz. Biopolitik* (Zürich: diaphanes 2012), 48–61.

SCRIPTIVE AND THE PREFIGURATIVE PERFORMANCE: SOME REFLECTIONS ON THE QUESTION OF TIME OF POLITICAL ACTION

A variety of political thought arising from the recent popular uprisings and activism in the aftermath of a protest could be gauged by one criterion: the time of political or social action.[1] The question of temporality here pertains to how action, doing, practice and operation in the political and social spheres relate to the present and how they project the future of the change they are aiming for. My inquiry will tackle three variant thinking models as they vie with each other around time and performance. I will start by briefly introducing the three models here. The first model is that of procedurality, which lies at the core of the mechanisms of formal democracy, and stresses presentism from normative and descriptive viewpoints. It informs us about 'how things go' or how they function, and how procedures describe, explain and help us understand the processes in policy- and decision-making and social practices, but also in the creation of things and thoughts, from scientific experiments and algorithms to dance performances, for instance. The emphasis on procedures as tools that orient and define actions and attitudes in general assumes an alignment with the given present, with the processes that are operated almost automatically, governed and mediated without critical contestation.

1 | The recent uprisings span from antineoliberal protests in Europe and the Americas to the Middle-Eastern 'revolutions' and riots against oppression. Activism considered here includes grassroots social movements (e.g. Solidarity movement in Greece or *municipalismos* in Spain) and smaller more specialised anarchist groups and collectives.

In opposition to procedurality, a politics of prescription of axiomatic principles has been formulated, which we will consider a second model here. By asking for a direct and urgent application of a principle (e.g. the principle of 'spatial justice' animating protests against privatisation of public space) instead of a procedure, the rising public anticipates its subsequent power and commits to the consequences of a changed political situation for which it strives without a guaranteed success. Prescriptive politics, which Peter Hallward developed after Alain Badiou's and Jacques Ranciere's political thought and further amended in his own conception of the political will of the people, entails a rupture and disalignment with the present.[2] From there on, it orients a long-term process of organising collective action towards a future anterior, by determining a political end for which the means are sought. A peculiar sense of conviction and audacity imbues this standpoint of political voluntarism for it to affirm the power by which the action 'will have produced' the anticipated outcome.

Prescription and emancipation through the political will as an inherent human capacity project the horizon of a revolution. Therefore, yet a third conception must be examined here as a pervasive alternative promoted through the 'prefigurative practices' of social activism today. The politics of prefiguration – in the view of its proponents – seeks to diminish the gap between the present and a revolution to come. The main claim here is that the present action or practice 'prefigures' the future of social change. It does so either in the symbolic sense, by imagining and enacting alternative social structures on small-scale experiments within a community or a local movement which will expand on a larger scale at a later moment, or in an actual sense, through embodied practices of horizontal social relations, whereby means equal ends and the building of self-organised counterinstitutions already counts as an actualised social change.[3] Whether symbolised or actualised, the timing of prefiguration is proleptic, as it represents change either before it is actual or as an early indication or version of it.

If we are to examine and compare these three models in how they conceive of action/doing/practice and project it in time, performance and dramaturgy appear to have analytical purchase. The aim of my conceptual

<hr>

2 | Hallward developed his conception in the following texts: "From Prescription to Volition", *The Politics of Alain Badiou*, special issue of *Politics and Culture* (September 2014): 1–16; "The will of the people: Notes towards a dialectical voluntarism", *Radical Philosophy* 155, (May/June 2009): 17–29; "The Politics of Prescription", *The South Atlantic Quarterly* 104, no. 4 (fall 2005) 769–89, and "Concentration or Representation: The Struggle for Popular Sovereignty", *Cogent Arts & Humanities* 4, no. 1 (2017).

3 | The theme of embodiment features in the earliest conception of prefiguration, in Carl Boggs, "Marxism, prefigurative communism and the problem of workers' control", *Radical America* 6, (Winter 1977). Boggs writes: "The embodiment within the ongoing political practice of the movement, of those forms of social relations, decision making, culture, and human experience that are the ultimate goal", Ibid, 100.

inquiry is to ask whether the procedural, the prescriptive and the prefigurative modes of operation could be accounted for as 'performative' and consequently, how their 'performances' differ. I will be looking in particular at how they 'dramatise' process in the course of operation. For starters, performing here is undertaken in the broad meaning deployed after Richard Schechner's definition as 'showing doing'.[4] Thus, it involves a certain degree of awareness of how an action is done, by virtue of which rules, conventions and actors, and how this doing implies social relations. The concept of dramaturgy lends us the logic of organising stages in a process with respect to cognition. It will help us understand how effects of operations can be qualified in time, and whether, for instance, a process entails a plot or unfolds a flat structure in time.

Weighing up the three models against each other, this analysis will catapult us into a fourth case: *Time Bombs* (2017), the film-essay made by the Croatian performance collective BADco. As a work that combines a theatre performance, a film shoot and a live gathering of citizens around a political question, *Time Bombs* redramatises the same concerns that animate both the prescriptive and prefigurative politics in drawing out material contradictions within the form and the production of film and theatre. Unlike the other three models, *Time Bombs* ties the future of the present struggles with the futurist imaginary of the past avant-gardes. Thus, it provides us with a counterperspective on the temporality of social and political action with regard to art production and history, which is missing from proceduralist and prefigurative operations. Therefore, I will conclude this brief investigation by recalibrating the proceduralist, prescriptive and prefigurative perspectives on time through the eyes of a film-essay, a tentative fourth model.

1 PERFORMING *PROCEDURALLY*

To unpack proceduralism and its performance, we will first approach it through its most robust discourse and a somewhat overdetermining register, that is, democratic proceduralism. Democracy is said to be a procedure. What does this statement mean exactly? Let us briefly convey the juridical account of it. The rule of law is formal, guaranteeing formal equality of everyone before law, and in that sense, it is agnostic about the content of law. The question arises as to how the political legitimacy of laws, policies, institutions, candidates for political office and so on, are to be judged. Two global orientations apply. According to the substantive view, decisions are judged by the substantive values realised in them. According to the proceduralist view, the main criteria of political legitimacy are accuracy and consistency of procedures implemented in a process. Following the extreme normative conception of proceduralism, 'democratic decisions are legitimate as long as they are the result of an appropriately constrained process of democratic decision-making'.[5] The legitimacy of the outcomes of a political process depends only on the fairness of the decision-making process (analogous to rules of the happy performative),[6] and not on the quality of the outcomes it produces. This view is justified by the claim that there is no shared standard for assessing the quality of the outcomes, and deep disagreement about reasons for and against proposals will always remain. The neoliberal version of the same arguments is, as usual, more compellingly instrumentalist than the liberalist tradition. Intercourse needs to be regulated even through imperfect norms, because the journey must serve a practical need. A collective process of creation or any kind of decision-making of a heterogeneous group of people is deemed an infinite journey, which, however enjoyable, still does not guarantee a desirable outcome. There is much to approve in proceduralism, in the words of its advocates, because it ensures decisions. It prevents participants from employing the strategy of infinite delay, and it avoids having 'energies consumed' by infinitely long discussions of an infinite variety of issues. 'Outcomes are by their nature open to dispute, but processes need not be.'[7] Proceduralism reaches farther than a legal mechanism of democracy. This is best illustrated by 'procedural rhetoric', a video game theory that extends beyond the design of video games as it seeks to account for the comprehension of social processes in general.[8] Taking procedurality to be the computer's defining ability to execute a series of rules with the notion of rhetoric as persuasive expression, Ian Bogost proposes 'procedural rhetoric' as a way of making arguments and expressing ideas with processes in general and computational processes in particular:

> *Procedurality refers to a way of creating, explaining, or understanding processes. And processes define the way things work: the methods, techniques, and logics that drive the operation of systems, from mechanical systems like engines to organizational systems like high schools to conceptual systems like religious faith. Rhetoric refers to effective and persuasive expression. Procedural rhetoric, then, is a practice of using processes persuasively.*[9]

5 | Fabienne Peter, "Political Legitimacy", *Stanford Encyclopedia of Philosophy*, April 29, 2010, http://plato.stanford.edu/entries/legitimacy/.

6 | See "Conditions for happy performative" in J. L. Austin's pioneering theory of speech acts, or *How to Do Things with Words* (Oxford: Clarendon Press 1962), 12–24.

7 | Stephen Chilton, "The Problem of Agreement in Republicanism, Proceduralism, and the Mature Dewey: A "Two Moments of Discourse Ethics" Analysis", *Steve Chilton's Home Page*, November 5, 2001, http://www.d.umn.edu/~schilton/Articles/Tilburg.html.

8 | Ian Bogost coined the term 'procedural rhetoric' in his video game theory: see Ian Bogost, *Persuasive Games: The Expressive Power of Videogames* (Cambridge: MIT Press 2007).

9 | Ibid, 3.

Bogost goes on to show how this 'design philosophy' can provide a framework through which to ask questions about what a particular social situation might demand.[10]

The Whiteheadian philosopher and cultural theorist Steven Shaviro raises a philosophical objection of ontological priority: 'All procedures are in fact processes, but not all processes are procedures'.[11] In other words, Shaviro's objection addresses the nature of process. If we are to follow the model of procedural rhetoric, the process is predetermined by an algorithm of steps thanks to procedures that unilaterally cause and determine a course of action. Procedures protect processes from uncertainty and unforeseeable change.

Another register of procedurality pervades the kind of knowledge acquired by artists and students of an increasingly professionalised art education. This know-how ranges from artistic methodology (methods for organising work, collaboration and, in a narrower sense, construction of a 'piece') to managing one's career through applications for projects and research grants or through recently developed academic (postgraduate) degrees in art.[12] Part of artists' self-performance is to set a promise of potential for a new creation, whereby to perform is to show the ability to use images, words and procedures that respond to a growing expectation of shaping the audience's experience.

The comparison of procedurality in the three registers above (procedural democracy, video game theory, artists' procedural knowledge) reveals the common ground of instrumental reason. Procedures stress the regularity of a process; they are the means and the norms of performativity when performing is equated with achievement (or *Leistung*, the German word for performance). Following a procedure ensures effectiveness, a way to control the future from the ability to predict it in the present. This is why presentism is the temporal horizon of procedurality with a kind of mechanical causality: the normal functioning of 'how things go', elections, parliamentary debates, stocks on the market or subsidy allocations all the same.

10 | The examples include videogames such as *Tenure*, which is based on scenarios typifying conflicts that occur between teachers, students and administration in U.S. high schools, or *Fat World*, which treats obesity in the U.S. as a social problem.

11 | Steven Shaviro, "Processes and Powers", *The Pinocchio Theory* (blog), *shaviro.com*, August 18, 2011, http://www.shaviro.com/Blog/?p=995 (last accessed May 24, 2019).

12 | Two statements capture the procedural knowledge in art methodology. The choreographer Eleanor Bauer writes: 'What do you do when you get in the studio? There's nothing to do there! The empty room gives us nothing, nothing but space and time. A sterile luxury. Advantages of having methods we are aware of using are that we have things to do when we get into the studio and that the work is stronger than the constant shifting of our interest, confidence, and motivation'. The choreographer Andros Zins-Browne remarks that 'most good pieces are the writing of a methodology in their production'. Bojana Cvejić, "In the Making of the Making of: The Practice of Rendering Performance Virtual" in *Goat Tracks of Self-Education*, special issue of *TkH*, no. 15 (2008): 29.

2 *PRINCIPLES* ASIDE FROM PERFORMATIVITY

Several voices in political theory have been explicitly or indirectly raised in critique of procedurality. For Slavoj Žižek, procedurality is a kind of ideology that prevents any revolt against capitalism.[13] He writes that our political consciousness is shackled by questions like the following, questions which form the legal framework of an empty concept of freedom: Does a country have free elections? Are its judges independent? Is its press free from hidden pressures? Does it respect human rights? The Marxist answer would be that the key to actual freedom resides in the 'apolitical' network of social relations, from the market to the family, which can be transformed not by any political procedure but rather by class struggle. We do not vote on who owns what or about relations in the factory, and soon – such matters remain outside the sphere of the political, and it is illusory to expect that one will effectively change things by 'extending' democracy into the economic sphere. [...] Radical changes in this domain need to be made outside the sphere of legal 'rights'. He thereby concludes that the acceptance of democratic mechanisms as providing the only framework for all possible change is the 'democratic illusion' that prevents any radical transformation of capitalist relations.[14]

A more systematic critique of procedurality is to be gauged in Hallward's call for prescriptive politics:

> *Against alignment with the way of the world, against withdrawal from engagement with the world, it is time to reformulate a prescriptive practice of politics. Prescription is first and foremost an anticipation of its subsequent power, a commitment to its consequences.*[15]

As we will see, prescription entails a whole different model of operation which breaks with procedures that perpetuate the status quo.[16] In place of procedures, a principle is applied as an axiomatic imperative. To use an example from Rancière's account of emancipation, when equality is assumed as an axiom, a point of departure rather than a goal, then another approach to learning is prescribed in which differences in knowledge and

---

13 | Slavoj Žižek, *Living in the End Times* (London: Verso 2010).

14 | Slavoj Žižek, "The Jacobin Spirit", *Jacobin*, no. 3–4, 2011, https://www.jacobinmag.com/2011/05/the-jacobin-spirit/ (last accessed May 24, 2019).

15 | Hallward, "The Politics of Prescription", 771f.

16 | Discussing the standard usage of the phrase 'the will of the people', Hallward comments that it 'usually amounts to nothing more than a token nod to "formal democratic" mechanisms for ensuring some sort of minimal choice in the selection of political representatives [...] apparent respect for the will of the people is an integral aspect of the status quo, and has been so for a long time'. The mainstream discussion of current affairs relegates the will of the people to the democratic procedure of political representation. Hallaward, "From Prescription to Volition", (*The Politics of Alain Badiou*, special issue of *Politics and Culture* (2014), published online 1 September 2014, http://politicsandculture.org/2014/09/01/from-prescription-to-volition-by-peter-hallward/ (last accessed May 24, 2019).

authority no longer matter.[17] Facing objections that prescriptive politics is abstract and universalist, unable to account for the concrete situatedness of contemporary political struggles, Hallward emended his model by elaborating the process of prescribing through the practice of the political will of the people. The main question here is how a dominated or a coerced group of people can free themselves from coercion and 'acquire the power they need to determine their own course of action, consciously, deliberately or "willingly", in the face of the specific obstacles and resistance this course will confront'.[18] In contrast to procedurality, the process of popular mobilisation does not follow a given set of rules. Although it is purposeful, willing a certain outcome, it does not rely on 'a fully formed solution in advance of engaging with the problem'.[19] The subjective commitment involves 'readiness to follow through on a decision and the principles that orient it, the willingness to do what is required to overcome the obstacles, both predictable and unforeseen, that may emerge over the course of its imposition'.[20] In contrast to prefiguration, the principle is prescribed and the end is anticipated, whilst the means is not. It is so because the political will is a capacity that must be renewed and constructed, rather than being an authentic expression of people's purported essence. Hallward outlines a laborious and thorny practice of association, combination and assembly: education, information, deliberation and debate through which a collective defines its priorities, goals and decisions, and many other practices that cultivate collective spirit and brace the gathering against the tendencies that will inevitably threaten to disintegrate it.

The politics of prescription and emancipation that Hallward advocates is largely modelled after past revolutions (French, Haitian, Russian, Chinese and Cuban) and projects a definite future in an indefinite time. The dramaturgy that could envisage it is a plot of linear accumulation, where the long and stumbling process of deliberation eventually leads to action and the effectuation of a systemic social change. This model affirms the effort of involvement as a commitment without representation, not to be measured or interpreted by 'external observers'.[21] It is a doing that can enact known conventions of gathering (the historical examples include Jacobin clubs and workers' councils), but does not necessarily have to be a 'showing doing', representative in its awareness and certainty about how things must be done. By invoking principles rather than procedures and norms, prescriptive politics evades the performativity qua *Leistung*. And it shapes the present as a long-term process towards a future without a guarantee.

17 | Jacques Rancière, *The Ignorant Schoolmaster*, trans. K. Ross (Stanford: Stanford University Press 1991).
18 | Hallward, "From Prescription to Volition", 1.
19 | Ibid, 7.
20 | Ibid.
21 | Ibid, 4.

3 *PREFIGURING* BY PERFORMING

In the prescriptive model, the mobilisation of political will resembles a perennial process of rehearsal for a revolution, a deliberate preparation of a political and ideological ground, of strategy and means for an act of popular sovereignty that will take place at a propitious moment. Even if revolution is never explicitly asserted as the form that the political action will take, it lingers through historical examples that Hallward draws upon. This is exactly the point of divergence from which another, more recently avowed model of political action constitutes itself. Prefiguration dispenses with the horizon of an event projected into a distant future, together with the 20th century model of vanguardism of an intellectual class that will lead the insurrection. Rather, it seeks politics in the reshaping of social relations during or alongside political protests. The 'square' or encampment movements are dubbed the playground of social practices in which social alternatives are imagined and rehearsed. During the occupation of the squares, restructuring of social life and social space was recognised as a feat just as important as the political demands of the protest.[22] As Valeria Graziano points out in her comprehensive account of prefigurative politics, the coming together of the people in the occupation of space expanded the scope of political struggle to include aspects of social reproduction, and not exclusively orienting itself towards the questions of production and political action.[23] Care replaces militancy in that it features reproductive labour in the self-organised activities in which people maintain social life on the streets during protests (food, sleep, medical help, etc.), which is transformed in the aftermath of protests into a regular practice of self-organisation. The significance of the shift lies, as Judith Butler commented, in the collapse of the traditional distinction between the private realm in which social life is maintained and the public stage on which political struggle is enacted.[24] The description of these gatherings as forms of *social* resistance brings together acting and living into one practice, where the conceptual valence of 'practice' discloses performance and temporality about social change.

22 | Mehmet Döşemeci critically examines the concept of revolution in the current social movements and their moments of uprising in Syntagma, Gezi Park and Tahrir square, arguing that people 'did a much better job' than the state organising the reproduction of social life in the squares. See "Don't move, Occupy! Social movement vs social arrest", https://roarmag.org/essays/occupy-revolution-mehmet-dosemeci/ (last accessed November 3, 2013).

23 | Valeria Graziano, "Prefigurative practices. Raw materials for a political positioning of art, leaving the avant-garde" in *Turn Turtle Turn. Performing Urgency #2* (Berlin: House on Fire Publications 2016). I consulted an earlier version of this text in September 2017, now available at https://www.academia.edu/30263516/Prefigurative_Practices._Turn_Turtle_Reenacting_the_Institute._Performing_Urgency_2_House_on_Fire_Publications_2016_

24 | Judith Butler, "Bodies in Alliance and the Politics of the Street", September 2011, http://eipcp.net/transversal/1011/butler/en (last accessed October 1, 2017).

'Be the change you want to see' is the famed slogan of prefiguration that captures the temporal and performative meanings of the practice. In Carl Boggs's early definition (1977), the ultimate goal of the social movement is to *embody* an ongoing political practice through its 'forms of social relations, decision making, culture, and human experience'.[25] Drawing on the legacy of anarchy, direct democracy and self-management of the workers in socialism, embodiment is an emphatic expression for the experience of political participation. One of the most vocal proponents of this model, Marianne Maeckelberg, testifies that only experience could teach her 'horizontality' and 'diversity' in learning by doing.[26] Activist and spokesperson of the grassroots solidarity movement in Greece, Christos Giovanopoulos describes the engagement of the citizens in Athens in the aftermath of the occupation of Syntagma. People took responsibility for the situation in which the welfare state disappeared and the public sector couldn't service citizens' basic needs. This doesn't only entail a reciprocal exchange of skills in organising pharmacies, clinics, kitchens, evening schools, time-banks etc. but also a horizontal process of decision-making.[27] Theorists of prefiguration have recourse to performativity to account for 'collective experimentation'.[28] In their understanding, performance is synonymous with a collective action *here-and-now*. It is also preoccupied with the 'how' just as much as the 'what' the mobilisation is for. 'Political action becomes prefigurative when it fulfils certain conditions in the way in which it is performed'.[29] The doing does in a similar fashion as saying is a kind of doing in performative utterance. Another constitutive characteristic that follows from the direct present of here-and-now is the immanence of means and ends.

'Practising prefigurative politics means removing the temporal distinction between the struggle in the present and a goal in the future; instead, the struggle and the goal, the real and the ideal, become one in the present'.[30] Process is considered to qualify the temporality of the means-ends equivalence. If it is diverse, prefigurative practice must unfold in an open-ended process: 'When goals are multiple and not predetermined, then prefiguration becomes not only strategic, but the best strategy because it is based in practice, in doing, which allows the people who are "doing"

---

25 | Cf. footnote 2.

26 | Marianne Maeckelberg, "Doing is Believing: Prefiguration as Strategic Practice n the Alterglobalization Movement", *Social Movement Studies*, 10, no.1 (2011): 1-20.

27 | See Alexander Koloktronis, "Building Alternative Institutions in Greece: an Interview with Christos Giovanopoulos," *Counterpunch*, March 11, 2016, http://www.counterpunch.org/2016/03/11/building-alternative-institutions-in-greece-an-interview-with-christos-giovanopoulos/ (last accessed July 2016).

28 | See Luke Yates, "Rethinking Prefiguration: Alternatives, Micropolitics and Goals in Social Movements", *academia.edu*, (last accessed in October 2017).

29 | Ibid.

30 | Maeckelberg, "Doing is Believing", 4.

to participate in determining the goals'.[31] Compared to procedurality, the process of self-organisation is more akin to a messy, inefficient improvisation in which principles have to be put at work before any protocol or procedure can be defined. Precisely, because the goals of prefigurative practices aren't predetermined and projected in time – another characteristic that differentiates them from prescription – prefiguration seems the most distant from instrumental reason.

The means-ends equivalence is either used as an argument for a positive account of the lack of clearly defined goals and demands due to a diverse and inclusive political practice[32] or it is regarded a serious deficiency curtailing the political effects. One of the persistent criticisms is that their indistinction allows for blurring individual motives and movement goals, protest and everyday life.[33] Another critique targets the dangers of alternativism, that is to say, the problem of the self-sufficiency of communities enclosed in their own practice and isolated from the society in which they seek to effectuate 'deep change' whilst they are simultaneously dependent on that society in ways they may be theoretically blind to. To counteract the charge of alternativism, prefiguration is said to be exemplary. A prefigurative practice imagines and symbolises the social relations that it seeks to instil. Graziano expounds a threefold function of imagination here: prefiguration unravels something which is no longer present, it symbolises that which is not yet there, and, lastly, it indicates that which exists only as a possibility.[34] The 'imaginal' dimension enables prefigurative practices to extend the process beyond the present through demonstration, a kind of 'showing by doing' of another social imaginary. Another manner in which prefigurative practices view their expansion beyond locality is through insistence on the distribution of the new collective norms born out of collective experimentation. This brings prefiguration closer to the goal of building alternative or counter-institutions, where social change wouldn't only be anticipated or indicated, but partly actualised.[35]

31 | Ibid, 13.

32 | David Graeber writes: 'This is why all the condescending remarks about the movement being dominated by a bunch of dumb kids with no coherent ideology completely missed the mark. The diversity was a function of the decentralized form of organization, and this organization was the movement's ideology', David Graeber, "A Movement of Movements: The New Anarchists", *New Left Review* 13 (2002): 61-73.

33 | The following statement from the interviews Luke Yates conducted with the participants of various organisations and platforms practising prefigurative politics in Spain illustrates how entangled collective social life and political action can be: 'For me, activism and my life are super-mixed-up, I don't know where one starts and the other ends, but at the same time I try to not let activism take over my life totally', Yates, "Rethinking Prefiguration", 18.

34 | Graziano, "Prefigurative Practices".

35 | Daniel Murray advocates counter-institutions as opposed to prefiguration: 'An overemphasis on the value of prefiguration can be debilitating, leading to a focus on internal movement dynamics at the expense of building a broader movement, and a focus on symbolic expressions of dissent as opposed to the development of alternatives to actually replace existing political, economic and social institutions. [...] Instead of prefiguration, we should redirect our efforts toward developing and linking democratic counter-institutions that produce and

In all accounts of prefiguration, terms and instruments of performativity and performing arts have been evoked in a tradition of thinking the social through aesthetic models, such as performance, rehearsal and practice. Some authors recognise the aesthetic mandate of art in general when they attribute to art (and artists engaging in social movements) the capacity to aesthetically shape care, in terms of attending to the senses through animation of the social life and political agitation. Such instrumentalisation doesn't differ in principle from how business and other sectors (education, scientific research, medicine, sports) regard the utility of art for their own purposes of aestheticisation today.[36] A more specific and decisive difference on the artist's role in protest can be found in the organisational capacity that artists and cultural workers use to mobilise citizens for a political concern. The Zagreb-based activist Teodor Celakoski shows how the cultural sector can initiate an intersectoral tactical cooperation around an issue of public interest. In the case of Right to the City, a movement of social resistance to the privatisation of the city infrastructures of Zagreb, independent cultural platforms have been orchestrating a campaign with people concerned by the issue. They help the movement involve actors with various expertise and necessary legal and media support, and they disseminate expert knowledge and experiences of other local struggles.[37]

In comparison with how procedurality associates political and artistic discourses, the notion of practice runs not only through prefiguration but also through the experimental segment of the arts today. Some similarities are striking. Speaking in a schematic manner, we could say that artists and activists of prefiguration privilege the practice over the production (of works of art) or goal-oriented political action, as they prefer practice as a regular activity in which perfecting the means (the how) of doing things is an end in itself. Repetition, rehearsal, effecting changes little by little instead of revolutionary strides, informs a moderate pace of sustaining work and existence fused in one. The insistence on practice without predetermined goals, an experiment with unforeseen outcome, orients the activity towards a speculative present: process, committed to continue and persist despite an uncertain future.

manage common resources'. See "Prefiguration or Actualization? Radical Democracy and Counter-Institution in the Occupy Movement", *Berkeley Journal of Sociology*, November 3, 2014, http://berkeleyjournal.org/author/daniel-murray (last accessed October 1, 2017).

36 | For artification, see 'Artification', Ossi Naukkarinen and Yuriko Saito (Eds.), *Contemporary Aesthetics*, special volume, 2012, https://digitalcommons.risd.edu/liberalarts_contempaesthetics/vol0/iss4/1/ (last accessed January 1, 2017).

37 | See interview with Teodor Celakoski, *Zemos98*, https://archive.org/details/TeocorCelakoski (last accessed January 2017).

4 *TIME BOMBS:* "INSTITUTIONS MUST BE CONSTRUCTED"

Having arrived at the end of this inquiry, I would like to reverse the perspective. Until now, we have observed how political action and its temporality might resemble or be best approached through the conceptual and aesthetic blueprint of performance. Now the same problems discussed under procedurality, prescriptivisim and prefiguration are recast in and through a work of theatre-cum-cinema (i.e. from an artistic perspective). Therefore, I will weave in here the fourth voice of a film-essay in which concerns with temporality, work and political action will be reinvestigated, and lastly I will probe the three models described above.

Time Bombs is a film-essay in the form of an experimental documentary made after three performance events organised by the Croatian performing arts collective BADco. At the end of 2015 and the beginning of 2016, the performing arts collective BADco. organised three twenty-four-hour events occupying former industrial, public spaces that were left to decay during recent decades in the cities of Rijeka, Split and Zagreb. The eight members of BADco invited other artists, cultural workers and activists, film crews and stage workers as well as spectators, film extras and clubbers to spend a full day planned and divided into eight hours of work, eight hours of culture and education and eight hours of rest or sleep. '8-8-8' evokes the popular labour slogan of workers in the 1880s who demanded the workday be limited to eight hours so that there would be eight hours left for sleep, and eight hours 'for what we will'.[38]

In times when artistic and most freelance labour has become atomised and extended to subsume the whole life of an individual twenty-four-seven under work, when artistic production is eventalised, that is, transformed by the experience economy of spectacular events, an invitation to the audience to attend and participate in the 8+8+8 day asks for an unusual effort. Moreover, paying them to participate – to watch a performance reconstructed before them and act as extras in the film that is being shot with them at the same time – is a somewhat quaint gesture, which the voiceover in the film reflects by referencing a custom from Ancient Athenian theatre. Everyone was paid there, comments the narrator, not only the actors hired by the polis, but also the spectators whose wages came from the public fund called Theorikon! Sharing the same etymological root for watching and contemplating (*theorein*) is no coincidence: the spectators were citizens paid to attend a theatre play which was a form of public political activity, a manner of participating in a discussion on political matters. BADco.

---

38 | The first recorded use of this slogan is thought to have occurred during a Federation of Organized Trades and Labor Unions rally in Milwaukee on May 1, 1886.

revives this custom by paying their spectators-as-extras to take part in all three eight-hour long activities, of which the time for culture and education corresponds to the hours in which they engage in discussions with the artists, cultural workers and cultural activists about the future of infrastructures in times of crisis. In the words of BADco. themselves: 'Our objective is to analyse and critically reflect, from an artistic point of view, the disintegration of institutions faced with austerity measures, lack of their responsibility for the endangered cultural sector as well as transition of institutions from the field of production to the field of presentation'.[39]

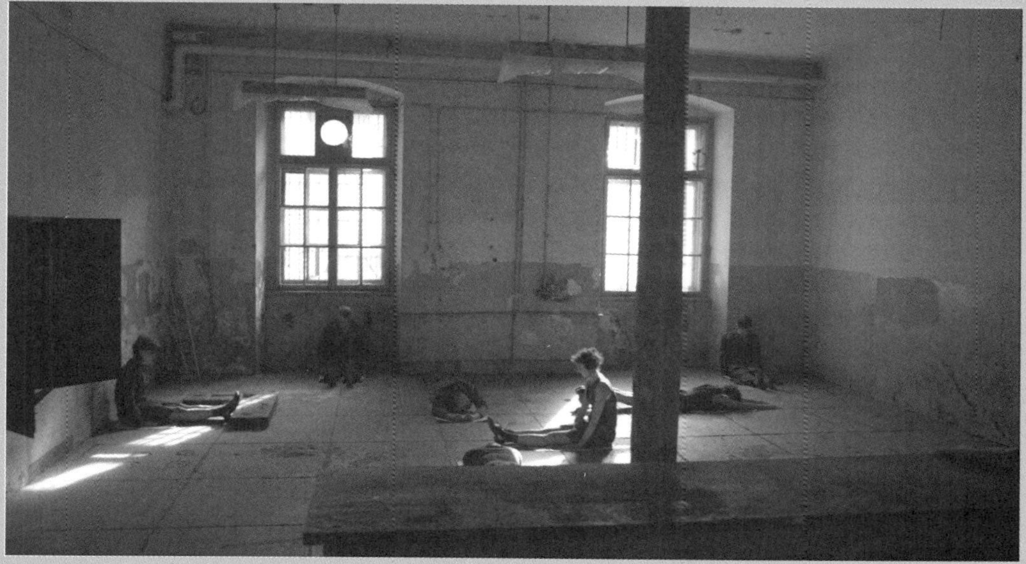

The spectators-as-extras are paid to work: they are watching an excerpt from BADco.'s performance *1 poor and one zero* (2008), a reconstruction of which they will thereafter take part in at the factory site in front of a film camera (shooting the future film *Time Bombs*). In a scene from this performance, BADco. are rechoreographing and performing live the first film by the Lumière brothers – the fifty-second-long film *Workers Leaving the Factory*, shot in Lyon – whilst it is screened above them (see figures 1 and 2). The analysis of the three versions of this movie, which differ in their gaze as well as in the organisation of the bodies of workers walking out of the factory gates, occasions a reflection on times of work and times of production. The refrain repeats like a circle: scenarios can turn into rehearsals, rehearsals can turn into fifty-second-long experiments and this short experiment can become an eight-hour endeavour. Time expands and

Figure 2.1 BADco., *Time Bombs*, 2017. Photo: Dinko Rupčić. Courtesy of the author.

39 | See http://badco.hr/en/news-item/institutions-split-zagreb-2016 (last accessed November 2017). Whilst extras/spectators were paid, artists and cultural workers invited to speak about the problematics of infrastructure today were not, which effects a striking reversal of paid and unpaid roles.

contracts, accumulates and dilates along the axis of poetics and production, as a story can turn into an essay, an essay can become a scenario and a scenario specifies eight hours of work, like the experimental documentary by the artist Tomislav Gotovac which envisages a worker filmed during eight hours of their work in a factory without interruption, in one static shot. But in the scene of the workers leaving the factory an allegory of the end of production is displayed. The image is taken as a visual trope for the 'interruption of work [which] becomes a new industry – the industry of free time'.[40] In a terse commentary, one of the performers of BADco., Tomislav Medak, says, addressing the spectators-as-extras in front of him (figure 3):

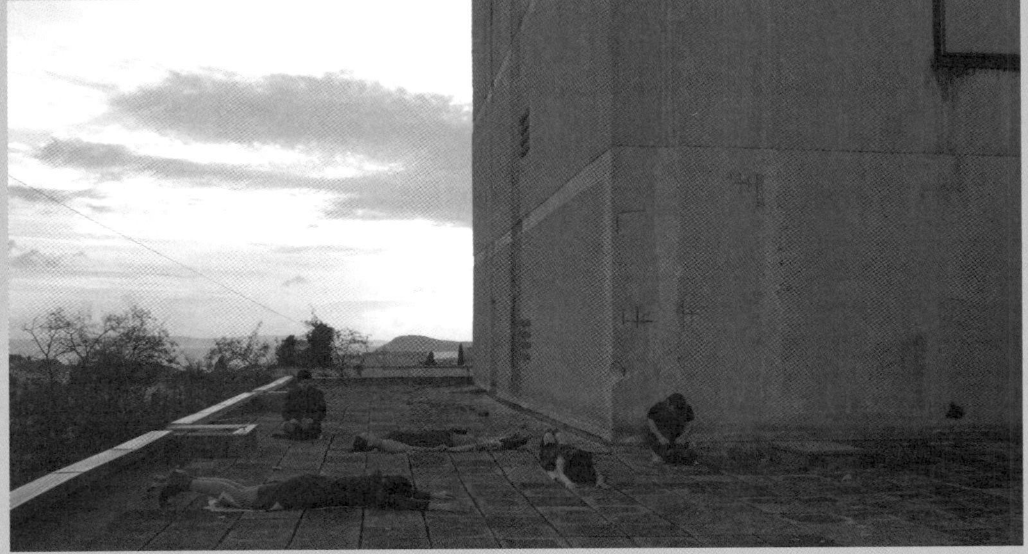

Figure 2.2 BADco., *Time Bombs*, 2017. Photo: Dinko Rupčić. Courtesy of the author.

'It is us – at the factory gates and THEM at the factory gates.
It is us – us now, a century of film history down the line, reenacting them – the Lumières and their workers.
It is us – us present, and them in celluloid and memory.
It is never us, it is always about her.
It is us – me, him, him, her, us and you too.
It is us, in so many ways not us.'

'Us, in so many ways not us' might be a poetic way of defining the gathering in proximity without belonging, a condition that the queer theorist of affect, Lauren Berlant, reserves for the commons: 'The crowded but disjointed propinquity of the social calls for a proxemics, the study of sociality as proximity quite distinct from the possessive attachment languages of

40 | All subsequent quotes from the film are taken from the English subtitles. The text is originally spoken in Croatian.

belonging'.[41] Amongst the many tropes it can hold, the famed scene of workers leaving the factory, for BADco., marks a shift from the situation in which cultural institutions were committed to the production of art and culture to the present moment when these institutions are primarily preoccupied with the management of the art recipient's experience. The factory serves as a pivotal metaphor for the vicissitudes of historical transformations which the institution qua apparatus of production and building on site has gone through. This account is told with a fatuous simplicity, as a nasty fairy tale, recounting 'turns' and 'returns' of property relations and divisions of labour:

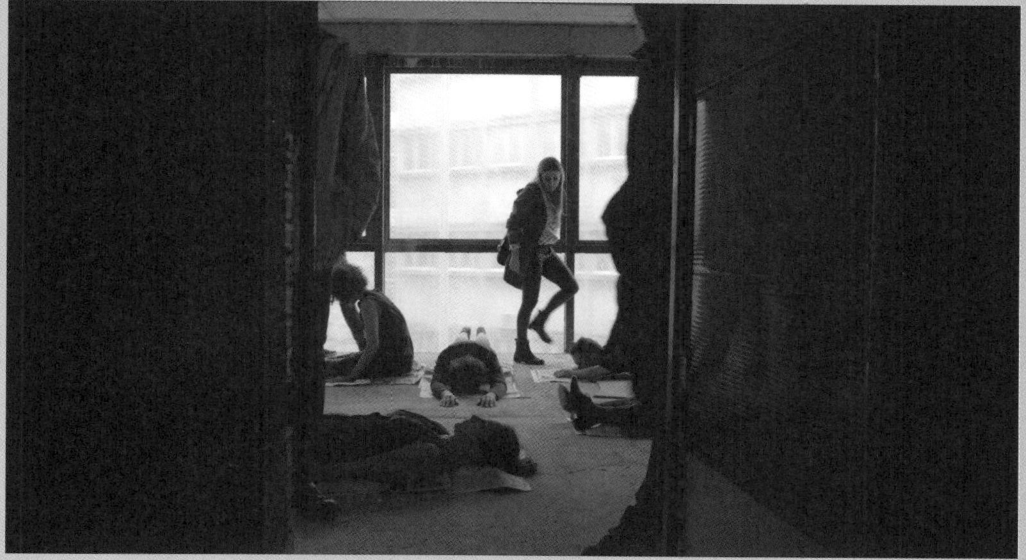

Figure 2.3 BADco., *Time Bombs*, 2017. Photo: Dinko Rupčić. Courtesy of the author.

'First we left the villages and went into factories. And they told us: "These are your hands, this is our factory". We left our hands in the factory but we didn't get the factory. They told us: "This is our factory".
We left to another factory trusting, however: "This is not our factory either".

Then we took matters into our hands and took over the factories and they said: "This is factory of all of us now".
Then we were returned to factories, and returned again, and they kept returning the factories to us, and finally to themselves. A constant returning. Several returns and several lay-offs. Several turns and several overturns.
And again, we left the factory and they said: "This is no longer a factory".
We left the factory for good and our departure is recorded in images.
We entered the image and made the image move.

41 | Lauren Berlant, "The commons: Infrastructures for troubling times", *Environment and Planning D: Society and Space* 34, no. 3 (2016): 395.

 # BOJANA CVEJIĆ – THE PROCEDURAL, THE PRE-

The history encompasses the passage from feudalism to industrial capitalism, then to socialism and self-management of the workers and lastly to the turbulent makeovers and takeovers during the period of postsocialist privatisation. It must be told together with the urban transformations that built and dismantled, deserted and isolated and eventually repopulated and revamped factories into cultural venues. Such is the destiny of the places in which *Time Bombs* are shot (the ex-industrial complex Rikard Benčić in Rijeka, Zagreb's POGON Jedinstvo – Centre for Independent Culture and Youth and the never completed Youth Centre in Split.) Recapitulating a

Figure 2.4
BADco., *Time Bombs*, 2017. Photo: Dinko Rupčić. Courtesy of the author.

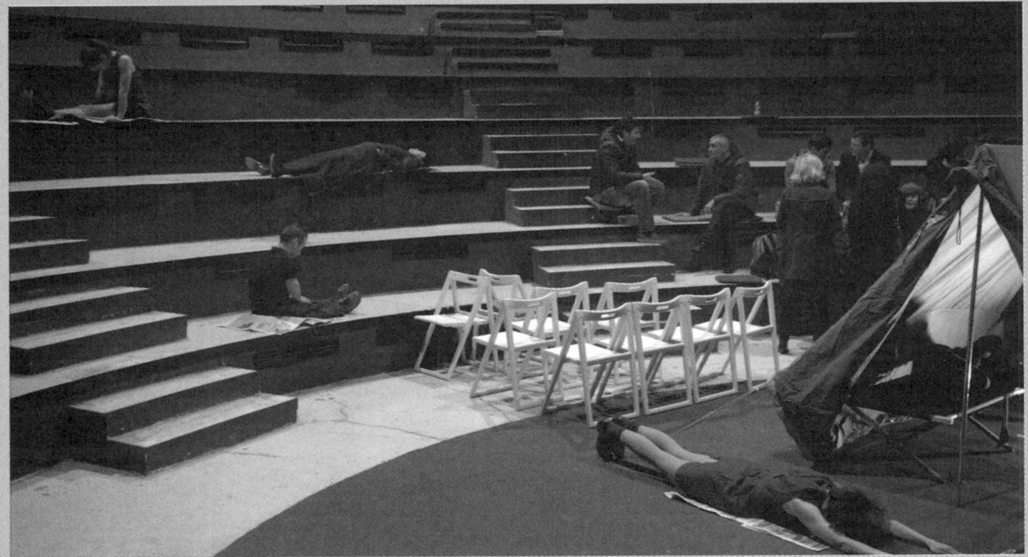

series of technological developments of production and reproduction from the 18th century, from which the first public theatres date, to the urban and cultural policies of the 1990s, the narrator concludes: 'Institutions are time bombs'. What is the temporality and the politics from which this work of film and performance acts?

In *Time Bombs* the occupation of the factory doesn't claim a future, a future of infrastructures that the artists, together with their spectators, attempt to imagine prefiguratively. On the contrary, it summons up history, as if the most important lesson is not to forget that past from which utopian promises haven't been fulfilled. The historical memory is rekindled by bringing forth the utopian revelation of the New Man in the Soviet Cubo-Futurist imaginary of the 1920s. Artists from those past times are compared to 'ufonauts', if UFO stands for an institution as a 'universal fictitious operation, universally-cultural futurologic operation'. Amongst many artworks from historical and postwar avant-gardes and conceptual art, we could recall Konstantin Melnikov's plan for a Green City and its building named *Sonata of Sleep* from 1929. This pre-Stalin-age project aimed to provide a place in which workers would rest and replenish themselves. Air and sounds were to be scientifically investigated in order to intensify sleep and dream. In the last five years, the U.S. Defense Department has been investing in the study of a species of birds that can survive for several days without sleep, the aim of which is, as Jonathan Crary has argued, 'the creation of the sleepless soldier', the precursor of the sleepless worker.[42]

Against the procedures that cultural institutions impose, and without the authority to prescribe or prefigure the future, artists can renew our capacity to reimagine and reconstruct the history we don't have to give up. As with buildings and customs, people can be dispossessed of their history too in the wake of neoliberal presentism, whilst that history holds in store the courage that is necessary to act in the present.

* * *

In a few closing remarks, the four thinking models I have shown can at last be juxtaposed. *Time Bombs* has gained us an acute sense of the present's vicissitudes. It puts to work art's capacity to renarrate the present situation with a discontinuous insight into the future as it has been imagined by the past. As a work of performance, it doesn't impel its audience to political action. Its remit lies in educating a public through the history of avant-garde and socialist experiments that are nowadays judged as unsuccessful and unrealistic projections. The recollection of the historical transformation of institutions as places of production (factory, theatre, cinema) is thought to license an attempt to reimagine institutions in the present crisis for a different future. Such displacements of past and future are expelled from both the proceduralist and prefigurative modes of action. Proceduralism affixes us to a present, barring both the past and the future from our imagination by the force of instrumental reason. Perform by the standard of these procedures or else you will lose your grip on the real!

Even if they share principles and values with the leftist avant-gardes, prefigurative practices part with that past on account of its inefficacy. The gap between the critical present and a utopian vanguardist future must be bridged by prolepsis. The present in which we act and the future in which our actions should bear fruit of deep systemic change are reconciled by representative performance. The ways we live and act now might be confined

---

42 | Jonathan Crary, *24/7: Late Capitalism and the End of Sleep* (London and New York: Verso 2013).

to small-scale experimental collectives or midscale social movements and punctual mobilisations, but by and large they are exemplary of social transformation. It only requires a leap of faith, if not imagination, to claim the future effectiveness of our present actions. By contrast, prescriptivism, and its successive account of political will, repudiates the present in its power to sustain a status quo. According to this model, a long way of political education, assembly and action is needed in order to transform society with equality and other principles of democracy. The process of forming the political will for political action doesn't rely on existing procedures and images, but searches and fabricates the means of struggle in its course. The threshold of political action is set high here, demanding a wide-reaching popular and collective engagement. And the future remains remote, without guarantee.

GATHERINGS: BETWEEN DEMOCRATIC AND TECHNOCRATIC EUROPEAN CULTURAL SPACE

One of the most outspoken critics of the recent political changes in Hungary and Eastern Europe in general, Gáspár Miklós Támás, explained once in an interview that 'what is missing from liberal democracy is socialism, what has disappeared is a working class'.[1] According to him, ruling elites could prosper so successfully in recent decades because they are not threatened anymore from within, there is actually no political adversary. Such disappearance of the tension and destruction of the political dynamic between classes which was crucial for the whole 20th century (and which also strongly influenced the relationships between art and politics), caused a destructive social system with the absolute victory of the rule of the market and the dissolution of all other alternatives. The result is a strange capitalist utopia in Eastern Europe, where the rule of market is actually more ruthlessly actualised than in some other Western European states (erasing every trace of the social state, political discussion about the notion of the public, the public role of art etc.), and it is deeply entangled with illiberal, post-fascist and nationalist tendencies. In this sense these political developments are disclosing the internal connection between neoliberalism and fascism, supported by corruption and privilege, nationalism and radical reevaluation of the notion of the public sphere. Performance practices and their institutions are offering us an interesting opportunity to study these

1 | Gáspár Miklós Támás, Political Critique, July 28, 2016, http://politicalcritique.org/cee/hungary/2016/the-rule-of-the-market-in-east-central-europe-is-absolute-interview/.

processes, not only because many of them came under attack from illiberal democratic movements but also because of their public aspect, the ways in which they enable gatherings and frame assemblies of the people. Here we can observe symptoms of the disintegration of the notion of the public, the ways the political understanding of the public is intertwined with post-fascist, nationalist, populist and illiberal tendencies.

Támár's statement about the disappearance of the working class is no nostalgic call for the return of socialism. Instead it helps us grasp the main features of the process of transition. Transition was one of the main political processes in Eastern Europe since the beginning of the 1990s, much celebrated by Western democracies as the main progressive political and cultural development. It can be described as a process of catching up, socially, culturally, economically, with the so-called developed democracies. In this process Europe functions as a specific ideological territory, which is still not there and has yet to be reached. In the transition, Eastern European citizens are perceived as innocent political children, ideal subjects without history who should be moulded for a renewed democratic beginning. Boris Buden describes how the 'repressive infantilisation of the societies that were liberating themselves from communism, is the main political feature of the so-called post-communist condition'.[2] The passage of the transition itself is not another particular historical epoch, but rather a transition to the time that is not yet there. In such a process, the subject is deprived of its own (historical) political dimension; it exists in innocence without any conception of its own political past. The notion of the East 'erases the political dimension from the Eastern past and achieves equal effects in the present'.[3] The outcome of such an infantilisation of (political) subjects, described by Buden as a feature of transition, can be found nowadays closing down the transitional process in a very cynical way through patriarchal, nationalistic and hierarchical populism. Populist and nationalist movements are retaining the ideological narrative of awakening their nations from their political infancy, operating through various processes of reevaluation, rebirth after the end of socialism, but the goals of these processes are far away from the agonistic dimension of democracy and the demand for equality and difference that characterised this process at the beginning of the nineties. The process of the transition didn't fail because the people were not yet ready for democracy; it was doomed to failure from the beginning. It is proceeding parallel to the erasure of autonomous (socialist, leftist, avant-garde) political histories of the past, taking away the autonomy of political subjects. In this process

2 | Boris Buden, *Cona Prehoda. O koncu postkomunizma* (Ljubljana: Krtina 2014), 36.
3 | Rastko Močnik, "Europe as a Problem", unpublished paper, quoted in Boris Buden, "The Post-Yugoslavian Condition of Institutional Critique", November 2007, http://eipcp.net/transversal/0208/buden/en (last accessed May 24, 2019).

of transition the communist past is translated into a cultural and not into a political phenomenon, and instead of the agonist history of different political forces, what stays at the end is a history of political inferiority. Nationalist and populist ruling elites are exploring and appropriating precisely that political inferiority which in recent decades constituted the relationship between the East and the West of Europe. In these processes inferiority is entangled with the celebration of nationalism and hegemonic cultural appropriation of history. This means that subjects of the cultural reformation are again not approached as political subjects but as infantile inhabitants who have to be transformed by the ideas of the political parties and leaders: either into the populist visions of the nations, governed by the fear of globalisation, or into the paternalistic state with its own idea of the pacified public, erasing oppositional voices and different forms of life in order to rule over the economy and to privatise without constraint.

This social and cultural background is crucial for the disentanglement of the paradoxes surrounding the positioning of performance and other artistic practices and their institutions in the environments governed by populist and illiberal understandings of political institutions. In this essay I am especially interested in the difficult processes going on in attacks on performances, performance festivals and other artistic events, attacks which all relate to the rise of populism. For example, the nationalist and conservative attacks on art institutions in Poland have the clear political agenda of resisting inter-nationality, equality of genders, openness of values and nonhierarchical approaches to the production of art in performance institutions. The results have been several severe cuts and radical reevaluations of institutions and festivals, like Malta in Poznan or Konfrontacje in Lublin in the year 2016, or populist and violent political attacks on the alleged moral decrepitude or lack of patriotism in the performances of theatre director Oliver Frljić in Croatia or Poland. This often happens together with the criminalisation of artists and the reevaluation of national and state institutions. But it can also be related to the series of austerity measures and cuts to nongovernmental cultural sectors, which are often used as series of reevaluations and adjustments towards a more hierarchical and populist understanding of art, throwing many artistic agents into invisibility and poverty and marginalising their already precarious situation even more. Therefore, the same paternalistic and populist discourse which characterises governance of citizens is also at work when observing the position of art practices and art institutions: space for the plurality of expression and alternative forms of art is rapidly narrowing, making way for strong interventions into the multiplicity of cultural expression and assembly and strong attacks on the aesthetic and political plurality of gatherings. These attacks can take various forms, such as the cutting off of government money for experimental forms of performance especially engaged with the equality of forms and expressions, with shifting between art, politics and education and opening up other ways of coming together. The field of creation becomes endangered and intentionally pushed into poverty, diminishing and mocking every argumentation in favour of institutional and economic equality. From the side of the cultural institutions, this is often interpreted as an ignorance on the part of politicians towards more experimental and alternative forms of art. But we have to read these cuts also as an open rejection of any idea of institutional public equality that would enable different kinds of gatherings, expressions and embodiments of the audience and their expressions of the political. With these processes, institutional hierarchies and privileges are strengthened, and some forms of coming together are more privileged than others, with many alternative ways of expressing becoming marginal, invisible and even criminalised. These attacks can also take the form of the stigmatisation of the cultural enemy and can demand the reevaluation of culture in general, which can also be transformed into a cultural war. Here artists and art institutions are becoming the enemies of the values defended by ruling populism as well as popular targets of rising post-fascist tendencies that celebrate the aestheticisation of cultural expressions and nationalistic reevaluations of cultural institutions as such. The common result of various attacks is then to disable every hint of institutional equality of gatherings and make such common practices invisible. The goal is to erase the infrastructural support which is needed not only for survival of those practices, but also for the continuity of autonomous political and aesthetic expression.

That's why I would propose thinking austerity cuts to government monies for alternative and nongovernmental art institutions in the same frame as open attacks on the values of various artistic practices, which go together with a reevaluation of the role of art and a need to wash it clean of multiculturalism, globalism, inclusion of the other. Even if these are varied approaches, they can all be thought together as the reevaluation of the public and the ways the public assembles, infrastructurally supported by the artistic institution. What is desired, then, is to close down cultural expressions which work towards plural and open public space, any space of various publics using parallel and nonhierarchical modes of production, expression and endurance; to silence the defenders of plurality of expressions and disable any imagination of other alternatives. On the surface, this can be detected as the moral condemnation of the lazy artist, who is not only dependent on public money (in Slovenian there is the expression *pri koritu*, meaning 'waiting to be fed like a pig') but is also, because of her or his laziness, also a corrupt personality whose sole interest is to steal taxpayer money. The ironic side of this accusation is that it directly exemplifies the creation of a scapegoat: the anger which should be directed towards the corrupt and privileged elite, the real beneficiaries of the process of transition striking, is actually turned towards marginalised artists and other social parasites, themselves much softer targets, easier objects of anger. An excellent example for this ironic twist is the case of Russian theatre and film director Kirill Serebrennikov, who faces up to ten years in prison on fraud charges. Serebrennikov, who was often openly critical towards Putin and his government, but also towards the orthodox church, was accused in the year 2017 of spending government money intended for his *Platforma Theatre Project* for himself. Even though *Platforma Theatre* presented the performances and there are many audience members who saw and witnessed them, the judges wouldn't change their argumentation: the performances were never created. This argumentation shows us the utterly cynical attitude of the government towards those audiences: the gathering is utterly invisible and marginalised; even if there is proof that it happened, it doesn't count anymore. In the same way, three Slovenian artists who renamed themselves Janez Janša, thereby officially taking on the name of the Slovenian right-wing populist politician Janez Janša, were accused of intended fraud by then prime minister of Slovenia, Janez Janša, who stated in a radio interview in 2010 that this name change was helping the artists swindle and rent out apartments in Paris under his name whilst the invoices were sent to him. Such moral condemnations are transforming artists very effectively into scapegoats, which turns the justified anger of artists and other marginal subjects who are dependent on state support towards the corrupt elite. This is also paving the way to the criminalisation and condemnation of other disobedient subjects of the state: people should be subjected to the new moral and political order, which originates from a dangerous mixture of market ideology, technocratic management and paternalistic nationalism.

At the same time, from the perspective of the growing populist and right-wing movement, art practices espousing alternative expressions are seen as symptomatic of a decay of culture, a devaluation of art and a failure of globalisation and internationalism often described as 'everything goes'. This can be read as the paradoxical outcome of the transition process, a finalisation of the transformation from political infancy to the political subjects who are yet to come. The transition failed, because from the beginning it was problematically grounded on the infantilisation of Eastern societies. Instead of democratic subjects, it formed new political subjects, not democratic ones but ones which are constituted around the erasure of democratic, Western liberal society itself, around the archaic, nationalistic and populist values and ideas of the nation. These populist movements actually adopted this belief in the infantilisation of socialist societies (no democratic practice, the erasure of the memory of the left, of socialist ideas and history), but they also approached it with paternalistic and authoritarian measures. So what the new populist and nationalist movements are doing now is actually to repair democratic, Western liberal society itself. In its place arises the idea of the moralistic, paternalistic and nationalistic state, an illiberal democracy where the main glue between the ruling elites is actually corporate brotherhood, the erasure of any social state, gender equality and the radical re-evaluation of what citizenship actually means.

In this situation contemporary art institutions (in this essay, especially ones which are related to performance) are not only under attack but also inhabit a difficult and ambivalent crossroads. Here I would like to introduce another dimension to the discussion, which can show to us why this political situation is also so crucial for the multiplicity of cultural expressions and gatherings. The cultural conflict that is often part of public discussions when cuts are made, when the institutions are endangered and artists come under attack, clearly signals the desire of the ruling elites for infantile and submissive political culture where political subjectivity would be obedient, passive and governed hierarchically and where values cannot be further examined, subverted or transgressed. But this is only one part of the problem; what is going on here is actually a hegemonic fight, a fight between different cultural articulations and the imaginations of how it is possible to live together, and not a conflict between conservatives and progressives, between institutionalised frames of culture and its nongovernmental part. These questions are very intriguing if we observe them from the perspective of the dynamic relationship between Eastern and Western Europe, especially from the perspective of the history of the cultural exchange between different cultural operators and actors in the cultural field. The transition period deeply marked the formation of artistic institutions, especially in the nongovernmental field, where almost all developed their structures through cooperations, networks (related to European cultural funding), festivals, residencies, coproductions etc. I would even claim, even if this has yet to be studied in detail, that the independent or nongovernmental cultural sector and its development in the West is tightly linked to processes of transition and the opening of the territory of Europe to the south and the east. European cultural politics, as we know them today, still owe a lot to their founding event, the fall of the Berlin Wall, but unfortunately not so much to the people who destroyed this wall, the people who were the cause of this event. This development is tightly intertwined with another historical genealogy, namely, the economic expansion of neoliberalism. In this sense the transitional development of cultural and artistic institutions is not so much related to their democratisation but much more to their professionalisation. The process of professionalisation is the crucial process of how artistic institutions were reformed, with the example of a few more collaborative and nonhierarchical formations. Professionalisation makes the nongovernmental institutions capable of applying for public money and should make them equal to others, but at the same time it also transforms them politically bringing them much closer to self-exploitative, flexible and precarious forms of work. In this sense, it is possible that the most exploitative forms of flexible work are instilled in these institutions, and collaboration is actually changing the institutions into competitive units. This competitiveness could even be measured by their progressiveness and their political context, which of course is an utter paradox, although it makes sense when being thought as a part of neoliberal cultural hegemony. That also helps us to understand why the contra-strategy cannot come anymore form the progressive and provocative agenda of art, because art institutions themselves and many artistic practices are very deeply entangled with neoliberalism and its commodification, with its destruction of the forms of alternative life, with the exploitation of a precarious working force. It is perfectly possible today to produce a radical political content with the most precarious and exploited working force, with governance over its subjects through self-exploitation. In the end, the outcome is competition between cultural agents and contest based on skilfulness in project management, networking and logistical operations through which differences are negotiated and turned into cultural products.

The way performance was produced and the way institutions operating on the field of performance and similar events supported assemblies of people, became more and more generic, especially in the time, paradoxically, of a growing interest in participation and other forms of convening. This has a lot to do with the efficient management and logistical organisation of the institution, by which they prepare for participation in various financial and political networks. The professionalisation then enabled the aesthetic production of differences on one side, but on the other it diminished the politics of those very differences, a diminishment mostly detected as the generalisation of cultural and political expressions. The live gatherings in events, festivals and other performances produced by these institutions, are becoming multiple but simultaneously also the same: their political content can easily be shared and fluctuates because it belongs to the general desire for emancipation and freedom, where we are mostly gathering to gaze at others gathering to emancipate themselves, then share their experiences, their images, their gestures etc. In this sense such circulation becomes a part of the smooth travel of cultural products, where gatherings of people are generalised in the same way as the global economy equalises its products, with the help of a cosmopolitan class of people. On the other side, labouring, immobile and particular material processes of production are becoming more and more invisible. That's also why innovative artists, when striving for recognition, cannot avoid the fact that it might finally only be either recognition on the market or a competitive winning of the biggest financial share of public money. The sad truth is that this can only bring safety to the very few; only a few artists can start temporarily working beyond everyday flexibility and precarious networks of friends. Many of those so-called 'progressive' institutions are part of the neoliberal hegemonic discourse which celebrates the difference but also the continuous flexibility of the working force, affirming innovation but also accelerating work through logistical, organisational and management procedures. They open up political discourses about art but at the same time erase them from their situational embeddedness, divide them from their always conflictual structure belonging to the here and now of practice. Artistic production works with political emotions and affects, awareness of political issues, problems, etc., demanding freedom of expression, but at the same time many artistic institutions make use of the precarious flexibility of workers of which they themselves are so critical. In this sense the artistic practice of work is similar to all other precarious working conditions, with the difference that it retains the symbolic value of working in the art field: a symbolic value of political awareness, criticality and friendship, which, paradoxically, instead of diminishing dependence on forms of exploitation, establishes it even more strongly. Cultural institutions are inhabiting a paradoxical position: they can despise the market economy and representation dynamic to which they belong, but at the same time with the inventing of critical and political contexts also often perpetuate the very same dynamic, especially with the submission of projects and new applications, with the optimisation of the organisation and flexibility of their workers. In the situation of the precarious life, where life is governed through precariousness and a continuous feeling of insecurity, current institutional work sometimes functions as a cruel optimism[4]: a belief in the very narratives that keep us going, even if they are at the same time utterly destructive for us.

Many cultural operators are suffering today under a repeated series of shocks originating not only from the continuous fight for survival and the burdens of their precarious situation, but also from the challenged political position of the cultural gathering as such, especially when related to the institutionalised frame of performance events: Why are people actually brought together? Why is there any gathering? What is the value of the

4 | See Laurent Berlant, *Cruel Optimism* (Durham: Duke University Press 2018).

events, festivals, networks, performances, ways that people are brought together, especially from that paradoxical perspective? Cultural gatherings enabled with the operation of non-governmental institutions, alternative festivals, performances and some exhibitions, are currently existing in this ambivalence. On one side, they are opening up the space for the not yet truly creative class; they are initiators of gentrification and the place for rehearsals of communicability and affectability for the future workers, mostly ignoring gender, race and class differences or at least abstracting them from their embodiment and situatedness. But at the same time, exactly these institutions are also enabling a significant and very important affective, aesthetic and embodied proximity to the issues and values of otherness, openness, equality, tolerance and solidarity, which are under attack from populist and nationalistic tendencies in political movements. They are researching infrastructural ways and forms of support for bringing people together and opening up possible political and aesthetic forms for assemblies, affectionately working towards another imagination of life and being together, but also reimagining the autonomy of another political history. That's why it is very important to address the value of those contemporary events, festivals, performances, networks, works of artists, research processes, and reexamine the political and social role of gatherings. This is especially crucial in a situation where institutions are confronted, on the one side, with the pressure of political populism and nationalism and, on the other, with the pressure to produce more and more through the use of flexibility and precarious ways of working. How to reflect in this situation upon the artistic institution as an imaginative construction, as an infrastructure for the imaginative and alternative gathering, with practical, situational and performative consequences for the ones who are willing to participate in the performances and other similar events? We should first critically approach the mechanisms which are producing generalisations of expressions and which are very tightly related to the ways these institutions are working, or to return to the words of Támás at the beginning of the essay, to the conditions of the disappearance of the working class. In most of these institutions work is done because of our desires, so most of the time we work voluntarily. There is nothing wrong with voluntary work per se, but its affective drive should be turned from the feeling of self-exploitation to emancipation in collaboration with others: to work and enable forms of life together. This would be a way to return to autonomous political practices and relate them to infrastructural knowledge and support of art institutions, rather than optimising them and making them even more successful in the struggle for the remains of public money. They should instead be transformed into other, maybe only temporary spaces that would, through their modes of instituting, challenge the general way art is produced today and also how it is related to its economic and political value.

We can learn something helpful here from the failed narrative of transition, something also helpful for environments that don't share the same political and cultural circumstances but are nevertheless confronted with the same populist turn in politics. What was crucial in this narrative of transition was an erasure of political autonomy, a denial of political subjectivation, a denial of the historicity of its own subjects, of the fact that there was a political history at work before the historic rupture, the fall of the Berlin Wall. Professionalisation functioned also as a replacement and generalisation of any political singularity and went hand in hand with neoliberal tendencies to generalise expressions and commodify culture. Institutionally organised gatherings like festivals, performances, events and other kinds of coming together slowly lost their political and situational embeddedness, their various temporal and imaginative practices, and they became more and more generalised in the commodified and inconsequential narrative about democratic emancipation. So, the false ideological promise of a common European cultural space as was so present in many professional developments of institutions, should be addressed and disclosed in its dependence on the power dynamic between the ones who are equipped with rich contemporary cultural history and the one who still have a ways to go before they get there, arising from political infancy. If we want to develop our thinking about processes of instituting, this political infancy at their core has to be disclosed as something actually derived from the neoliberal and technocratic idea of the European cultural space, which is also at the core of the new nationalist and populist movements. This is what these different movements have in common: they both need a political subject who is never awoken from his or her historical invisibility, neither as subject of radical commodification where histories are continuously reinvented nor as a subject of nationalistic pride, where he has to be reinvented as a member of the community.

The political battle against populism will not yield results if at the same time the generalisation and flexibility of work in artistic institutions is not addressed. The institutions have to be thought more as material processes of production with different temporal and spatial dynamics; not so easily exchangeable, they should be opened up as a vivid political space of different adversaries. What I mean with this is that we have to think about possible temporalities of institutional and instituting work, which would not be subsumed under the temporality of the project, logistical excellence and management organisation but would instead work through an infrastructural dimension: supporting and enabling practices of coming together in their political, embodied and temporal singularity, deeply entangled with the micropolitical environment. I would think about the live gathering here as a contingent sum of many different, also contradictory, forces that are simultaneously only accessible through multiple, but at the same time singular, political dynamics. There is something interesting in the micropolitical dimension of the gathering, which can strengthen the contingent and paradoxical coming together of different social and cultural forces and make it possible to imagine expressions that would not be easily shareable and exchangeable in a global scope but would nevertheless circulate as a complex and demanding process of translation. This way of thinking is of course far away from the logistical idea of optimisation and flexibility, which today is so strongly grounding the ways gatherings are made public and how their aesthetic expression is shared. Many performances are shared the same way other political gatherings are, with a lack of complexity of their translations and a demand for instant satisfaction. They are shared through the circulation of instant images, documents, circulating affectionately around macropolitical gestures of emancipation, but without the complexity, antagonism and difficult processes of political subjectivation. This process of political subjectivation would, namely, demand another temporality and engagement with the event, acknowledging the failures, ruptures, misunderstandings and deep ambivalence of the gathering itself, of coming together, without an easy identification with either us or them, but nevertheless continuously being-with.

If imagination today seems to be colonised by the right and the right seems it could win the hegemonic battle, this also happens to be the case because of the ways capitalism works on our subjectivities and their desire to belong. What would be important to admit when we are thinking about performances and their gatherings is that the field of imagination is a conflictual and agonistic field where aesthetic expressions and creative changes and ruptures play a significant role. However, these expressions are not projected onto the future, but already practised *as if*, as if the changes are already there. This performative moment in the instituting process should also be important when thinking about gatherings and their value; it can be also be thought as the imaginative practice: doing as if. With such imaginative practices it is possible to develop strategies and representations, articulations to address hegemonic consciousness, to subvert images and representations fed to the cultural imagination and to resist the ways these representations are produced. Performance is not progressive per se, but it has this radical micropolitical capacity for aesthetic invention and poetic playfulness that can open complexities and show us the paradoxes we are living with today – when it brings a group of people together. Performance can then open expressions for alternative ways of living and incite displacement in already existing structures, opening up discourse and initiating change – but this can only be possible if it can be made, produced and endured as a set of various multiple practices, temporalities, collaborations and not as a generalised and managed mode of production. To imagine and come together as if it is possible to radically change the value of that which is yet to be done in a valuable and very present way, right now.

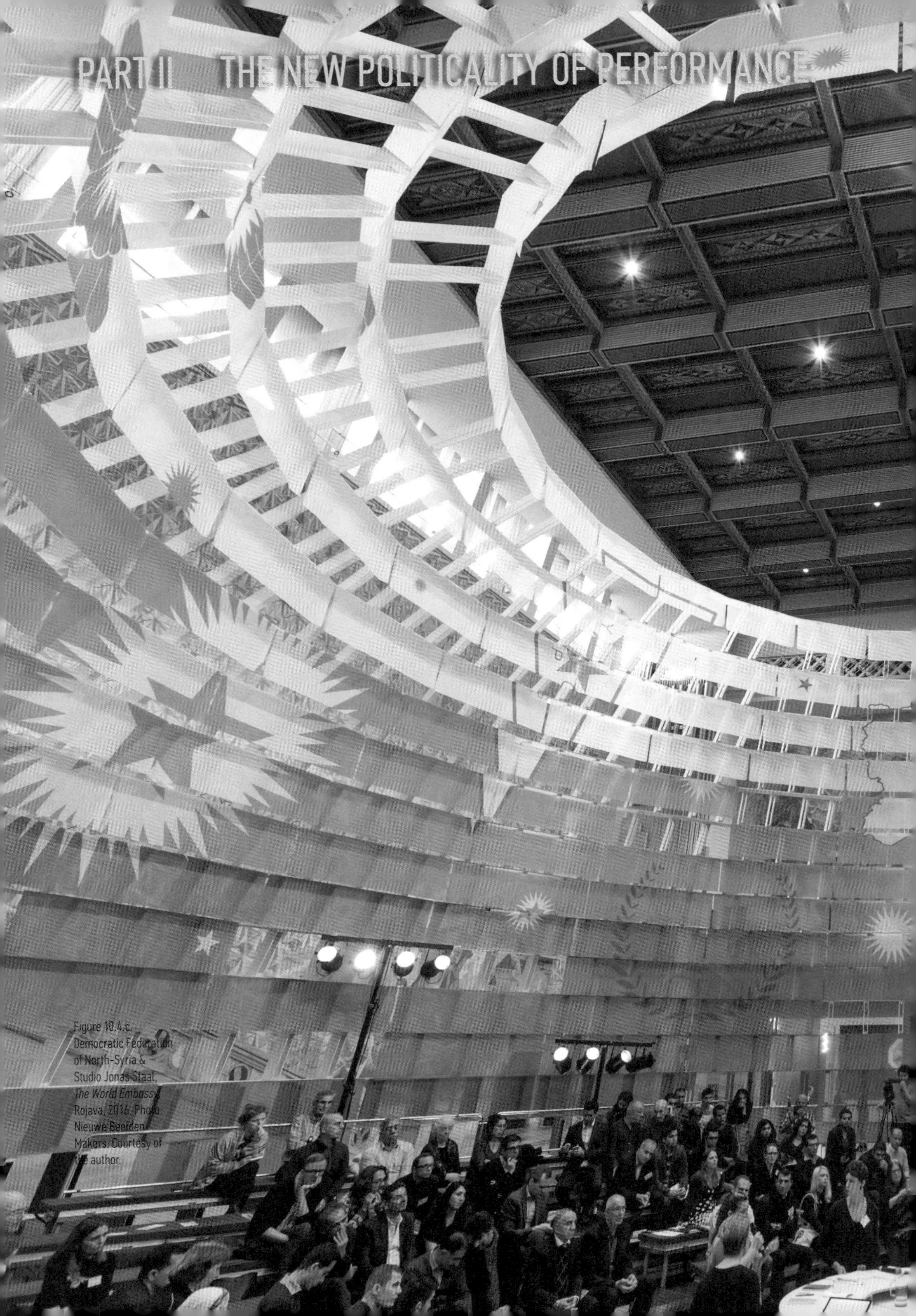

Figure 10.4.c. Democratic Federation of North-Syria & Studio Jonas Staal, *The World Embassy of Rojava*, 2016. Photo: Nieuwe Beelden Makers. Courtesy of the author.

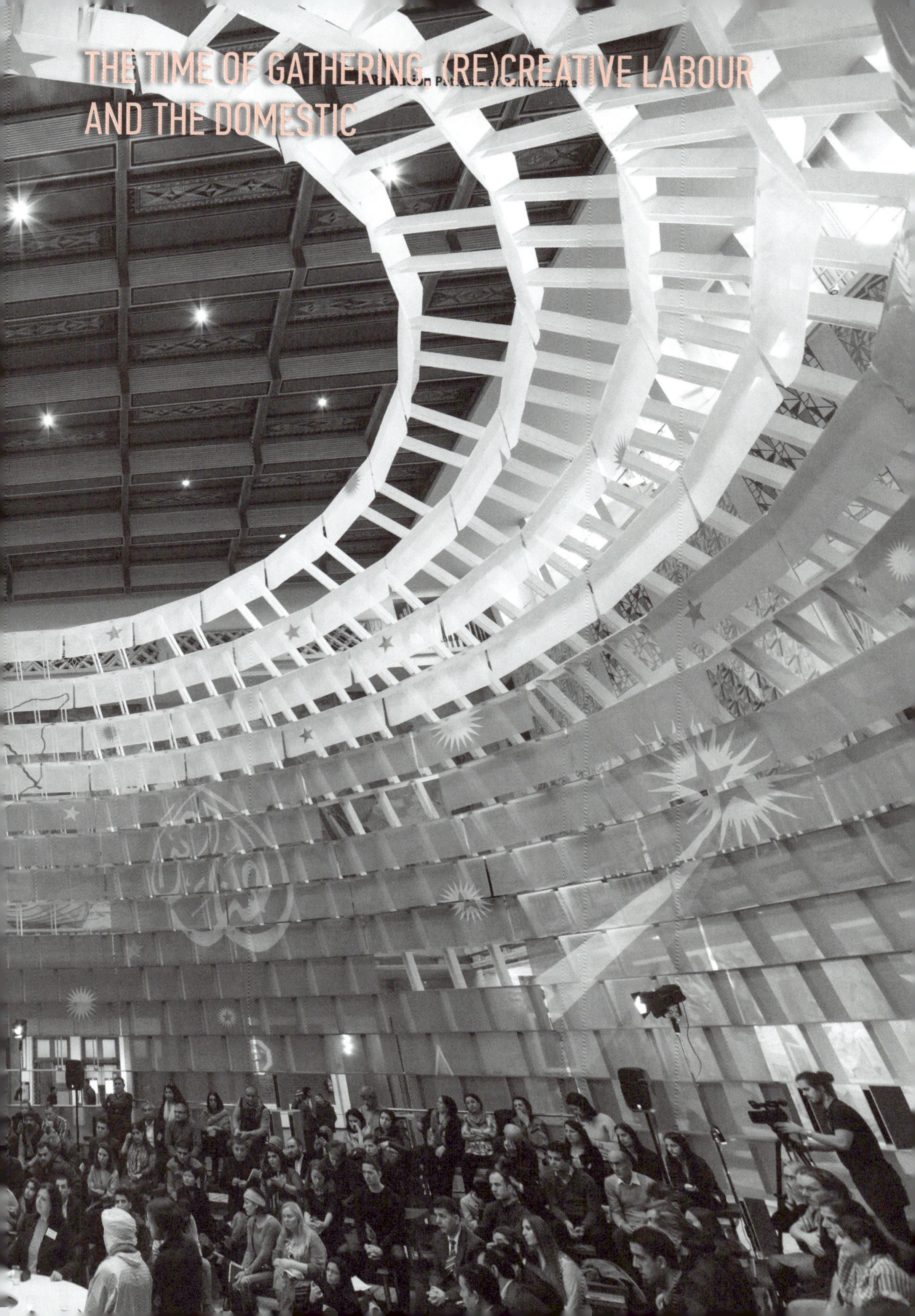
THE TIME OF GATHERING, (RE)CREATIVE LABOUR
AND THE DOMESTIC

STINA NYBERG

A.

APOLITICAL

The apolitical is a regularly longed for myth, often claimed by artists in order to dodge questions about their work that they find 'uninteresting'. Rather than seeing their work being criticised from a political standpoint, they perceive their own work as apolitical. There is no such thing as an apolitical book, apolitical speech, apolitical art work, apolitical room or apolitical practice. And if people seem to have forgotten this, we need to repoliticise these spaces and point to the politics of every situation. The political lives in every situation; it resides in the structures, histories and actions that make up every space. The live gathering can be the political action of meeting others and discussing the society we live in, acknowledging the preexisting politics of the space, proposing the politics for the future or radically rearranging how politics are made. (see: Uninteresting)

B.

BALLPLAYER

Every group needs a certain amount of compromise and confirmation in order to function and move things forward. The experience of swinging ball after ball to a player that just won't play is the experience of a dysfunctional group work. On the other hand, every politically relevant group occasionally needs the person who just won't play ball. Who will call out a bad hand and refuse to reply, but who will call for a change of the game altogether. In any gathering, the ability to play ball is as crucial as the courage to let the ball drop when needed. (see: Apolitical, Dysfunctionality)

C.

CELEBRATION

Is an unbeatable strategy for a live gathering to sustain itself. After weeks of criticality, self-reflection and internal

debate, a balloon, a milkshake and a shakedown is needed. Any gathering that does not acknowledge the importance of what they do and celebrate each other for it will eventually wear itself down and quit. If you do not have a boss that gives you a cake on your birthday, do it yourself. If you do not receive a retirement vase from your institution, buy one for yourself. Do you always feel like you could have done better? You did good, now go get yourself a fancy margarita.
(see: Kindergarten)

D.

DYSFUNCTIONALITY

All gatherings are dysfunctional. There is no assembly of people, no matter how small or big, diverse or homogeneous, ambitious or lazy, that is fully functional. Every gathering will limp, stutter, be narcoleptic, contract a wide array of stress symptoms and suffer from chronic anorexia. So rather than assuming that a group is functional from its outset (and only later falls into dysfunction), it is advisable to assume that every group is dysfunctional in its very formation. And within every dysfunctional group, a bunch of dysfunctional characters reside, and for a gathering to sustain itself it needs to make space for difference. It can help to accept that other people are always idiots, but that they have their reasons. Maybe they are sensitive to body contact? Are slow readers? Maybe they are ashamed of their incapacities, exhausted due to crappy relationships, consumed by sadnesses and sicknesses and need to work differently than you

do because of that? This does not have to be a problem. It is just a special need and although it is not your need, you can cater to it with as much caring as they will cater to your needs. If we can avoid the norms of functionality, to be dysfunctional can become less of a stigma and more of a fact of life, even a constituting factor of it.
(see: Ballplayer, Family, Gymnastics)

E.

ESCAPE ROUTE

To allow insignificant details to grow into the thing you are focussing on, you need to find an escape route. Or, to notice a diverging path and choose it just for the simple reason that it makes itself available for you. Insistence, determination and focus will only take you so far, for the rest you need to deviate. When working in a group this can be a way to move intuition into collaboration. Since collective intuition takes decades to grow, taking an unexpected escape route can serve as a fast way to insert the unforeseen into group work. You set a plan, and then you just escape, escape, escape until you have moved into a direction that neither of you in the group were aware that you were taking.
(see: Lucky side effect, Practice)

F.

FAMILY

Families are a special group within the performing arts. It is traditionally most well used within the field of circus,

but has lately been a growing category within the dance scene. As more and more performers work in a constant flux of place and space, they meet other artists more often than they meet other people, and so sometimes they start to build families together. As an extension of this tendency, several families start working together, creating joint artworks, as a strategy of being able to keep a family while working within the artistic field. Since at some point a family could prove a counterpoint to the dull labour of the workplace, or the workplace a refuge from the demands of family life, the close intersection between work and family are in most cases problematic.
(see: Kindergarten, Nepotism)

G.

GYMNASTICS

Throughout history, gymnastics have been a recurrent form of live gathering. Meeting up on fields and squares to collectively bend and straighten the knees; often as an expression of the healthy body in a healthy state, it holds a special role in the history of social choreography. As of today, there are numerous groups meeting in public to perform collective exercise; tai chi in the park, military training up and down a slope, outdoor gyms with log lifting, running groups and triathlons. Group gymnastics in the outdoors continues to mirror contemporary political ideas, but also, very physically, rehearse them.
(see: Modalities)

H.

HASHTAG

Is an online gathering live? When the #metoo -movement started to spread in Sweden, statement after statement popping up in my feed and interrupting daily life with testaments of abuse, it definitely made me experience a movement as it was happening. People in my vicinity bearing witness to actions that no woman was surprised by but had not talked openly about. In closed groups, in friendships, in courts and in confidence, yes – but in the semi-public, semi-private space of Facebook? Suddenly we were part of a live situation of solidarity, stolen or facilitated by a Hollywood star and mediated through a multimillion dollar company, which slowly seeped into the media, into public debate and into schools, theatres, companies, courts and the heart of the Nobel Academy. And then men started to lose their positions.
(see: Nepotism, Issues, Witness)

I.

ISSUES

A gathering needs to gather for a reason in order to avoid the fetishisation of working in a group. When we gather, we gather because we have a shared friendship with each other, but we also share a friendship with certain issues. At numerous occasions have I been asked about why it is important to work in a group. And I can give you a million reasons:
because other people know other things
because other people are in general better than you are

because you can share your sorrows
because someone remembers to bring
milk to the coffee
because you can have a bad day
because you have someone to motivate
because you have to argue for your cause
because you get surprised
because you have to work with
differences
because you learn new words
because there is always someone
remembering why what you do is
important
because you have to meet the killjoy
because someone is waiting for you
because you have someone to celebrate
with
because you have someone to call when
you need to call in sick
but most of all,
it is just common sense. Working
together is not something specific to the
performing arts, on the contrary many
other fields have even longer experience
with this. People do it all the time. It
does not make it less important or great,
but let's stop pretending that what we
are doing is somehow 'experimental',
'underground' or 'cutting edge', or even
'interesting'. It is what we do in order to
do what we do in the best way possible.
And regardless of, or maybe because of,
the fact that I find it so important to work
(be, talk, touch, think) together with
others, I wish to avoid that the 'working
together' becomes a thing in itself.
Working together is not a thing we do in
order to work together. But it is a crucial
prerequisite for doing the things we want
to do together.
(see: Apolitical, Practice)

J.

JOIN POWER

We need to group up in order to form
stronger alliances. In order to support
each other's individual work without
highlighting the individual work.
To make structural impact possible
through the force of many signatures,
of being not one person with some
thoughts but a group of people who
have already criticised each other's
work and thus can stand in one,
diversified voice.
But we also need to acknowledge when
our group has become a power factor in
itself and the support for each other tips
over to becoming a gentlemen's club.
When the already-strong are having
the back of the other equally strong
ones, we are just making an exclusion
of others from the positions we hold.
Now, these positions are not easy to
recognise. The art facilitator Anna
Efraimsson always says: 'recognise
your power and then use it for what you
believe in'. We need to acknowledge
that in every situation, in every complex
web of interrelated power hierarchies
between money, class, race, background,
gender, looks, sex, sex appeal, age,
language, education, weight, hairiness,
muscle tonus, vocal chords and CV,
we always hold one position of power
over one aspect of another person in
the room. Recognise that privilege,
that power, and then use it to help the
situation. Sometimes this recognition
stops at the recognition, at seeing one's
privileges and being apologetic. Or
even worse, seeing them and getting
busy with shame, often ending up in
a statement that I do not have to be

ashamed over my privileges. No, you do not. But if you see them, don't abuse them. Use them for yourself and others.
(see: Hashtag, Nepotism)

K.

KINDERGARTEN

A kindergarten is many people's first encounter with a live gathering. It is a place where people who have the most power over you, your parents or caretakers, are absent and replaced by a few representatives of the ruling class, a.k.a. adults. In the kindergarten, the first experiments of collective action can be practised and played out. This is the (play) ground where humans learn things their parents didn't teach or have 'protected' their children from. In the kindergarten, there is an opportunity of learning from kindred spirits rather than from masters, in a collective gathering governed by rules different than those of the home. There are very few places where children are relieved of their families in a similar way.
(see: Family, Join power)

L.

LUCKY SIDE EFFECTS

One of the most rewarding parts of gathering with others are the lucky side effects. Every time we plan to do something we seem to always end up doing something else than that, as a kind of positive collateral damage. In many cases these sideline activities, emotions and actions become equally important aspects of our gathering. As Fred Moten

and Stefano Harney describe it in *The Undercommons* (2013): 'What's interesting to me is that the conversations themselves can be discarded, forgotten, but there's something that goes on beyond the conversations which turns out to be the actual project. It's the same thing I think in the building of any kind of partnership or collectivity: it's not the thing that you do, it's the thing that happens while you're doing it that becomes important and the work itself is some combination of the two modes of being.' If we allow these happy side effects to affect our groups we will after a while no longer know who actually proposed what or whose idea it originally was, until the sum of the parts forms something else than the whole. A gathering can support this inherent unpredictability of being together.
(see: Celebration, Escape route, Opacity)

M.

MODALITY

Crucial for any live gathering I have been in is the possibility of shifting modalities during the time of the gathering, or between gatherings. To write, sing, dance, sleep, eat, think or talk gives different people different possibilities of expressing themselves, or feeling at ease. It also makes time manageable, as it gets cut up into reasonable proportions, and the information each modality gives feeds into the next modality. As a kind of parallel practice, or a juxtaposition of learning activities, they stop you from feeling that any single way of action is too important to let go of.
(see: Celebration, Gymnastics, Kindergarten)

N.

NEPOTISM

There is a thin line between unconditional support and nepotism. A disproportionately large amount of groups are formed simply in order to cover each others back, which more or less consciously leads to keeping others out of whatever power they possess.
(see: Family, Issues, Join power)

O.

OPACITY

In order to collaborate with people we do not already know, others with different backgrounds, languages, knowledges, experiences and longings, we have to accept the fact that we will never be able to completely understand anyone else. But that does not mean collaboration does not work, we just have to live with the unknown realms of collaboration. The unknown, the opaque, the hidden beneath communication, constitute a major part of our daily life, and that is not necessarily more mysterious than anything else. It's just how life is constituted and it's a necessary prerequisite for any form of collaboration.
(see: Lucky side effect, Transparency)

P.

PRACTICE

The workings of a live gathering can never be conceptualised without practice. As with any other practice, its knowledge is deeply implicated in its very materiality; or in other words, learning through *doing*. If the doing we are busy with is the matter of gathering, what a gathering can do and how it works, there is no other way of figuring it out than to simply do it. If we want to get better (whatever better means) at reading, we learn it through reading. If we want to get better (question virtuosity) at dancing, we learn it through dancing. If we want to get better (remember dysfunctionality) at gathering, we learn it through gathering. As a consequence, reading this will not teach you anything about gathering unless you read it with others.
(see: Kindergarten, Questions)

Q.

QUESTIONS

In many situations, meetings tend to live their own life, and although you are acutely aware of this you might end up in a bad collaboration at any moment. In 2015 I met up with my long-time collaborators Sandra Lolax and Rosalind Goldberg in order to figure out whether we wanted to work together again, or just stay friends and not work together. We ended up writing questions that we found crucial to ask oneself when being in a gathering with others, then passed the questions to each other to edit, and ended up with a list of questions we wanted to continuously ask ourselves when working together. Here is our list of questions:
Do we feel reasonably well?
Are we building from where we are right now? From our concrete situation, experience, sensation?
Are we taking the time we need?
Do we dare to stay in a mess, in the place

*where we do not know where we are going?
Is it fun?
Are we trying to do something that does
something? That is making a change in the
line of our opinions and not allowing for our
opinions to passivise us.
Are we taking care of each other?
Are we giving each other cred?
Are we being explicit, specific, straight
forward, straight on and clear? Without
unnecessary hassle but not necessarily
according to a known logic.
Are we respecting each other's differences and
inability to always understand each other?
What did we learn today?
What are we fantasising about and are our
dreams big enough?*
(see: Practice, Transparency)

R.

RELIEF

A live gathering is a space for relief from
being an individual.
(see: Celebration)

S.

SAFE SPACE

Gatherings sometimes need to be sealed
of from the public in order for us not to
risk badmouthing each other in front of
a much larger enemy, and in order to not
get harassed by insignificant questions.
Although we come together for a shared
cause, we disagree on the details of
the cause and the means of making it
happen. Within an expert room, where
only the narrow us (us as in shared
experience, knowledge, oppression etc.)
can experiment in a safe environment.

Because we will fail, but we don't
want to be afraid to try. This smaller
gathering can practice politics with each
other, knowing that the basic premises
are already held, and no unassuming
questions need to be answered. Then,
when we have sharpened our arguments
and pirouettes in a friendly battle with
each other, we turn them outwards.
(see: Transparency, Opacity, Modalities)

T.

TRANSPARENCY

Transparency is a necessary prerequisite
for any form of collaboration. Since we
will never truly understand each other,
we need to be transparent about the
politics we practice. In order to avoid
unspoken power structures, blurry gangs
of cool and uncool, a belief in 'you know
what I mean' or 'common sense', we need
to be transparent about what we mean.
Practice saying 'No, I do not know what
you mean' over and over again.
(see: Opacity)

U.

UNINTERESTING

To name something uninteresting is an
effective way of cancelling critique. It
functions as a means of avoiding counter-
arguments in favour of undermining
the whole discussion in itself as being
uninteresting. It is not wrong, or
misinformed, it is just not so interesting.
Like, yesterdays news. In many cases, it
is used by people in power to cancel a
discussion on their position and actions.
Examples are: 'I just find it uninteresting

to bring up the race question right now,
we are dealing with philosophy, right?'
'To discuss my position as a white male
is just uninteresting in this situation'. Or
a personal favourite: 'We all read Judith
Butler, right, but by 2017 identity politics
has become uninteresting'. Or allow me a
longer example:
Sometimes, when you are supposed to
make a collective work, some people
'propose' a method or a situation to
depart from. Usually this is a good
departure point; a clear proposal makes
everyone know what they are getting
into. But in certain situations, the
person or group of persons proposing
the situation simultaneously claim
it is a *collective* work between all the
participants. Maybe they simply say
that they have spent their unpaid
time to work for your sake, to prepare
this thing during their evenings and
nights, and that all they wanted is to
stir an interesting discussion. Yet, this
interesting discussion always seems to
have a way it should go, according to the
prepared few. And if some people have
set the rules that others are encouraged
to break, this break can only happen
within the expected field in order to be
recognised as an 'interesting' critique.
Otherwise, the people organising
it find it uninteresting. A failure, a
breakdown, a reason to close it off at the
end to another potentially interesting
project which turned out to be ... just ...
uninteresting.
(see: Apolitical, Transparency, XYZ)

V.

VOICE

Every situation you experience involves
a context: a place, a situation, a body,
a state. It is not possible to listen to
all impressions at once, and we are
constantly separating out *noise* from *voice*.
The background sounds from the sounds
we listen to. Through focussing on the
practices and habits which determine
what is considered noise and what is
considered voice, we pay attention to the
political aspects of listening to every
situation. In *Caribbean Discourse* Édouard
Glissant describes how Caribbean slaves
disguised their Creole language to
make themselves unintelligible to their
overseers. By sounding like noise in the
colonists' ears, their Creole was perceived
not as a language but as something
unimportant, something that did not
need to be listened to. It made possible
the use of this language – this noise – as
an act of resistance. The awareness of
what we see as noise *and* as voice can be
a conscious way of listening differently.
(see: Uninteresting, XYZ)

W.

WITNESS

As in the case of the recent #metoo
movement, to bear witness to a situation
can become a powerful source if the
witnesses choose to gather. One single
testimony can be questioned, it can be an
exception, an exaggeration, and if I would
rather forget about it myself – it is easiest
to keep quiet about it. But thousands
of witnesses giving the same account
form a critical mass of testimony. The

online live gathering easily slides into
a representation of political awareness.
A means by which to show your
engagement to others, regardless of its
actual effect. But at moments, to simply
tell the story of being one of the many,
can be an act of support strong enough to
cause real effects.
(see: Apolitical, Hashtag, XYZ)

XYZ.

XYZ

The XYZ are the people that never count.
The bottom of the credit list, the not-
worth-mentioning, the ... and so on. This
book was made possible by Important
Person, Interesting Character, Intelligent
Philosopher and XYZ.
(see: Nepotism)

A speculative wonder of democratic society is that inside itself it opens up a vibrant space of the proximity, sometimes even the continuum between performance and politics. That space is located somewhere in the public sphere. It is densely populated with citizens as the *public*, who gather not only to watch and listen but also to speak and act. The continuum between artistic performance and politics has never been smooth and undisturbed, and for that reason it would be an exaggeration to say that democracy is an aesthetic, artistic invention insofar as the artistic imagination in democracy has a nature of political dreams about possible worlds.[1] Allow me a little bit of hope that this may partially be the case, and I will readily admit that there is a concern of greater importance to be explained here. Namely, in democratic society the social imaginary enacted in a performance as cultural-artistic event is or is to be taken seriously as the imaginary of the people gathered in the event who are enfranchised to actualise that imaginary in wider social realm if they want, because it is *their society* and it is they who rule it (*demos-kratia*). Plato's hostility to theatre comes exactly from his fear of the social power of its imaginary. He recognised theatre's perverting and subverting aspects, which could give a crowd 'a crazy idea'

[1] | I clearly see the exclusivity of democracy and will soon get back to that problem. Nevertheless I must emphasise that here, in this text, I don't speak about an ideal society but about democracy. Problems and challenges of performance in dictatorship, anarchism, monarchy, tribal society, or oligarchy are different from those characteristic of democratic society, which are my present concern. Thus I will leave them aside.

that their world is not the best and that other worlds, where an ordinary man wears 'myrrh on his head', are possible. Moreover, in difference to other art forms, theatre or dance as a live art let the people imagine and indeed experience these fictional worlds together whilst creating a public social situation in and around the performance.

However, as a cultural worker involved in the art scene and not only academic theory, I can easily see that the social imaginaries we create in performance events are usually far from bringing any remarkable social change. The inference about that can be a source of deep frustration. In the case of artists concerned with sociopolitical matters in particular, the frustration derives from a sense of being politically paralysed as artists-citizens. At the same time, there are some far-reaching theoretical writings that insist on that proximity between performing arts and politics, which recurrently increases our political ambitions and hopes. In a historical perspective, it seems that it was possible, relevant, even necessary to speak about cultural and artistic performance as a model of political practice in some earlier democratic societies. It was demonstrated by Hannah Arendt's and Richard Sennett's analyses of performing arts as *a public practice of citizenry* in Athens in the fifth and the forth centuries BC and European bourgeois society of the eighteenth century.[2] However, it may be exactly this historical perspective that should prevent us from generalising that status of performance. Instead, we can see it as a signal that the classical discourses formulating the political practice of performance are indeed limited within the borders of these particular social contexts and cannot be applied to democratic society in general.

While focussing on the knot that obstructs the political practice of performance in today's European democracy – which is identified as representative – it could be noticed that a significant obscurity lies in the new relationship between politics and production in a society which is not only democratic but also neoliberal capitalist. In that context, it may be that, instead of speaking about the *performance as a model of politics*, we should speak about *performance as a model of production*. This would change the terms of the discussion, but only for a while: my hypothesis is actually that today we should look at the performance as a model of production if we want to grasp its political dimension. That detour to politics via production – limited to the already huge context of Europe and its contemporary performing arts scenes – will be the main move with which I would like to contribute to the debate opened by this book.

2 | Hannah Arendt, *The Human Condition* (Chicago: University of Chicago Press 1998); Richard Sennett, *The Fall of Public Man* (New York and London: W. W. Norton 1976).

PERFORMANCE AND THE DETOUR OF POLITICS IN NEOLIBERAL DEMOCRACY

When speaking about the politicality of performance in today's European context, we face a few problems that appear along the process of integration of the social imaginary proposed by performance into our ways of socialisation, and that seriously limit or even hinder that process. First of all, we mustn't neglect the fact that virtual interactions by digital technologies are ever more dominating, while the political scene is configured by the system of representative democracy. Therefore, it is a sheer fact that physical public space and live performance – on which performance in art and culture, in difference to democratic politics, still insists – are not current social paradigms; the main paradigms are representation and mediatisation. These paradigms methodologically and procedurally correspond to the new representative democratic system, based on political rituals and procedures. However, apart from that procedural disqualification of performance from politics, we mustn't neglect a keen and growing interest in performance on the part of the art world, the media, marketing and the sphere of production. In an attempt to think these two processes together, I would hypothesise that the new social role of the performing arts is to be a model of production instead of a model of politics. This does not mean that the performance is apolitical or politically irrelevant, but that its politicality is now usually indirect, tacit and in fact dubious, predominantly operating in the register of the 'political unconscious'.[3]

Reasons for that indirect and dubious politicality of the performing arts should be found in a wider socio-economic process of today's neoliberal society not only in Europe but in the entire so-called Western world. The point is that therein, politics has already been immersed in capitalist production, which is post-Fordist and post-industrial. That phenomenon has multifold causes and consequences. In order to disentangle it, I will now unfold the twin processes of the economisation of politics and the politicisation of production.

ECONOMISATION OF POLITICS

According to Hannah Arendt, in modern capitalist society, starting with the French Revolution, politics has increasingly taken an interest in so-called 'social issues', whereby it legitimised the entrance of private interests and

---

3 | Fredric Jameson, *The Political Unconscious: Narrative as a Socially Symbolic Act* (Ithaca: Cornell University Press 1981).

distribution of goods into the public sphere.[4] For Arendt, politics involves speech and deeds of free citizens interested in the organisation of the *polis*, performed on the public stage of society. It concerns current performances on that stage (*appearance on the public stage*) as well as the performance of those stages themselves (*appearance of the public stage*), whilst politics is never concerned with issues pertaining to the *oikos*, private life, personal interests or material goods. For Arendt, the socialisation of politics and its approximating economics spelled its demise, since in her key writings she looked back in history at the Athenian model of direct democracy, where politics was a form of human activity called practice. Practice (*praxis*) is not geared towards fulfilling citizens' existential needs and reproducing life (as is everyday labour), and unlike production and creation (*poiesis*) it does not produce material objects which are investments into human civilisation (as do arts and crafts) but is rather realised and exhausted in itself, affecting current social relations. Political practice in democracy is therefore a public activity performed by free citizens, driven not by their existential needs or interest in material goods but by the will and desire of human beings as political beings to organise relations between humans. From that perspective, Arendt saw the entrance of social issues – private issues that have become publicly relevant, such as the distribution of goods – onto the public stage as what led to the instrumentalisation and therefore also demise of politics in the classic democratic sense.

In neoliberal capitalism, predicated on the collusion between protecting individual rights, globalisation and corporate capital, this far-reaching critique of modern democratic politics is manifested on an unprecedented scale. Still, Arendt neglects a more careful consideration of the complex relationship between the economic and the political, that is, the private and the public, which have been structurally entangled on several levels at least from the Second World War onwards. Without that, Hannah Arendt's conclusions remain somewhat schematic as well as problematic, in overlooking the fact that the right to participate in politics was rather exclusive in democratic Athens, even though it was a participative democracy. It was extended only to free citizens, which kept a majority of Athenians off the public stage: the women, the slaves, the foreigners, the freed slaves and those who had lost their citizens' rights. Therefore, if we widen the perspective or take the perspective of the people excluded from citizenry, the introduction of social issues into the public scene appears also as an indicator of a higher inclusivity on the part of modern democratic societies, which gradually extended suffrage to those who worked and produced, to women and to other previously excluded social subjects.[5] In

4 | Hannah Arendt, *The Human Condition*.
5 | Jürgen Habermas committed the same oversight when he concluded that the supposedly glorious epoch

order to establish themselves as citizens, they had to penetrate the already existing public sphere, break the basic political consensus and bring in their own interests, which were seen as private because they hadn't had their place in the public sphere.

The theses expounded above form the theoretical ground on which Arendt brought forth her famous thesis on the performative character of political practice and on the political dimension of artistic performance alike. The thesis draws from the accomplishment which lies in the very action, a need for the presence of others and a publicly organised space, which she found both in performing arts and politics.[6] With her idea of performing arts as a public practice close to politics, she sets a challenge for the entire Western understanding of artistic creation as poiesis, especially when it comes to its political aspirations. The Austrian artivist group WochenKlausur have offered a provocative and critically elaborate response to this challenge by their 'artistic practice' of interventions in lieu of the 'artistic production' of objects.[7] As is the case with many artivist initiatives, WochenKlausur's interventions closely approach politics, so much so that they function as certain social and public services and actions which are at the same time artistic and political, such as *Medical Care for Homeless People* (1993), *Civic Participation in Public Space* (2000) or *Renovation of a Refugee Hostel* (2016). However, Arendt's explanation of the similarity between performance and politics skates over historical changes in concepts of poiesis, praxis, politics and art as well as their current relations.[8] On the one hand, Arendt overlooks procedural differences between the political practice of Athenian direct democracy and the official political practice of modern society, that is, representative democracy. On the other hand – and this is even more important for my present discussion – whilst critiquing politics for its economisation as previously explained, Arendt fails to subject the performing arts to the same materialist critique. Observing them from a

of the egalitarian and liberal bourgeois public sphere was followed by a decline of the public sphere in the nineteenth century, because the public scene was penetrated by various social groups that had interests different from the consensual one(s) and some of them demanded protection by the state; see Jürgen Habermas, *The Structural Transformation of the Public Sphere: An Inquiry into a Category of Bourgeois Society* (Cambridge: MIT Press 1991). A number of feminist theorists later brought that problem into sharper focus, and an important critical contribution came from Jacques Rancière as well, who introduced the distinction between the concepts of police and politics, whereby politics begins precisely when the *plebs* penetrate the public sphere; Cf. Jacques Rancière, *The Politics of Aesthetics: The Distribution of the Sensible* (London: Continuum 2004) and Jacques Rancière, *Disagreement: Politics and Philosophy* (Minneapolis: University of Minnesota Press 1999).

6 | Hannah Arendt, *Between Past and Future* (New York: Viking 1961), 153–54.

7 | See http://www.wochenklausur.at/, especially "From the Object to the Concrete Intervention".

8 | Cf. Giorgio Agamben, "Poiesis and Praxis" and "Privation Is Like a Face", in *The Man Without Content* (Stanford: Stanford University Press 1999), 68–94 and 59–68. Since Agamben's claims would make a digression here, I will only mention that a 'return to practice' doesn't necessarily repoliticise art today, because practice itself is no longer what it was in ancient Greece, but instead has been understood as an expression of individual will and creative power since the nineteenth century. Cf. also Ana Vujanović, "What do we actually do when... we make art", *Maska*, no. 127-130 & *Amfiteatatar*, no. 2 (2010): 47-86.

very distant position of a political theorist as well as an audience member, she ignores the fact that today they, too, are a form of production, that performance is a commodity and that virtuosic performance is a job like any other.[9]

An indicative example of that is a new, 'soft' form of *censorship*. Nowadays it is a forgotten word on the European performing arts scenes, incompatible with neoliberal democratic vocabulary. And indeed, censorship as a policy/police activity whose purpose is to prevent certain artworks from being presented in public on the basis of being politically unacceptable, looks as if it's been thrown into the dustbin of history altogether with undemocratic political regimes. However, what we have today is 'censorship by other means', or to be precise, censorship as an economic measure of control instead of political/police measures of discipline.

One illustration of this mechanism is a censorship embedded in grant-giving policy for artistic and cultural projects from former Yugoslavia which emphasise their Yugoslav framework. To be sure, that region has seen intense and vivid communication and collaboration amongst cultural workers on the independent scenes throughout the 2000s and 2010s. There are many reasons for that, from common history to leftist aspirations, to easily communication in Serbo-Croatian and similar languages, to sharing worries about the transition towards capitalism, to a willingness to look back into Yugoslav socialism as a still valid repository of social ideas. However, it is symptomatic that this interest and the affiliation were blurred in the 2000s by being present mostly through the geopolitical toponym of the Balkans, especially in larger networks and projects. I could mention for example the biennial festival Balkan Dance Platform, launched in 2001; the Balkan Dance Network and its program for education and production Nomad Dance Academy (NDA), initiated in 2005; and the network and web portal BalCanCan Contemporary, which started in 2010. I cannot fail to notice here that apart from the fact that the memories of Yugoslavia and its bloody ending were too fresh and confusing in the 2000s to use that toponym frequently in public, international foundations – such as the European Cultural Foundation, Swiss Cultural Program / Pro Helvetia, etc. – who have been the main financial supporters of contemporary art in that region, promoted the notion of the Balkans and offered special grants for collaborative projects in that region. Later, the foundations started to promote the new geopolitical entity of South-Eastern Europe, and then the Western Balkans. Only the toponym Yugoslavia never seemed desirable for

---

9 | Here I would like to mention recent theoretical writings by Bojana Kunst that are almost entirely dedicated to current modes and conditions of work in the field of art as a sociopolitical matter; cf. Bojana Kunst, *Artist at Work: Proximity of Art and Capitalism* (London: Zero Books 2015).

official cultural policies. Therefore, without opening a fierce public debate, burning books, imprisoning artists or exercising any political/police force in suppressing performances and performing arts initiatives which had a Yugoslav orientation, these foundations, together with local cultural authorities and public funds, silently and softly managed to discourage the appearance of Yugoslav projects, networks and initiatives, and Yugoslav collaborations have existed only through informal, provisional and unofficial tendencies and alliances. In a similar fashion, we can analyse the methods cultural policy uses to assess European countries, which support their artists in dealing with certain topics or regions – for instance, the wars in the Balkans, the Middle East or the Refugee crisis –, and by the same stroke, by rejecting to support unfit interests, they prevent many other artworks from being made. The main measure of that economic censorship is not violent and loud in the way we know from history, and it basically assumes a simple and transparent measure of grant giving – or not.

A radical case of censorship by economic means is the Malta festival in Poznan (Poland), which was heavily censored by way of pure financial punishment.[10] Namely, in the application the festival team submitted to the Polish Ministry of culture in 2014, it was stated that the theatre director Oliver Frljić and the dramaturge Goran Injac would be the co-curators of the Balkan section of the festival's program. The festival got a three-year grant, while the contract for money transfer was to be signed on an annual basis. Unrelated to that, the premiere of Frljić's performance *The Curse* at Teatr Powszechny in Warsaw in February 2017 was a public scandal and the producers were investigated by local prosecutors. After that event the Ministry of culture didn't use the classical political/police measures to eliminate Frljić from the position of Malta festival co-curator; it only refused to sign the contract for this year's edition of the festival if Frljić remained in that post. And he did. A similar scenario was repeated in many other festivals and theatre houses in Poland that presented Frljić's controversial performances.[11]

The censorship by economic means may be an unexpected case in the present discussion, but exactly here, in that step beyond Arendt's inattention to the economic side of the performing arts, a new correspondence between

10 | The report on this case is based on my interview with Marta Keil, Grzegorz Reske and Marta Krawczyk in Vordinborg, Denmark, on August 23, 2017.

11 | As Marta Keil further explained, withdrawing ministerial support from the Malta Festival led to a situation where almost none of the most important theatre festivals in Poland decided to present *The Curse*, or if they did it, as in the case of the Dialog Festival in Wrocław, they did it on the basis of private resources, such as enormously expensive tickets to be paid by the audience. For other examples of economic censorship of festivals in Poland – where censorship, both the new and the good old variety, is apparently not a forgotten measure of regulating the performing arts sphere; cf. Marta Keil, "The Institutional Practices of a Festival", *Polish Theatre Journal (PTJ)*, 1-2 (2017), http://polishtheatrejournal.com/index.php/ptj/article/view/98/495 (last accessed October 23, 2017).

performance and politics emerges and concomitantly a new understanding of the political practice of performance: it is now easy to deduce that if politics in neoliberal capitalist democratic society is already economised and performance belongs to the realm of production, then its political dimension is inscribed in its mode of production. But there, it is a default condition of art making rather than a deliberate decision of the artist. In other words, since politics is present in production in a latent form, a form that is not discussed, whereby production has become a public matter tacitly, the performance's politics of production commonly functions as its collective or political unconscious.

POLITICISATION OF PRODUCTION

To discuss further the political unconscious of contemporary performing arts on the European scenes, I would add that apart from being latent and tacit – as 'the repressed and buried reality' of the history of class struggle[12] – the politics of performance's mode of production also means a restructuring of the classical Marxist relation between the economic base and the superstructure. We cannot say that politics and performance today simply shifted from the superstructure to the base, because parallel to the economisation of politics the process of politicisation of production has taken place. Therefore, Althusser's interpretation of Marx's division between base and superstructure, which posits them as interdependent and grants relative autonomy to the superstructure while still insisting that economic factors are in the last instance determining, still seems to be valid.[13] Moreover, Jameson's contribution to the debate seems to be even more valid today since in his reading of Althusser's model, he diagrammed a horizontal network of interrelated social practices where the notion of the mode of production expands into the structure itself.[14] The latter thus comprises but is not limited to specific relations and forces of production. They are seen only as its narrowly economic element, alongside the political element, the juridical element, culture and ideology, which all form and are being formed by the social structure. In that constellation, the mode of production (the structure) – with its history, which is 'in the last instance' still economic – is never fully visible as a solid element of society; it rather features as 'an absent presence', inevitably and unconsciously piercing through all 'cultural texts':

12 | Jameson, *The Political Unconscious*, 20.
13 | Louis Althusser, "On the Materialist Dialectic", in *For Marx* (London: Verso 1969), 161–218.
14 | Jameson, *The Political Unconscious*, 35–36.

> *'This is the sense in which this "structure" is an absent cause, since it is nowhere empirically present as an element, it is not a part of the whole or one of the levels, but rather the entire system of relationships among those levels'.*[15]

One interesting and complex example of how the mode of production operates in the register of a collective, political unconscious of contemporary performing arts is Xavier Le Roy's performance *Project* (2003). Before I look closer into this already fifteen year old performance, I would like to briefly present or remind the reader of some basic theses on today's capitalist mode of production, of which this performance can be seen as expressive. While Hannah Arendt is important for understanding the process of economisation of politics and its consequences, Italian post-Operaist theorists such as Maurizio Lazzarato, Antonio Negri and Paolo Virno, amongst others, have extensively discussed the process of the politicisation of economy. Since this theoretical platform is considerably determined by its interest in biopolitics and by the concept of immaterial labour – or, better still, cognitive and creative labour – those authors set out from the fact that the boundaries separating politics and economy, praxis and poiesis as well as public action and private life, have been blurred in today's capitalist society. They assume this blurring as the initial condition and thereby give a reply to the question that Arendt left unanswered: How and where do we practise politics today, after it ceased to exist as a distinct social practice? According to them, post-industrial and post-Fordist production in the West has itself integrated elements of political practice, so we are talking here about politicising production. From that perspective, the disappearance of politics actually means that politics has migrated into various social spheres and activities, from the economy via art and culture to everyday forms of life, which are all situated in the structure's network of mutual relations.[16] This is how and where it is now practiced. Virno explains:

> *'I believe that in today's forms of life one has a direct perception of the fact that the coupling of the terms public-private, as well as the coupling of the terms collective-individual, can no longer stand up on their own, that they are gasping for air, burning themselves out. This is just like what is happening in the world of contemporary production, provided that production – loaded as it is with **ethos**, culture, linguistic interaction – not give itself over to econometric analysis, but rather be understood as a broad-based experience of the world'.*[17]

In his seminal article 'Immaterial Labour', Lazzarato advanced the crucial thesis that the core of capitalist production today, based as it is

---

15 | Ibid, 36.

16 | Cf. Michael Hardt and Antonio Negri, *Empire* (Cambridge: Harvard University Press 2000); Maurizio Lazzarato, "Immaterial Labour", 1996, http://www.generation-online.org/c/fcimmateriallabour3.htm (last accessed October 21, 2017); Paolo Virno, *A Grammar of the Multitude* (New York: Semiotext(e) 2004).

17 | Virno, *A Grammar*, 26.

on what Lazzarato used to call 'immaterial labour', is not the production of commodities but of their cultural-informational contents: standards, norms, tastes and – strategically most important – public opinion, produced by means of cooperation and communication as its basic work activities.[18] Thus issues that become central to production are political issues *par excellence*: those pertaining to the organisation of the social condition, whose principal content is the production of subjectivity. Art thereby gains a new political position and performance acquired a special role to play there.[19] Namely, in the mode of production organised in this way, management is based on the slogan 'become subject' (of communication) and grows totalitarian in its bid to draw the worker's entire subjectivity into the production of value. Therefore, in the capitalist, Western world, in any line of production, workers are no longer obliged merely to get the job done but also to be virtuoso performers: eloquent, open and communicative. 'One *has to* speak, communicate, cooperate, and so forth'.[20] In performance studies, Jon McKenzie has been striking a similar path. His theorisation of performance, as laid out in *Perform or Else*,[21] is predicated on extending the concept of performance or on positing it as existing simultaneously in culture and art, in high-technology and in business, whereby it becomes a universal social imperative: 'Perform or else!' For that reason, McKenzie considers performance an onto-historical category that marks today's entire capitalist society, which fundamentally questions the liminal and transformative social potential of cultural-artistic performance, including its political effectiveness in a narrower sense.

Let's now look at Le Roy's performance *Project*. It is a group piece which consists of sport-like games played by a large group of performers: dancers, artists, curators, choreographers and theorists. Their performing mode is 'pedestrian' and as protagonists they act literally as game players. Therefore, one can identify the game as Le Roy's main choreographic configuration, whilst the curiosity and playfulness of this choreography lies in its players playing several games at the same time. Moreover, they belong to several teams at the same time, which differ from game to game. For instance, a performer wearing a cap and pink T-shirt plays a football-like game with others wearing caps whilst simultaneously playing a four-corner-like game with others wearing pink T-shirts, some of which are also teammates for football (those with caps) whilst others are rivals (those without caps). The identities of the players are not substantialised; they are determined by the games the players play and the teams they play with. Moreover,

18 | Lazzarato, "Immaterial Labour".
19 | Cf. "Exhausting Immaterial Labour in Performance", *TkH* 19 & *Journal des Laboratoires,* August (2010).
20 | Lazzarato, "Immaterial Labour".
21 | Jon McKenzie, *Perform or Else: From Discipline to Performance* (London and New York: Routledge 2001).

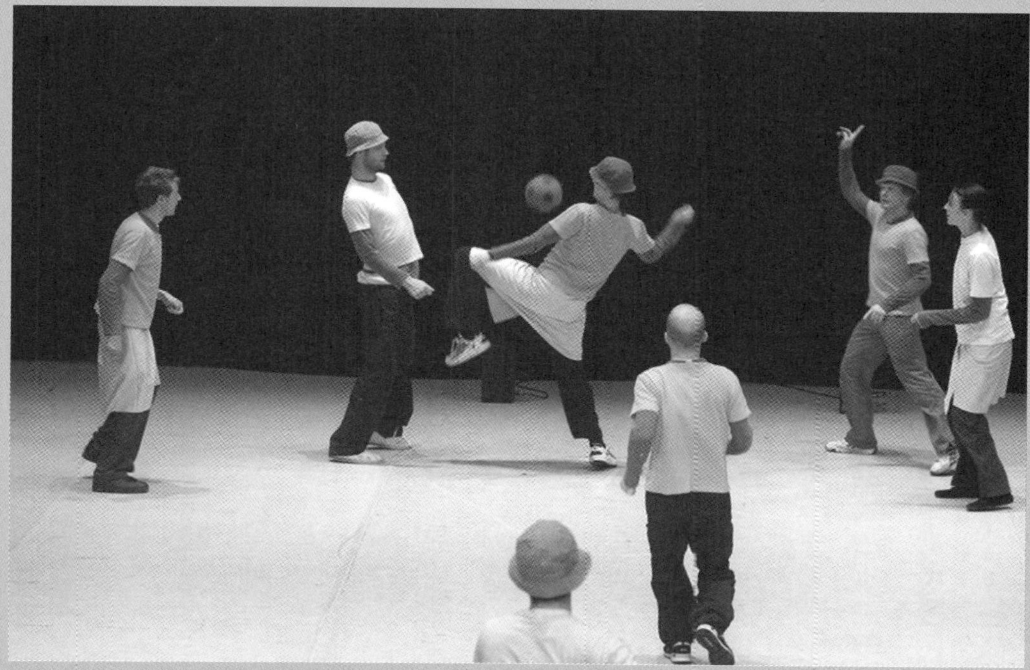

Figure 6.1
Xavier Le Roy, *Project*,
2003. Photo: Kathrin
Schoof. Courtesy of
the author.

since that backdrop is multilayered, unstable and constantly shifts, these identities are provisional and multiple. We can even say that the players are so busy navigating through the game system that it doesn't leave them time for creating and remaining in any identity. At the same time, with the arbitrariness of signs (pink or yellow T-shirt, cap or bareheaded) the performance leads the concept of identity into the absurd, which is further enforced by the multiple game structure, where the winner in one game can be the loser in the other, one that is skilful in one game is sloppy in the other and so on. Le Roy's primary choreographic tool in the group configuration here is inter-individuality, in the sense that *Project* creates the group starting from the already formed individual who will never become a group individual. Individuals thus appear on stage as givens, independent and fully developed artists, and the performance engages, challenges and exploits their capacities and skills. And let's look at how the inter-individual group(s) are created in game-playing so that individuals remain unaffected by being grouped. Firstly, having several teams simultaneously discards the idea of group identity and group spirit, which is to a large extent formed not only by internal similarities and kinship ties but also by negating the surroundings (other groups included). In addition, by the necessity of playing in several teams, issues of belonging and loyalty are discarded as well. Speaking about inter-individuality, we can further these two thoughts and say that an individual player actually does belong to a group, but by belonging to several groups at the same time they are not loyal to any individual. A teammate in one game is a rival in the other. In addition, individuals don't have a need to negate other groups (because they might be their own other teams in another game), whilst they instrumentalise other individuals from game to game for the purpose of their own game playing. Don't we eventually find the players of *Project* in the midst of that dense, curious and multilayered network of social relations alone, left on their own to navigate through the system? Indeed, what is unfolding on the playful stage before our eyes is an ongoing competition of all individual players on all levels.

In *Project*, sport games and their competitive character contribute to that 'group loneliness', especially because the game and the play resemble work, labour. Even in the title of the performance – *Project* – the social imaginary and the mode of production are collapsed into one. Speaking precisely and with hindsight, this performance is thus not a critique of the working conditions of the 'creative class' or a proposal of different modes of production; it is rather a witty diagnose thereof. Namely, it engages the performers' communicability, flexibility, multi-tasking concentration and capability to improvise ('general intellect') in the play, which takes place on stage and which is at the same time the labour of these performers. Although as spectators we tend to see them only as the players of that game and not as workers, there is proximity, almost overlapping between the staged play and the labour of the people playing that play. The proximity emerges from the fact that the game playing corresponds to the current organisation of work in post-industrial production and becomes expressive of its political imaginary. Through this lens, in Xavier Le Roy's *Project* we can observe how today's living labour (the work of creative and cognitive labourers) uses the general intellect (creativity and human cognitive capacities) and relegates it to the means of capitalist production of surplus value, which will be privatised and unequally socially distributed. As Virno explains, 'post-Fordist living labour has verbal thought, the capacity to learn and communicate, and the imagination – in short, the distinctive faculties of the human mind – as its raw material and instrument of production. Living labour therefore incarnates the "general intellect"'.[22] Today we can see that this operation is especially problematic because it leads to alienation and commodification of generic human capacities, which are their common, historically created potentialities, such as creativity and intelligence.[23] But

22 | Virno, *A Grammar*, 60. However, post-industrial and post-Fordist production is not a global phenomenon of the world ruled by neoliberal capitalism. And the selection of performers in Le Roy's *Project*, whose bodies are young, well-maintained and white, demonstrates the class and geopolitical situation of the subjects of creative and intellectual labour while implying the missing others who are condemned to industrial labour.

23 | I would just briefly clarify that in Marxism there are in fact three understandings of the general intellect and human common capacities. One comes from early Marx (who saw them as biologically given, as species-being), whilst probably the only point where humanist and Althusserian Marxists of the 1960s would agree is that these capacities are historically created possibilities, although Althusser practically rejected this notion as ideologically

Project was made in 2003 when the idea of the creative class still looked promising, or at least challenging to many, and we must historicise that artwork properly.

The problems 'appearing on the stage' of *Project* as an artistic performance reoccur in another register of contemporary performing arts scenes in Europe, the register of the production process itself. In that register theses developed in post-Operaist theory have been mostly taken as a promise of political relevance of the art, because they (seem to) suggest a simple equation: art is political insofar as it belongs to the domain of immaterial production, which today includes politics. In other words, these post-Operaist and biopolitical claims have been welcomed on contemporary European performing arts scenes by many artists and cultural workers as the tools for shaping new, more open and more flexible, experimental, innovative and inventive ways of working and producing. Evidence of this can be found throughout European scenes between 2000 and 2010 in numerous brochures, websites and curatorial texts for festivals, gatherings and public programmes that had been celebrating networking, flexible working hours, nomadism, informal 'encounters' and 'gatherings' as public programmes, merging private life, friendship and work, etc. One well-known early example here is the 'environmentalist curating' of the ten-day performance event *BSBis* by BDC/Tom Plischke & Friends, organised in 2001 at the Beursschowburg in Brussels.[24] However, the problem is that these ways of working and production in the performing arts can hardly be extricated from their implications in the experience economy, affective economics in marketing and post-Fordist organisation of production on a grand scale, which is exactly where their dubious political practice lies – sometimes or even quite often in spite of the different ideas, wishes, visions and imaginaries that form their 'political conscious'. And thus, looking from the standpoint of 2018, it seems obvious that these post-Operaist theses are quite disturbing in fact, because they approach Hannah Arendt's problem from another side and imply that the very configuring of the social in the context of neoliberal capitalism has been largely privatised and capitalised and that it is more about simulating politics than generating public space for an open, multi-voiced and risky political discussion. The performing arts, with their new ways of organising festivals, residency programs, project management, European systems of international coproductions in dance, etc., are symptomatic of this macro-process, which, as I hopefully

constructed. In my view, and here I mostly follow Virno, we cannot afford to reject these capacities since they are a strong argument against both individualism and exploitation, and I would posit them as historically created human potentialities that might be actualised by individuals as transindividual ventures of common good, if not privatised and commodified. On that basis, I call to reclaim creativity and human intelligence.

24 | Elke Van Campenhout, "Curating as environmentalism" (2011), *N.O.W.*, November 16, 2013, http://www. nowperformingarts.eu (last accessed November 9, 2017).

made clear, can also observed both on stage and in creating the conditions for the stage itself. To boil it down to the everyday life of art making, I am referring to the limits facing every critical author whose work is produced in the capitalist system of the performing arts without real power to disturb it, as Bojana Kunst polemicised when discussing contemporary participatory performances.[25] In that respect, the prevailing politicality of contemporary performing arts in Europe, structurally belonging in that system of production as part of the tertiary sector, turns out to be not only indirect and weakened but also often complicit in and contributing to the dominant mode of production. Because of that, this new political relevance is not something to celebrate or have great expectations for, since the politics integrated in capitalist production is structurally normative – that is, intended to strengthen the neoliberal capitalist mode of production – and thus operates as regulatory *police* rather than interventive *politics*, to use Jacques Rancière's well-known terms.[26] It is not impossible to change that situation; however, this is the prevailing state of affairs.

PERFORMANCE AS A NEGATION OF THE NEGATION OF POLITICS

Due to their neglecting to look at the performance as a model of production, many attempts to politicise and repoliticise performance as well as analyses of its political dimensions fail to create antagonisms, without which there is no politics. In European neoliberal democratic political discourse, saturated – still – with terms such as plurality, difference and tolerance, it is indeed not easy to create the antagonism. However, since that democratic society is still capitalist, it assumes exploitation, competition and domination, and thus the antagonism does appear as soon as we turn to the mode of production as a wide and never fully present system of relations among various social practices. Therein, self-entrepreneurship in the economy, for instance, resonates with a self-creative performing of the self in everyday life's socialisation on social networks and with stardom among sportswomen, musicians, or scientists, and most of social elements are *by default* haunted by exploitation, competition and domination as much as they contribute to these principles. Every time we invite 'big names' to contribute to our book or conference – which we do only if we have money, since paid time for research and the discovery of new and unknown authors is ever shorter – we supplement the dominant mode of production. We do so by giving more visibility to those who are already prominent, whereby we increase bias in productivity and visibility among active authors in the field. Every time we get envious when we see a colleague's sudden success on

25 | Kunst, *Artist at Work*, 53-72.
26 | Rancière, *Disagreement: Politics and Philosophy*, 21-43.

Facebook – which we do since the ideology of individualist performing the self teaches us that it is an indicator of our personal failure – we strengthen the dominant mode of production. We do so by believing that subsuming everyone under the market is fair play and that domination is a social fact. Every time we pay an assistant to work on our new museum performance, which we sell for a price of which the assistant's fee is just an unremarkable fraction – which we do since we have evidence that we're big artists whose work is more valuable than the work of our assistants – we justify the dominant mode of production. We do so by allowing a 'pumping out' of producers' unpaid labour to those who control the means of production[27] and by rejecting to call it by its name: exploitation.

This whole argumentation apparently sheds a gloomy light on the political dimension of the performing arts today, where creative and cognitive workers in post-Fordist production undergo a proximity, even an overlap between the aesthetic production of imaginaries in performance and work. However, we can also turn it upside down conceptually in a negation of negation. Thinking in these terms, I would close this article with another speculation, one that meets again the speculative wonder of democracy whilst going backward from the opposite direction. The thought I would like to unfold is that we can eventually consider performance, with its anachronistic political aspirations and paradigms, as a litmus test measuring how democratic our democratic society is, yielding the result that it is the society in which capitalist production takes priority over living people gathered to discuss and imagine the society they live in. The democratic society that is actually not so democratic. In continuation, I'd speculate that the contemporary performing arts, with their immersion in neoliberal capitalist production, could in fact be a political practice of resisting and changing that mode of production. Attempts to do so already exist, especially on local independent scenes throughout Europe, where artists, theorists in the social sciences and humanities, and activists try to analyse and then change the ways they work and live together. Here I would mention PAF, the Performing Arts Forum in St. Erme (France), which has existed and persisted since 2005; the transformation of the French Coordination des intermittents du spectacle into Coordination des Intermittents et Précaires (CIP) in 2003; Croatian network Clubture fostering collaboration projects and exchange (from 2001); and also some recent initiatives in Greece, from the Solidarity movement to Embros Theatre and the Green Park initiative in Athens. Besides, if we refocus again on what is presented on stage and compare the performers' 'capital relation' in *Project* with more recent propositions from Doris Uhlich's *More than naked*

---

27 | William C. Dowling, *Jameson, Althusser, Marx: An introduction to the political unconscious* (Ithaca: Cornell University Press 1984), 47.

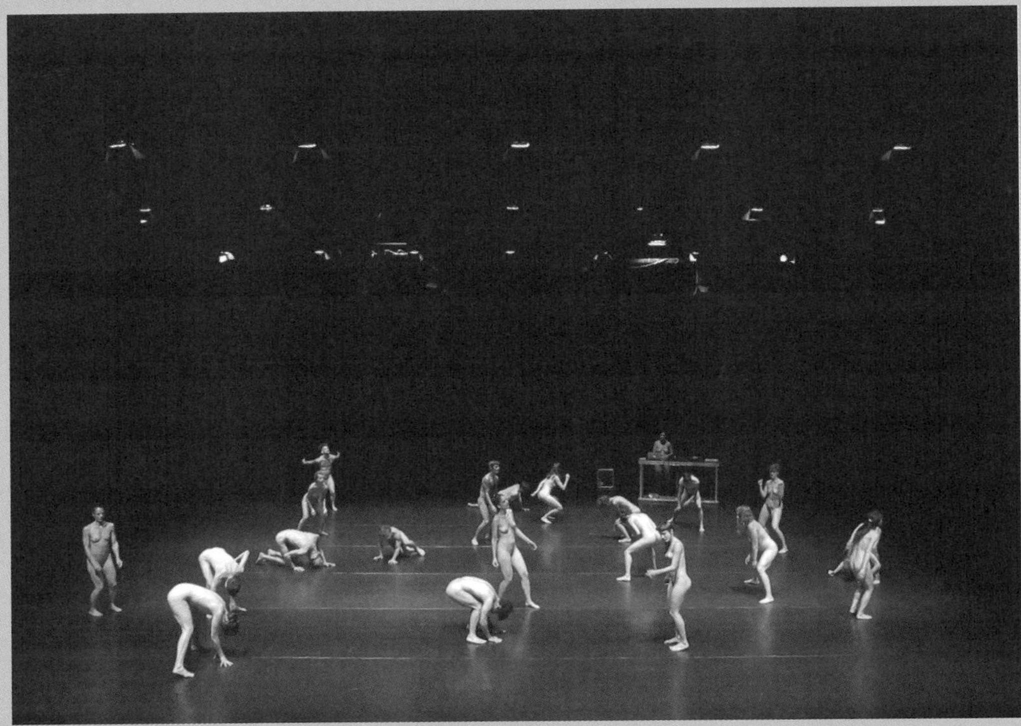

Figure 6.2
Doris Uhlich, *more than naked*, 2013.
Photo: © Theresa Rauter

(2014) and Ivana Müller's *Edges* (2016), we will see a subtle yet principal shift in thought on the contemporary production of subjectivity and the relationship between the singular and the common. New choreographic thoughts are certainly not extricated by miracle from the dominant mode of production, since, as Jameson held, 'culture and ideology viewed as a whole [...] exist to hold the repressed at bay or "manage" its threatening eruptions'.[28] And yet in these performances the postulates of neoliberal capitalism are somewhat suspended in how the performers are present on stage, relate to each other and create social imaginaries, which I would regard as intriguing propositions for *walking through ourselves populated with others*. In both cases, in addition, there is a subtle feminist perspective on the competitive labour market and the (neo)liberal capitalist idea of possessive individualism.

More than naked is a group performance, which consists of 20 naked dancers moving, exploring how their bodies move, and dancing on music, alone or in provisional group formations. The choreographer herself is present on stage, in the first part as a half-naked DJ behind a DJ set positioned in the third plane of the stage, and – in some versions of the piece –later as one of the moving people on stage. In this performance Uhlich takes as a

28 | Ibid, 36-37.

point of departure that which is common to all performers, which is in this case a capacity to move their bodies, and starting from that premise the performance then examines and displays how twenty performers actualise that generic capacity differently in singular interplays between their body shapes and movements. The dramaturgy of the performance is 'to and fro', and like a loop it goes from individuals emerging from common capacities and melting back into them while losing their individual specificities again and again. Curiously, when speaking about the politicality of this performance in common terms, we could see that thanks to that dramaturgical approach, the performance doesn't go farther and the rudimentary and changeable group on stage doesn't progress towards a more structured formation: eventually, there is no strike, revolution or a happy commune organising on stage. These people are just there and stay there, without a common achievement on the horizon. However, another intriguing point here is that, when compared to *Project*, the group in *More than naked* is constituted on stage not by an interaction between individuals which doesn't affect them – which I named 'inter-individuality' – but by individuals' participation in the common, which could be named 'pre-' and 'trans-individuality'. That participation – which at the same time is that which we preliminarily share as humans and that which individualises us – cancels the condition of possible exploitation or competition, and that is where we should look for the social imaginary of Uhlich's performance.

In *Edges*, Ivana Müller proposes to change the perspective on society and its history, which we habitually watch from the viewpoint of main actors, agents, if not winners. Müller brings invisible people on stage, film extras, to unfold the history they have witnessed and from which all central and most spectacular events are missing. The performance starts with an empty stage over which fog is hovering. The introductory dialogue of two interlocutors, which we hear in voiceover, goes like this:

> *JB: Last night I had a dream.*
> *A: Really?*
> *JB: Yes.*
> *A: And what was happening in your dream?*
> *JB: Well, I was dreaming I was inside of a painting.*
> *A: How strange.*
> *JB: Yes. It was one of those paintings with many details, many people, many animals, also with objects, houses, trees...*
> *A: Mmh mmh... And how was it?*
> *JB: It was good. It was very ... lively. A lot was going on. Except that very soon I realized that I was... invisible...*

> *A: Mmh… Invisible to whom? To those who where in the painting with you or to those who were looking at the painting?*
> *JB: Actually, for both.'*

Can you imagine a world from which all main actors suddenly disappear? The world given to the invisible ones? While leaving us, spectators, like this to watch the performance from a deleted point of view, Müller in fact provokes us to watch it together. In a slightly humorous way, the performance fosters our recognition of ourselves, invisible *publicum* in the film's extras, and we indeed follow the performance never fully understanding the scenes, since what is offered are only their margins, traces, leftovers. Again, this reserved and in fact humble way of gathering brings a challenge to the principles of competition and domination, by inviting us 'to share a view' on history as well as on stage, which is at once individual and communal.

These attempts may not be very radical, and they maybe don't reach very far beyond themselves as staged artistic performances, for instance by radicalising the ways they are produced; even their primary social situations are set traditionally, and the audience sits in the dark on tribunes, observing what is happening on an illuminated stage. Nevertheless, they can be seen, together with the initiatives dealing with working conditions in performing arts, as expressive of a new understanding of the political that seizes democracy from capitalist production and thinks it from within the relationships amongst people that are underdetermined in terms of power and possession. On that basis, I regard these performances as experiments with creating ourselves while being populated with others. To spread and strengthen these attempts, an elaborate discourse of the political economy of art is urgently needed. Only with its help can performing artists in their artworks and other artistic-cultural practices start systematically negating their collective unconscious, their policy that repudiates politics; by making the absent cause, exploitation, competition and domination visible and thus a matter of antagonism and dispute. To develop that discourse and become politically conscious (again) we don't need the lights of the public stage and must dirty our hands with the problems of capitalist production, such as violence, predation, corruption, nepotism, mobbing, complicity, abuse, sexual abuse…, problems much shadier and quieter than those of the public sphere, free speech and citizenry, which we inherited from the glorious history of European democratic politics.

GIULIA PALLADINI — ON COEXISTING, MENDING AND

IMAGINING: NOTES ON THE DOMESTICS OF PERFORMANCE

In this text, I propose a small shift in addressing the relations between performance and politics, or for that matter, the politics of performance. To start with, I shall drop one of the terms involved in this binomial, 'politics', and put forward another one: 'domestics'.

This expression does not quite exist in English, or rather it is not a term anybody would use in a standard sense, as a signifier immediately associated with a distinctive sphere, as opposed to 'politics'. Speaking of 'domestics' here, I encourage language to conjure something it would not usually mean: that the set of activities associated with organising, maintaining and inhabiting a house constitute a category in its own right, and that – just as much as the organising, maintaining and inhabiting of a *polis* – this category is not a given, but a field of struggle and imagination. Dropping the term politics, at least in the space of this text, I do not mean to deny the political potential of performance. On the contrary, I would like to suggest that for exploring such potential today, we need to first overcome a certain linguistic saturation which came to characterise this binomial. This is not only a question of terminology: it is the relation between the 'political' and the 'domestic' that needs to be carefully reconsidered, in politics as much as in art.

In what follows, I start sketching out a meditation on the possibilities that a shift from a 'politics of performance' to a 'domestics of performance' would imply, and put forward scraps of a connecting tissue that, hopefully, could be used for further weaving of thought and praxis. For this reason, this text is written in the form of a reconnaissance: as if taking out clothes from a chest of drawers, my own and those of others, washing them, trying them on, playing with their combinations and their possible use, mending them, piling them up and sitting on them, building precarious castles or temporary beds out of them, packing them up for future travels.

THE DOMESTIC AND THE POLITICAL

As I am typing these words, a particular strategy of denigration is being performed on social medias against María de Jesús Patricio Martínez, better known as Marichuy, the independent candidate who had registered to run for the presidency of Mexico in the 2018 elections, designated and supported by the joint forces of the Fifth National Indigenous Congress (CNI) and the Zapatista Army of National Liberation (EZNL). Marichuy's candidacy is an extremely relevant political fact. Not only is it the first time since its foundation in 1991 that the EZNL supports a candidate in presidential elections (so far, the Zapatistas had scorned competition for state power, privileging a strategy of local struggle and progressive acquisition of autonomy and indigenous control over regional resources); moreover, she is an indigenous woman, in a country where both indigenous people and women have been systematically abused, exploited and murdered for centuries. Born in Tuxpan in the state of Jalisco, Marichuy is an herbalist and a traditional healer, and she has been politically active for twenty years in the indigenous movement.

The strategy chosen to denigrate Mariuchy on digital platforms like Twitter is to suggest that she looks like a cleaning woman. Various ironic remarks are associated with this comment: how suitable she would be for 'cleaning up' the country from corruption, how odd is to imagine her running an electoral campaign instead of making a good soup. The racist class prejudice at work in this denigration campaign is indicative of a certain relation between the 'political' and 'the domestic', appearing first of all on the level of representation, but also entailing specific conceptions and value judgments in terms of capacities associated with these two domains. This very strategy is also relevant to the 'going public' of domestic violence, which the immateriality of social networks easily allows. Marichuy's political performance, on its part, is relevant to a specific force of the field of 'domestics' which this text attempts to address.

It is true: Marichuy looks like many domestic workers employed in Mexican houses, who are, just like her, women and indigenous. This is neither an insult nor a secret which is suddenly revealed, but the index of a shameful reality on which Mexican society, as much as many others, is based: the gendered and racial division of domestic labour. This resemblance is therefore a political fact: the very association brought up by these racist comments is one of the reasons why it is so important that an indigenous woman runs for president in Mexico. To stick to the level of representation, her brown body, her dress code, her way of speaking are a scandal. She is making it possible that such comments in reaction to such a scandal, expose a simple fact: 'the king is naked'. This points to domestic labour in a house, but the political problem Mariuchy's presence signals is much broader: the abuse and exploitation characterising domestic relations also corresponds to the state's expropriation of land and destruction of natural resources, which for centuries have been damaging, in Mexico and elsewhere, the lives of indigenous populations, who have been signalling the danger of this conduct for the planet long before climate change became a 'political issue'.

Making explicit the association between Marichuy and a domestic worker aims at questioning the candidate's capacity to be a politician: the underlying assumption, on the part of her denigrators, is that she is not able to run a country because she is an outsider to politics. Ironically, when someone with a distinctive professional identity outside of politics – for example, an entrepreneur like Trump or Berlusconi – had stepped into an electoral competition, the status of the 'outsider' was emphasised in media that were supportive of them, according to the argument that someone who was able to successfully run a company would be capable of successfully running a country. But apparently someone who can successfully maintain a house would not be as capable to successfully run a country: she – and many other women 'looking like her' – might well be useful in the private sphere, but cannot work in the public sphere.

Marichuy, however, does not work as a cleaning woman, although the skills she brings into politics, the expertise that she has gained in her militant background are definitely not fine-tuned to the way politics is conceived as a competition for state power. Indeed, she brings into the field of politics distinctive domestic capacities, in that she has been struggling for the past twenty years – and inherited the same struggle from her family members – to define what kind of home her community could imagine in a territory which was progressively made unfamiliar and toxic by the violence of investors and big corporations, backed up by the fatal embrace between criminal and state power. She embodies a capacity to *become a house* even when the house is stolen, disrupted, violated – a capacity of renewal which indigenous people have been practicing for centuries, and which international medias have only recently started to name 'political'. Becoming a house means also becoming a chamber of resonance for other voices: it is not surprising that, in line with the Zapatist communicative strategy, Marichuy always appears surrounded by other indigenous women who anticipate her first statement with the choir: '*Todas somos Marichuy*!': we are all Marichuy. The 'rebel dignity'[1] which Mariuchy stands for does not function in a logic of politics, not, at least, if politics is understood within a temporality of the event. She functions neither in a logic of representation nor in what came to be known as participatory democracy. Marichuy both presents and represents herself, and a millions of others, because she *is* millions of others: her domestics works not only for them, but through them. She is all the domestic workers who are conjured by those racist tweets, even if they won't vote for her. She is all of them, although she is not representing an identity but a subjectivity in the making: a political subjectivity which is taking shape and transforming as it faces new urgencies.

She is also all the women who will be killed from today on, during the long electoral campaign, before 2018, one after another, as continued to happen in Mexico for decades, one after another like in the incredibly long, terrifying, redundant, clinical description of female corpses found in the Sonora desert, piled upon one another in a seemingly infinite series of pages in Roberto Bolaño's novel *2066*: one after another, too exhausting a spectacle to imagine, which the author made difficult for the reader to bear so as not to allow her to forget how impossible it is to even speak of it, read of it, think of it.

Marichuy will not get close to achieving the presidency of Mexico in the elections: she did not collect the number of signatures needed in order to run for president, and she will therefore be excluded from the electoral competition. But her own 'domestics' functions according to another temporality: it cannot be measured according to parameters of efficiency or success. It is a process of apprenticeship and building solidarity, not only within her own country but also far beyond it, on an international level. Her domestics delineates different borders of reality, marking the public sphere with the collective effort to name a reality of the possible, which has been happening already for a long time in what was never recognised in public. Going public, then, is a performance of this 'domestics'. Such collective effort, which is embodied today in Marichuy's political performance, functions beyond language, or more precisely, works to *un-limit the language*, that of words and that of bodies, towards what maybe is still unthinkable but is in fact perfectly possible.

FOR A NON-DOMESTICATED NOTION OF DOMESTIC

Originally stemming from the Latin word *domus*, 'house', the adjective *domestic* literally defines that which 'belongs to the household'. 'Domestic' is also used to identify those activities taking place within a nation, as in the case of domestic flights. Yet another meaning results from the term's association with the practice of 'domestication', the taming of wild animals and adapting them to intimate associations with humans. Moreover, in various languages the word 'domestic' is used as a noun: it names a professional role, and it refers to a person employed to take care of a house, traditionally the household servant.

'Domestic' is a term loaded with a long history of disregard: strongly associated with a gendered and racialised division of labour, it is an adjective particularly devaluated in capitalist patriarchy. It is also inscribed in a linguistic order grounded in a seemingly naturalised series of dichotomies, which are themselves historically constructed, but seldom seen as such: for example, the distinction between private and public, between local and global, between reproduction and production, between untamed creativity and everyday banality.

As Elke Krasny has insightfully suggested, at least since industrialisation, and with the simultaneous explosion of urban growth, the organisation and representation of men's creative activity in public life has thrived upon the ideological and practical separation between the urban and the domestic spheres. It relied on the one hand on a rhetoric staging mobility, unpredictability and freedom as intrinsic qualities of public life (Baudelaire's *The Painter of Modern Life* being emblematic of this rhetoric) against the safety, the routine and the stability of home life, and on the other on the supply of a massive domestic labour force, which was – ironically enough – constituted primarily by women on the move: persons who had left their homes to work as domestics in other people's houses in the city.[2] This is a process we are well familiar with, as it persisted to this day: the global migrant workforce constitutes one of the backbones of international economy.

2 | Elke Krasny, "The Domestic is Political: The Feminization of Domestic Labor and Its Critique in Feminist Art Practice", in Anna Maria Guasch, et al (Eds.), *Critical Cartography of Art and Visuality in the Global Age* (Newcastle: Cambridge Scholars Publishing 2014), 161–76.

As much familiar is the unpaid domestic labour which women have performed in their own houses for centuries, during their supposed free time: a work of reproduction to which, at least since the 1960s, feminist activists and theorists (such as Silvia Federici and the *International Wages for Housework Campaign*) and artists (such as Mierle Laderman Ukeles, author of the 1969 *Manifesto for Maintenance Art*) have given visibility to and addressed as a crucial political issue, in society as much as in art.

I want to reclaim the word *domestic* taking into account such burden of historical disdain and countering the idea of the 'domestic sphere' as something opposed to creativity, anomaly, estrangement and the unknown. As Kresny suggests, today more than ever we need to reaffirm that 'the domestic is political'.[3] At the same time, in putting forward the idea of 'domestics' I also wish to open up the domestic to what it does not usually mean, and what it might, in fact, stand for: a domain of radical immanence, a possible alternative to the globalised flexibility of relations and labour, an outpost to rethink what a home might be. I want to invent a different politics of use for the domestic, mending the fate of its predicament and imagining a possible future of redemption for all the activities which this word might evoke.

I also wish to uncouple the idea of domestic from the notion of 'domestication', understood as a process of restriction, control and limitation, according to the meaning which is emphasised, for example, by Deleuze and Guattari, who often ridicule the 'domestic' (in particular, but not only, when discussing animals) in their conceptual landscape, counterposing 'a domesticated individual to a wild multiplicity' and associating the domestic with traditional family and psychoanalysis.[4] Here, I wish to call for a *non-domesticated domestic*, for a wild domestic, for an imaginative and unpredictable domestic. I wish to conjure a domestic beyond family and psychoanalysis, a domestic that already in fact exists in many realities, one built, defended and sustained by a multiplicity. A domestic not based on identity, but on a mode of being which makes human life possible and desirable.

On closer observation, actually, the idea of a non-domesticated domestic might well be seen as kindred with what Deleuze and Guattari called a 'refrain' (*ritournelle*): a temporary being at home where 'home does not pre-exist',[5] the drawing of a circle that marks an interior space in which

---

3 | Ibid, 161.
4 | Gilles Deleuze and Félix Guattari, *A Thousand Plateaus: Capitalism and Schizophrenia* (Minneapolis: University of Minnesota Press 1987), 3.
5 | Ibid, 311.

a deed may take place while at the same time opening onto a future 'as a function of the working forces it shelters'.[6] Like 'the house of the tortoise, the hermitage of the crab' – anomalous domestic images which Deleuze and Guattari evoke to conjure different strategies of territorialisation – the idea of a non-domesticated domestic also aims to keep 'at distance the forces of chaos knocking at the door',[7] creating a shelter of linguistic and critical distance from the predominant state of affairs.

In thinking about a 'domestics of performance', I wish to prompt the imagination of a domestic that is queer like the house on the hill which the two protagonists of Albert and David Maysles's 1974 documentary *Grey Garden* – once-upon-a-time aristocrats now living in rags – inhabited, surrounded by raccoons and feather boas, enacting hallucinated strategies of survival between a patina of dust and impossible glamour, precariously making their way between abandonment and autonomy. Or else, the domestics of Jack Smith, who staged in his apartment a radical political and poetic struggle against what he called 'the rented world', mobilizing theatre as a technology of time against the abuses of capitalism over space: the incomprehensible phenomenon he called *landlordism*, the interminable (and to his opinion illogical) demand to 'pay the rent that can never be paid', or finish a work (which can never in fact be completely finished) so that it can be positioned in a museum, in a book, in a programme, and be associated with a name, becoming a piece of property. The domestic, in this sense, is also the space of autonomy of work before it could be considered a product in a distinctive market.

I wish to call for an imagination of the domestic which is as enigmatic and historically loaded, as complex and incandescent as the scene conjured in the theatre piece *Lippy* (2014) by the Irish group Dead Centre: the scene includes four woman who, for seemingly unknown reasons, closed themselves in a house and committed a collective suicide, or rather died alone but in proximity, united in the pact to starve themselves to death. This is a scene which Dead Centre picked up from the news; it is a fragment of an unknown domestic life; it is the impossible fantasy of the death scene of four strangers, whose bodies are, on stage, the creative matter of a particular domestic phantasmagoria. 'In 2000 in Leixlip, [...] an aunt and 3 sisters boarded themselves into their home and entered into a suicide pact that lasted 40 days. We weren't there. We don't know what they said. This is not their story',[8] Dead Centre simply comments in their program notes – but clearly, much more is suggested by the performance itself.

6 | Ibid.
7 | Ibid, 320.
8 | Cf. Dead Centre website, https://www.deadcentre.org/projects-1#/lippy/ (last accessed May 24, 2019).

Beyond psychoanalysis, beyond the possibility of even making a distinction between an individual and a multiplicity, conjuring on stage those bodies who chose to die in proximity to each other strangely makes present a specific domestic history: hunger, which is so central to the history of Ireland; hunger as a metaphor for and effect of misery, but also as a signifier of political resistance, as in the many hunger strikes which have punctuated Irish political history over the last century. I am not sure whether *Lippy* would be presented, programmed or even conceived as 'political theatre', even by its own authors. But there is something about its politics which interests me by virtue of a mobilisation of a certain domestics. It interests me precisely because 'this is not their story': the women in question are not given as an object of knowledge, nor are they chosen to represent a particular biography or the political history of a country. They do, however, participate in the making of a certain knowledge, which gets done in bits and pieces, using domestic instruments, tools that perhaps are not made for a certain use; the same as what happens in a house when certain objects, which would be considered old or out of use in a market, function perfectly, entering another order of imagination for their use. In other words, the same as what happens when an economy of use comes to substitute an economy of value, and unexpected forms of expertise and knowledge are forged almost by accident, not at work but 'at home'.

FEELING 'AT HOME'

The field of domestics I am thinking of is not a given, just as the idea of a house is not a given: a house is a complicated thing. It can be a matter of privilege, of survival, it can be a burden, a hope, a limit, a grave and many other things. The recognition and configuration of what a house is and how it is managed and sustained, the question of who has the right to a shelter and under which conditions, are all both immaterial and utterly material matters in that they entail questions of affect and representation as well as instances of physical engagement and exclusion. Today in a time when major funds are allocated to support massive exhibitions on 'the housing question'[9] and large research projects investigating slums whilst people are evicted every day from whatever shelter they desire to call home, be it an abandoned building, a square or a bridge; today, in a time in which once again places are being occupied, however temporarily, making the idea of 'home' once again a public issue: buildings, theatres, forgotten private properties – today more than ever, 'what a house is' also stands as a central political issue in life and in theatre.

9 | For example, at the House of World Cultures in Berlin in 2015, inspired by Friedrich Engels' 1872 essays. For more cf. https://www.hkw.de/en/programm/projekte/2015/wohnungsfrage/programm_wohnungsfrage/veranstaltungen_108606.php (last accessed May 24, 2019).

Which idea of 'home', however, is at stake in our 'domestics'? How to speak of home far from sentimentalism, far from nationalism, far from a dangerous horizon of identity? In this endeavour, it is helpful to draw on some reflections advanced by Suely Rolnik, who, writing at the end of the 1990s and facing today's globalised world and globalised ways of living, denounced the disappearance of a particular affect: that of feeling 'at home'. She did not refer to a physical shelter (although it is undeniable that an increasingly large number of human beings on the planet find themselves deprived of a place to live) but of 'home' understood as a 'a subjective, palpable consistency – familiarity of certain relationships with the world, certain ways of life, certain shared meanings [...]. The whole globalized humanity lacks this kind of house, invisible but no less real'.[10] According to Rolnik, one of the main issues at stake in experimenting with different modes of subjectivation through artistic production and critical thinking, is to articulate a possible 'vaccine' against neoliberal domination of bodies and subjects, detaching 'the sensation of subjective consistency from the model of identity'; displacing 'oneself from the identity-figurative principle in the construction of an "at home"'.[11] Proposing to call 'home' a different subjective consistency means to question both the stability and the idea of borders delimiting one's territory as well as to conjure alternative practices of perception and habitation of the world:

> *'To build an "at home" nowadays depends on operations that are rather inactive in modern Western subjectivity familiar to the anthropophagous mode in its most active actualization: to be in tune with the transfigurations within the body, resulting from the new connections of flows; to surf the events that such transfigurations trigger; to experience concrete arrangements of existence that incarnate these palpable mutations; to invent new life possibilities'.*[12]

In a similar spirit, I propose to call 'home' a structure of affective intelligibility and recognition in which a coexistence might be imagined. This seems particularly important when thinking seriously about migration, and even more so in relation to the way the latter is treated as a topic but hardly confronted as an issue in contemporary art: the issue of mobility in this context reveals a deep problem of class, which might be stretched to even encompass more or less conscious forms of neocolonialism. In fact, whereas a 'global oligarchy'[13] of curators, artists and people working in different capacities in the cultural sector move and work freely between

---

10 | Suely Rolnik, "Anthropophagic Subjectivity", in *Arte Contemporânea Brasileira: Um e/entre Outro/s* (São Paulo: Fundação Bienal de São Paulo 1998), 137.

11 | Ibid, 142f.

12 | Ibid, 143.

13 | I borrow this term from a brilliant article recently published by Sven Lutticken on the occupation of the Volksbühne Berlin: "Art as Immoral Institution", *Texte Zur Kunst*, October 3, 2017, https://www.textezurkunst.de/articles/sven-lutticken-volksbuhne-occupation/ (last accessed May 24, 2019).

different national spaces and contexts, quite often migrants are extended a questionable invitation to 'represent themselves' on stage so as to make identity and subjectivity coincide and expose them to the public sphere. Hence, seemingly two different regimes of mobility and representation exist for what is curated, spoken of and written about, and what is displayed and represented in artistic work.

Furthermore, how the hegemony of such global oligarchy in the international art scene is affecting the 'local' contexts is hardly ever problematised, and it is again something symptomatic of a necessity to rethink the idea of 'domestics' in relation to both performance and the spaces where this practice takes place.

An almost emblematic example is the case of the nomination of Chris Dercon as the new director of the Volksbühne in Berlin, a theatre which for over a hundred years has stood as a home for political theatre, and a political theatre of a specific kind: grounded in a distinctive socialist tradition. Furthermore, this theatre occupies a significant part of the city, being located on Rosa Luxembourg Platz, the centre of an East Berlin whose social fabric has almost completely disappeared, eaten up by simultaneous processes of gentrification and historical erasure. Having served for a decade as a repertory theatre, the Volksbühne has also entertained over time a very specific relation with a local audience, a relation which will undoubtedly be interrupted with the arrival of the new director: a curator who has very little to do with theatre, and even less with the idea of repertory theatre, something that, by its own nature, has a distinctive relation with a local context, functioning in a continuity of artistic production and consumption. Dercon's program, instead, has a distinctive 'cosmopolitan touch': it is not only characterised by the prominence of global English as well as by dance performances (hence eradicating the linguistic component) but is punctuated by productions mostly developed elsewhere, showcased in the Berlin house as in a permanent festival as 'events' rather than multiple stages of a continuing process. Highly experienced as a contemporary art curator, with a remarkable résumé and endorsed by both the global cultural oligarchy and local politicians, Dercon's nomination was intended to lead Berlin towards its role as 'global cultural capital'. This episode is indicative of a substantial transformation in the mode of production of contemporary performance, openly welcoming some strategic features of neoliberal economy. An analysis of such transformation, and of the specific case of the Volksbühne, exceeds the scope of these pages. It is worth mentioning, however, that the instalment of Dercon at the head of the theatre was countered by a series of important actions which, in different ways, reclaimed an idea of 'home' for this theatre, interestingly re-signifying the nowadays normalised use of the term 'house' in relation to permanent theatres: the first was an open letter signed by all the workers employed in the theatre, which appeared in Spring 2015, asking the mayor of Berlin to reconsider Dercon's nomination, and the second was the occupation of the theatre by a group of activists, which happened in September 2017 and forced the city to face a public discussion on what the transformation of this theatre is really about and on the cultural politics implemented on all levels throughout the public sector. I do not read those actions as defending the status quo but rather as standing for a certain idea of what a 'theatre for the people' could be, first of all in terms of production. In this respect, some important questions were raised: how to defend a continuity of collective work and production for contemporary performance as well as a relation between production and consumption which is not *prêt-à-porter*? How not to let the mode of production of contemporary art cannibalise the mode of production of theatre, using dance and performance as fatal weapons in this process? And even more importantly, how to recognise and invent different forms of being at home in the theatre?

I suspect that such questions would be vital if we want to step beyond an excessively easy discussion about what is local and what is global, what is national and what is cosmopolitan, what is innovative and what is traditional. I also suspect that considering the fabric of certain practices of making performance, and the very domestic setup and arrangement of social relations which surround and sustain such practices, is vital to the possibility of building an 'at home' in the theatre, understood as a structure of affective intelligibility and recognition in which a coexistence might be not only represented but also concretely experimented with.

A DOMESTICS OF PERFORMANCE

This text strives to articulate an intuition: that the idea of domestics might be useful to reflect on performance, as a technique for figuring ways of living and working together not in terms of democratic consensus but rather in terms of proximity, organisation of material subsistence and modes of dwelling, in time and space. This intuition has to do with a necessity, which I feel strongly, to claim the stakes of performance as a laboratory for social reproduction, as well as a site of production, crucially holding that these two concepts are in fact not separated but intimately connected, integral to each other. This also means to affirm, if it is still needed at all, that performance's ephemerality does not cast it outside of exchange value, but makes it very suitable to contemporary neoliberalism, where immaterial goods are especially valuable on the market and work demands increasingly flexible subjectivities, putting their own exposure, behaviours and communicative capacities on sale.[14]

Reclaiming the word 'domestic' for a reflection on the political potential of performance also means to counter, at least on a discursive level, a certain tendency to conceive the practice of performance primarily as a site of critique or meta-comment on what exists: on neoliberalism, on immaterial labour, on institutions, on gender, on racism and so on. In other words, to counter an increasing reduction of the politics of performance to a glossing over the wrongdoings of neoliberalism, while at the same time mirroring its dynamics in terms of organisation, division of labour and production of cultural and symbolic capital. Even more worrying, this mirroring also implies that discourses on production and on work have progressively come to substitute production and work.

Thinking a 'domestics of performance' means to recuperate, for the domain of performance, a material attentiveness which characterises the practice of building, inhabiting or defending a house, and characterises as well the numerous and important struggles for housing which have taken place over the last decade, significantly led, organised and carried on by migrants: people whose home supposedly lies outside of the space they have to inhabit. With this idea, I am not so interested in addressing 'domestic performances' – performances happening in private houses, or valorising the domestic dimension over the public sphere. What interests me instead are performance gestures, images and circumstances which undo precisely that dichotomy in which the domestic has been historically constructed and confined: I am interested in gestures which uncouple the idea of 'home' from the realm of private life and make it an instrument to think and build public life.

DOMESTICS AS THE AREA OF DESIRE, OR THE MARVELLOUS REAL

Although hardly used in English, the word 'domestics' is not my linguistic invention. I have encountered it in a particular text, and I want it to retain the resonance of a distinctive politics of use. The text is the English translation of Roland Barthes' book *Sade, Fourier, Loyola*.[15] There, Barthes discusses in

14 | These arguments have been made and extensively discussed before me by various authors. A classical reference by now is Paolo Virno, who has defined the performer as an emblematic example of immaterial work in *A Grammar of the Multitude*. Cf also Claire Bishop, "Black Box, White Cube, Public Space", *Out of Body* (Spring 2016) Skulptur Projekte Muenster 2017.; Giulia Palladini, "Il disagio della performance: per una tecnica poietica del lavoro vivo", *Operaviva Magazine,* April 25, 2017, https://operaviva.info/il-disagio-della-performance/ (last accessed June 14, 2018).
15 | Roland Barthes, *Sade, Fourier, Loyola*, trans. by Richard Millet (Berkeley: University of California Press 1989).

parallel the work of these three authors – the Marquis de Sade, Charles Fourier and St. Ignatius of Loyola – attempting to extract their writings from the traditional economies of meaning in which they are commonly received and normalised (namely, sadism, political utopia and religion), and he addresses them first and foremost in light of their common trait: their respective formulation of new linguistic systems. The creative invention Barthes recognises as characteristic of the writing of Sade, Fourier and Loyola is also the base for these authors' world-making gestures: it is the display of an excess which, in a sense, forces the world to confront a radical otherness, in terms of imagination, behaviour, affects and language. Such creative invention, Barthes suggests, is not only valid on an aesthetic or conceptual level. It is also vital to the social positioning of the text, which, as any text, is never neutral or innocent, as it is always already condemned to take place (just like performance) within the space and the language of bourgeois ideology:

> *'The social intervention of a text (not necessarily achieved at the time the text appears) is measured not by the popularity of its audience or by the fidelity of the socioeconomic reflection it contains or projects to a few eager sociologists, but rather by the violence that enables it to exceed the laws that a society, an ideology a philosophy establish for themselves in order to agree among themselves in a fine surge of historical intelligibility'.*[16]

In the case of Charles Fourier, such 'violence' corresponds to the radical refusal to cope with both the language and the structures of what existed in the society in which he lived, and from within which he articulated his text. One of the expressions of such refusal is the choice to conceive his utopian project not in the domain of politics (*la politique*) but in that of 'domestics' (*la domestique*). These two terms, however, have to be grasped according to a specific meaning in Fourier's thinking, which Barthes spells out as such: 'the area of Need is Politics, the area of Desire is what Fourier calls *Domestics*'.[17] This is the resonance I feel it is important not to lose when we speak of 'domestics'.

Choosing domestics over politics meant for Fourier to approach the question of living and working together outside of most common understandings of both work and life, in the attempt to reverse the relation not only between desire and need but also between private and public, family and community, material and immaterial, real and unreal. The real within the domain of 'domestics' was beyond both reality and realism. It was what Barthes, with his distinctive interpretative touch, calls 'the marvellous real': 'The marvellous real very precisely is the signifier, or if one prefers "reality",

16 | Ibid, 10.
17 | Ibid, 84.

characterized, relative to the scientific real, by its phantasmatic train'.[18] It is in this sense that Fourier's refusal does not equal a refusal of reality but is rather a quixotic attempt to look at 'reality' in its excess.

Domestics, therefore, served Fourier not as a field of stability, but as a field of invention in which he could articulate his own utopian organisation of a society behaving, or so Barthes suggests, like a child who 'vomits up politics', if politics is to be understood (as it is necessarily to be understood, according to Barthes, at least after Marx) as a purge to regulate the indigestible misbalance between desire and need.[19] Fourier turned the 'domestic' into a technology: in one of the many programmatic statements which punctuate his books, he declares that his intention would be to 'demonstrate the extreme facility of exiting from the civilized labyrinth, without political upheaval, without scientific effort, but by a purely *domestic operation*'.[20] The political revolution which Fourier foretastes, which he predicts and prepares in his writings, does not have the quality of an event: it is the persisting labour of making visible, and usable, the 'marvellous real'. This revolutionary turn is not precisely an action, at least not if we understand this term as proposed by Hannah Arendt, who considered action a central category of politics, something the human animal is intrinsically capable of, opposed to both labour (which Arendt saw as the necessary task of subsistence or reproduction) and work (which she understood as 'producing', making, including the making of art). The central activity in Fourier's domestics, as well as the domestics we may wish to make our own, might be figured instead as a persistent 'doing': a temporality which disavows both the horizon of the event and a messianic notion of futurity. It is a radical immanence of social production which takes into account the necessity to encompass both the bliss of sensual delights and the execution of repugnant and filthy work.

The starting point of Fourier's effort to conceive another societal organisation was the acknowledgment that what he called 'civilisation' had reached a state in which it was incapable of overcoming its own contradictions. To his eyes, the 'civilized world' appeared not only unfair and exploitative, based on men's oppression of women and on the repression of pleasures, repetitive and boring, but also 'unproductive'. Or to say it differently, it appeared as the enemy to what production essentially is, outside of the monster of civilisation.

I am inclined to see such imagined production pretty much in terms of what the young Marx of the *Economic Manuscripts of 1848*, and later

18 | Ibid, 96–97.
19 | Ibid, 88.
20 | Fourier (I. 1 2 6), quoted in Barthes, *Sade, Fourier, Loyola*, 87, fn. 10.

Bertolt Brecht, will articulate as an horizon of 'production' whose main enemy is productivity: a production conceived outside and beyond what this concept has come to stand for in capitalism. Essentially, this is an idea of production as a process of transformation of creative matter, an intrinsically material and human activity matching together individual and social time, prolonging and moulding a world.

Since the world of 'civilisation' was soaking in its own contradictions, in his oeuvre Fourier decided to *remake the world*: not trying to correct existing patterns of an unfair order of things, but imagining how things could be thought and done otherwise. If the phantasmagoric organisation of work according to pleasure, which Fourier describes in great detail in his books,[21] is hardly imaginable as a political programme, it can well be understood as a magic lantern figuring possibilities for a different *coexistence*: the latter involved not only humans but also animals, objects, plants and even planets. Key to such an operation is a temporality – a temporality of writing and a temporality of social coexistence – in which 'the domestic detail of the example and the scope of the utopian plan' themselves coexist: they contribute to configure an 'imagination of detail', which is perhaps 'what specifically defines Utopia (opposed to political science)':[22] a passionate dwelling on the materiality of pleasure on which different forms of life could be based.

Whereas Fourier's bizarre meticulousness in describing the objects and forms of his new model of coexistence – including excursuses on melons or peacocks, theoretical lingerings on bergamot or pears, or particular agricultural practices, or the figuring of inventive ways to train a Juvenile Legion of youngsters aged nine to sixteen to do dirty jobs such as picking up garbage – has often been ridiculed by political thinkers (starting with Marx and Engels in *The German Ideology*, continuing with Adorno), in his material attentiveness and feverish curiosity towards the things of the world (as creative matter to mould another world) I see a radical overturning of the procedures and language of politics as well as a possible key to address what 'a domestics of performance' could be.

Significantly, in fact, Barthes calls the technique chosen by Fourier to realise his domestic operation *theatricalisation*: a technique that consists not in 'designing a setting for representation, but unlimiting the language'.[23]

---

21 | See in particular Charles Fourier, and Gareth Stedman Jones and Ian Patterson (Eds.), Fourier: *The Theory of the Four Movements*, Cambridge: Cambridge University Press 1996).

22 | Barthes, *Sade, Fourier, Loyola*, 105.

23 | Ibid, 5f.

UNLIMITING THE LANGUAGE: ON MENDING HISTORY AND DOMESTIC TOOLS

How to unlimit the language? What sort of theatre of the domestic might appear through such operation? What kind of tools would a domestics of performance require?

A scene comes to my mind. It is the opening scene of Mapa Teatro's performance *Los Incontados: a Tryptich.* This is part of a trilogy on the anatomy of violence in Colombia, a long journey composed by various performances, installations and artistic drifts around episodes imagined and dreamed of, remembered and invented anew in the Colombian history of the last fifty years, all of which focus in different ways on the relation between violence and festive celebration. This history is stained with blood; it is a history which on the international level is both very well known through the spectacularised version of 1980s Medellin and the legendary figure of Pablo Escobar, and at the same time very little known, as it is blurred for many in the nebulous mist of social and political unrest in which many Latin American countries have been writhing over the last century. It is a history which arrives on the European stage as an echo, seemingly too far away and too 'domestic' – in a sense, too internal to the nation to possibly hail a non-Colombian spectator. And yet, it is precisely by virtue of a domestic operation that the scene I shall describe in a moment succeeds to open a crack in theatre time, making it possible that a truly political potential unfolds in the live encounter with spectators.

The scene is that of six children sitting in what happens to be a domestic space, a living room, which is adorned as if a party is about to start: the image itself is a quote of a photograph by the Canadian photographer Jeff Wall, one of those photographs which are too real to appear realistic, or too realistic to be regarded as slightly close to any reality. The children sit quietly, each of them holding an instrument which they will play later on before marching off-stage as a small festive band: all of them but one little girl, who will remain on stage throughout the show, as a privileged spectator to this history, as if the performance that follows is done for her – a work about the fantasy and the sorrow of a revolution which never took place, a hallucinated journey into a tunnel of history which finally will disrupt the quiet domesticity of the living room she sits in.

In the first scene there is a grown up woman who sits amongst the children, holding a drum, taking part in the scene almost as a child among other children. She is the one who activates an old radio that stands at the centre of the living room, on stage, and starts transmitting a voice. The radio plays archival broadcasts from Radio Sutatenza: a radio founded in Colombia in 1947 with the prime purpose of providing informing to the working class and contributing to their political education. Mainly, the transmissions were conceived to reach peasants who were living in rural areas and had little access to the news or to education. The broadcast voice coming from the radio, overlapping and interweaving with strange sounds that will slowly take over the stage, reads from a political dictionary, spelling out the meaning of certain words: it spells out the different meaning that words like 'oligarchy', 'violence', 'revolution', or 'popular press' have for different social classes. The voice coming from the radio, on stage, takes the time to articulate those words, again, in a public sphere, but it does so in the theatricalised space of this domestic audience: a gathering of children who are at the same time the consumers of these sounds and the producers of future sounds for the 'real' audience, as it were, the audience watching the scene from their theatre seats.

The words coming from the radio are those of the priest Camillo Torres, a legendary figure in Colombian history, who preached and practiced class struggle and land expropriation and later radicalised his position, becoming militant, and was found dead in his first action in the NLA armed struggle in 1966. 'El Cura Guerrillero', Camillo Torres' affectionate nickname, is the figure of an infancy of revolution for Colombia, a time whose memory glimmers from behind the smoke of the armed conflict that has affected the Colombian population for almost sixty years and has not always been led by poetic and generous figures, as the guerrilleros also found themselves very much implicated in shameful episodes of land control as well as in close proximity with criminal organisations. The armed conflict is to this day still an open wound in Colombia, above and beyond the ongoing peace process celebrated on an international level, for which the current Colombian president Santos gained a Nobel prize in 2016.

Besides resonating in the 'domestic' history of this country, I want to suggest that this image has the potentiality to reverberate in multiple other directions. It resonates with other militant radios, with other ideas of radical pedagogy, with other attempts to reclaim language as a weapon in class struggle. It resonates with other domestic spaces in which the presence of radio broadcasts have made a difference in terms of information, activating processes of political subjectivation, occupying immaterially through the air a material space of living, the domestic space of everyday life, with the aim of transforming it.

This scene does not represent the scene of those who listened to Radio Sutatenza back them. It evokes this reality through what Barthes would call its 'phantasmatic train', but first and foremost it constructs a situation in which spectators cannot help but listen, again, to those words, once again allowing this dictionary to question one's aural space. This scene creates a 'feeling at home' that is cross-temporal and cannot be limited to a national context. To a certain extent, this scene resounds, at least in the echo it makes in the pages of this text, with the political call articulated by Doreen Massey in the *Kilburn Manifesto*: a call to find strategies to carefully reconsider the use of certain words which are not simply side-affects but part and parcel of the naturalisation of specific economic and historical processes:

> *'Underpinning the apparent common sense of these elements of our economic vocabulary [...] is the understanding that markets are natural: that as either external to society or inherent in 'human nature', they are a pre-given force. The assumption is all around us. There is the language that is used to describe the financial markets as they roam Europe attacking country after country — an external force, a wild beast maybe, certainly not the product of particular social strata and their economic and political interests'.*[24]

According to Massey, building a different vocabulary for economy and for the life in common which economy should serve, is one of the main political tasks we face today whilst living in a condition in which 'neoliberalism has hijacked our vocabulary'[25] and intoxicated our way of speaking, so much so that it has also affected a certain understanding of possible ways of coexisting.

The children listening to the radio at the beginning of *Los Incontados* are at the same time 'real' and 'unreal': they are the children who might have listened to those broadcasts, and those who listen to them today, on stage. They are those black and brown girls and boys wearing a school uniform; they are those children studying history at school and possibly learning that words have only one meaning, to be learned once and for all; they are those very children standing there, holding a musical instrument which they might start playing; and there, during rehearsals, performances and international tours, they listen to a voice coming from the radio saying that words might perhaps mean different things, move bodies differently. The children are, in a sense, both who they are and who they stand for; they are for a moment all the children who are growing up in a language they might want to undo. In their attentiveness, in their dynamic stasis, these children might be seen as holding in their bodies the very revolutionary capacity which Asja Lacis and Walter Benjamin described

24 | Doreen Massey, "Vocabulary of the economy", in Doreen Massey, Stuart Hall and Michael Rustin (Eds.), *After Neoliberalism: The Kilburn Manifesto* (London: Lawrence & Wishart Ltd 2013).
25 | Ibid, 15.

in their *Program for a Proletarian Children's Theatre* as a counter-force to pseudo-revolutionary bourgeois theatre: children who are beyond any idea of domesticity, children whose infancy is not domesticated, bodies still capable of incandescent gestures of political potentiality.

It is perhaps the very 'domestic' nature of this image which makes it possible for it to unlimit the language, that of performance and that of political discourse; it is its concern not to let go of the attachment to a local context but to foster the capacity to make it stand for a much broader spectrum; it is its care for a particular history and memory, for the way the latter are reproduced through theatre. This scene is not only, and not primarily, celebrating a nostalgia for a preparatory work for revolution – today, when a revolution has not taken place. It is instead a way of mending history in a public space: mending holes and accidental tears like one would do with an old sweater, convoking not the private sentiments attached to it, but the public affects which have interwoven the thought and praxis of a possible revolution in Colombia or elsewhere, which have left traces that official memory is keen to erase, which have developed accidental techniques that perhaps will be lost and perhaps can be recuperated for different uses. It is perhaps a way of mending this history's ruptures of its own future, which is now already past, and exposing it to possible echoes of whatever other future might be out there.

It is by virtue of this domestic concern, by means of this domestic operation taking place in public, in the theatre, that these words might be listened to again, not as mere memorabilia but as a call to the present, a questioning of its contradictions. It is by means of this domestic operation that these words can be sorted from the chaos of history, organised and staged in a structure of poietic and historical intelligibility, used not to build an illusion but to enlarge a possible idea of reality, a possible 'home' for certain thoughts and political techniques. What is at stake in the particular domestics unfolding in this scene is also the materiality of a certain theatre production which neither glosses over history nor conceives of itself only or primarily as critique of the present. It is a scene taking the risk of conceiving itself as production: a production which reclaims its status of activity beyond notions of productivity, in that – perhaps in Fourieristic fashion – it uses and transforms the things of the world as creative matter. It awakens a use value of forgotten materials. It dwells in the meticulousness of details, in a material attentiveness to the possibility of wonder, in theatre as much as in politics. This scene could be seen as an expression of the 'marvellous real' that a domestics of performance might display: a micropolitics of detailed actions which are, however, part of a continuous doing and imagining.

HOW TO COEXIST WITH PERFORMANCE

Fourier's domestic utopia, his quixotic attempt to create a system based on excess, was an important reference for Roland Barthes' own reflection on the question of co-existence: something which kept him busy in different forms towards the end of his life and which emerges with particular relevance in one of his last seminars: *Comment vivre ensemble: simulations romanesques de quelques espaces quotidiens*, given at the Collège de France from January to May 1977. Rather than sketching a politics of coexistence, Barthes' seminar focussed on various literary scenes which, to his mind, expressed a certain domestics of coexistence: the particular coexistence which might take place between subjects of different sorts, including what he called 'a text' and its reader. What Barthes considered the most profound pleasure of a text was, in fact, the achievement of a form of co-existence between the author and the reader, a co-existence which was, interestingly, imagined as a contagion of sorts: I would like to call it a *contagion of doing*. In Barthes' thought, this was achieved when a particular writing succeeded to 'transmigrate into our life', to generate from the pleasure of reading a desire to write. This is, in a sense, the gist of the Fourieristic utopia of eliminating any distinction between producers and consumers. A utopia to which Brecht's theatre also aspired and which he neared in his invention of the *Lehrstück*, or 'learning play'.

What would a form of coexistence with performance be?

Perhaps the activation of a particular desire of 'doing' outside common understandings of production, perhaps the intensification of a certain temporality of *remaking the world* which is not limited to the time of the event but functions beyond performance time, beyond representation, in small as much as in great details, on a utopian scale: but can utopia be anything *other* than domestic? Barthes asks with slight irony, 'can a utopia ever be political?'[26]

Perhaps a domestics of performance is a form of inhabiting and anticipating the 'marvellous real'. It is the triggering, for spectators, of ways to extend themselves beyond the encounter with performance: techniques for inventing different ways of 'feeling at home' in a live gathering, albeit not safely, not protected from conflicts but in touch with palpable possibilities of recognising a distinctive social space.

Perhaps it consists in figuring out ways to finally uncouple once and for all the idea of home from the realm of private life, and using performance as a

26 | Barthes, *Sade, Fourier, Loyola*, 85.

laboratory for inventing concrete arrangements of existence in which the proximity and movement of humans and things might find a shelter from the generalised homelessness of neoliberal subjectivity.

CODA: DOMESTIC DISTURBANCES

Years ago I was contacted by an art historian I had never met before who worked in the university where I used to work and had been given my contact by someone who knew my work on queer performance and the 1960s New York scene. The art historian asked me for a Skype meeting in order to present to me a project he was inviting me to 'collaborate' on, a project focussed on the politics of appearance of the queer subject in 20th century Italian art history.

The Skype conversation very quickly turned into an interrogation, an attempt to mine me for ideas, lines of inquiry, bibliographic references and possible professional contacts. For quite some time during the conversation, I answered the art historian's questions, suggesting ideas, names and titles of books which were relevant to the subject of his proposed project: thinking out loud, putting my own knowledge and intellectual capacity *in the service* of what I imagined was the beginning of a collaboration. Especially in view of the political affinity which the project topic seemed to promise as well as my thinking that I was setting up a relation of collaboration, I did not hesitate to share my ideas; nor did I think it was necessary to protect the value of the information I was providing him with.

At some point during this conversation, some noises started to come from the back of the room where the art historian was sitting: a typical bourgeois living room with an arty touch and a big bookcase full of dusty volumes, as in many academics' houses. As I was speaking I started to notice on the background of the screen, behind his middle-aged, white, male head, a brown figure moving around, cleaning. It was she – the Filipino domestic helper who was working in the house during our Skype meeting – who was producing those noises, I realised, while dusting off books and vacuum-cleaning the carpet.

The art historian, who was busy taking notes as I was speaking, took a while to notice the noises and the presence of his cleaning lady, who was now visible to me on the screen. When he did, he simply said: 'Sorry, I shall now move with my computer to the other room because there are some disturbances here'. Once in the other room, he sat down to continue the conversation, but for me the interruption had been more than a pause:

it had opened the time necessary for me to realise what this situation really was. Not surprisingly, when I stopped talking and asked a bit more about the conditions of the project he was inviting me to collaborate in, I found out that what the art historian was proposing to me was to gratuitously sketch out a research project for him, starting with compiling a bibliography and building up a scholarly network, and further allowing him to apply for potential research funding that, in the future, might also involve a scholarship for me.

The unease and indignation I felt during this Skype meeting endured in me long after I closed, quite abruptly, our conversation, long after I sent him an email explaining how shameful I found his attempt to exploit my labour. In my memory, such indignation bound the labour of the woman working behind the professor's back, in the house, to the gratuitous labour which he felt completely entitled to expect from someone who, although he did not even know her, appeared on screen as a rather young, female, precarious cognitive worker.

This association was obviously inaccurate, and can hardly be considered a bond between the two of us: on the one hand, I can imagine that the professor's domestic helper was paid for her labour, whereas I was not and would not be; on the other, I am fully aware that the differences between the two of us in terms of class and race (and how these two things matter in contemporary capitalism) make it much more complicated for her than for me to negotiate working conditions, or simply to shut the door and go whenever facing an unjust treatment. In truth, I also ignore the nature of her working conditions: perhaps she is well paid for her work and she has a good relation with her employer. One thing, however, I know for sure: in my presence her employer hardly acknowledged her labour and disregarded it as a mere 'disturbance' to his meeting. In very much the same fashion, I can imagine that my own withdrawal from the nature of this conversation was quickly filed away by the professor as a mere 'disturbance': a background noise in the setting up of a shelter for his project, an annoying and hardly understandable whim in the frame of the exploitative economy of knowledge which, especially but not exclusively in Italy, constitutes an unwritten rule of academic work relations. In a sense, I can well imagine that within the 'economy of the promise'[27] in which this academic is accustomed to work, his proposal of collaboration functioned, in fact, as an offer for me to invest in view of a potential future payoff.

<hr>

27 | The expression 'the economy of promise' and the dynamics it names is explored in the collected volume *Economia politica della promessa*, Marco Bascetta (Ed.) (Rome: manifestolibri 2015).

Both the labour of the domestic helper and my own (or, for that matter, that of another researcher who would agree to work for free) is key to the daily renewal of the art historian's life and productivity. It is this labour which makes up the conditions for the execution of his own work: for this reason, perhaps, it is vital that such labour – whether corresponded to by wages or by the promise of wages – is made invisible and rendered unrecognisable as labour. It is for this reason, perhaps, that whilst the art historian might think of his research project about the appearance of the queer subject in Italian art history as a contribution to thinking or writing on art and politics, or on the politics of art history, he completely fails to understand the profound injustice of his own 'domestics'.

I couldn't resist to share this little story because it is so strikingly exemplary of something which, to different degrees, is quite common in contemporary academia, and which, unfortunately, does not involve only men but also women: most of them likely women who in their scholarly research are busy with 'political' issues but likewise hardly question the organisation of their domestics – neither in terms of the management of their house, nor of their research projects. At the time of this episode, I wondered what sort of political solidarity might have taken place between me – a white, educated, European woman precariously working as a producer of knowledge – and the professor's domestic helper – who I cannot describe in as much detail, although I can imagine her having a background of migration and I know she is currently performing domestic service in a white man's house. The leap between us seemed very large, although I could already see clearly how close our collaboration could possibly be in boycotting this man's life.

This question is not easy and of course is also not new: how hypocritical it is to fill this gap on a conceptual level is an issue which Audre Lorde used to spell out loud and clear in many of her interventions, especially in conferences organised and monopolised by white middle-class feminists. In the same spirit, bell hooks pinpoints the question of 'work' as a major problem which the feminist movement has faced since the 1960s, when, for example, white, middle-class feminists like Betty Friedan emphasised the emancipatory potential, for women, of working outside of the domestic sphere while neglecting the fact that many women of colour were already working hard daily outside the house (and for that matter in the house too), and that this was not always emancipatory work but often just degrading toil. This question also necessarily points to the fact that a great amount of material labour still exists today, in and outside of the art field, alongside the immaterial labour which is a prominent topic of our discussions within the art field when thinking about performance and politics. The fact that most of this material labour is performed by racialised bodies or by women is another aspect hardly negligible in political struggle as much as in critical reflection.

After many years, I still do not have the answer to that question. Perhaps a possible answer lies precisely in the 'domestic disturbance' which, albeit involuntarily, our coexistence during this Skype meeting produced: a short but significant coexistence which was for me a source of knowledge, if not a posthumous form of subjectivation. The awareness of this possibility of coexistence does not pass through political discourse, but through inventing ever new forms of domestic solidarity, in praxis as much as in discourse, in production as well as in representation. Perhaps Marichuy, with her marked body and the *longue durée* of her domestic and political work, with her potentiality to delineate the borders of an unthinkable, marvellous real, is a very good place to start.

LIVIA ANDREA PIAZZA — PERFORMANCE AND

I

In the opening scene of Bela Tarr's *Werkmeister Harmonies*,[1] we see a small town bar at closing time. The atmosphere is bleak and decaying, when Valuska enters. Younger and sober than most others but equally shabby, he is invited to show something to the others. He puts a man at the centre of the room, says 'You are the sun' and instructs another – 'You are the earth' – to circle around him. He is going to explain something about immortality: 'Here we only experience general motion and at first, we don't notice the events that we are witnessing'. Soon, we see a group of half-drunk peasants performing the solar system. They rotate around each other until 'a dramatic change' occurs, a total eclipse. In the high-contrast black and white scene, Valuska tells the others about the terrible effects of the darkness on people and animals to show, then, how the change might have been not so dramatic, rather temporary and inscribed in the planets' orbits: slowly things go back to the norm. The men in the bar learn something about immortality and we, as spectators, are faced with the reality of our actions and their chance to have consequences on the society we inhabit.

A similar sense of powerlessness characterises the art fields, where questions regarding the political relevance of art are recurring, questions about the way we represent the world and the way we act in it as cultural

---

1 | *Werkmeister Harmonies,* directed by Bela Tarr, Hungary, 2000.

workers: these questions often have to do with the possibility of change. At the broader level, a reason for the recent reappearance of these issues can be found in the close-knit, paradoxical relationship between art production and neoliberal capitalism, in which artists and cultural workers produce immaterial value in a context that is premised on its exploitation, in a circle that both affects the conditions of production and limits the borders of imagination.

The scene described above constitutes a very powerful representation of the way we perceive our actions and their consequences within neoliberal capitalism also because they expose the present time as we feel it: it appears ephemeral and ungraspable in the everyday, and yet seems eternal and unchangeable in the long run. Setting our action against this backdrop puts us in a position to ask, and ask urgently: how to use the time? In this article I would like not only to stress the importance of the politics of the use of time in order to define performance's role within the current context, but especially to argue that what performance can do is put us in a position to ask not so much how to use the time, but rather how to build it.

'How to use the time? How to build it?' The prominence of these questions lies in the meaning of temporal processes that developed throughout the western modern regime of linear time.

On the day of one of the last solar eclipses, Aleida Assman gave a talk in the frame of *Thinking Together – Politics of Time* at the Berliner Festspiele, in which she tried to reconstruct and identify some characteristics of the current time regime. Working on Fernand Braudel considerations, she notices how the positioning of the clock in public space at the end of the Middle Ages became a symbol of modernisation in the shape of the chance to order and use time systematically. In that moment, time shifted from being dictated by organisms and natural cycles to being produced and measured as a resource. From then on, 'a sense of time as a scarce resource penetrated society and created a new temporal habitus and life style. Using time effectively and not wondering why it became a status symbol and a visible mark of a new habit'.[2]

We use the time that the clock provides us with, but the clock is not creating modern time itself, as Assman specifies. Rather it is used as instrument within a cultural framework characterised by specific values and ways of constructing meaning. In this sense, she defines western modern time as a time regime, a system constructed culturally and reproduced every

2 | Aleida Assmann, "Shapes of Time. Transformations of the Modern Time Regime", in *Vol.1 How to Build a Manifesto for the Future of a Festival. Build the Time* (Santarcangelo Festival Teatro 2015), 59.

day in societal institutions as well as in the feelings of individuals. As such, it informs the way we act, think and even imagine: 'A time regime is habitualised and deeply internalised, it works with the normative power of the factual, which means that it is generally considered as normal, without alternative and requiring no conscious reflection'.[3]

This cultural construction of time is, in David Harvey's perspective, closely related to neoliberal capitalism's mechanisms of time production. In *The Condition of Postmodernity*, he studies capitalism's developments by looking at what he defines as 'space-time compressions': 'processes that so revolutionise the objective qualities of space and time that we are forced to alter, sometimes in quite radical ways, how we represent the world to ourselves'.[4] In this perspective, the production of time is a driving force of capitalism – and of resistance to it – unfolding in the knot between the material conditions of time production and the way in which we represent time. Today this knot produces a paradoxical situation in which we cannot get a grasp on our present time, which feels ephemeral, accelerated and fragmented and simultaneously seems determined to reproduce itself for eternity, dismantling the present as a possible shelter for life, work and political action.

A similar account of our perception of the present time appears in Virno's *Déjà Vu and the End of History* as the 'affirmation of an eternal present, a centripetal and despotic actuality' nurtured by the prevailing feeling that 'as Bergson put it – the future is closed'.[5] This perception of the future is caused, according to Virno, by the way we tend to look at history in the moment of 'the end of history'. Virno aims at responding critically to this idea, summed up in the figure of the déjà vu as a false recognition of a moment in the present, never lived before, in the guise of a time already lived: past and thus unchangeable. The problematic consequence of this way of looking at history is the price we have to pay in terms of agency, which is disappearing in a deterministic mechanism: whatever we do in the present seems to be destined to be repeated exactly the same way in the future, just as it was in the past, with no room left for change.

There is an interesting assonance between Assman's and Virno's thinking as regards our present time. According to Assman, linear time was affirmed as a temporal regime also through a strong deviation from embodied time; it became 'natural' by means of a disembodiment: 'linear time has the tendency to become disembodied, neutral and empty in order to provide

---

3 | Ibid, 60.
4 | David Harvey, *The Condition of Postmodernity* (Oxford: Blackwell Press 1989), 240.
5 | Paolo Virno, *Déjà Vu and the End of History* (London: Verso 2015) 9.

a more schematic model for organising human action and experience. Losing its anthropomorphic touch, it becomes an abstract framework for new constructions of orientation and meaning'.[6]

In this way, the dominant time regime is not only internalised so much as to be perceived as given and unchangeable, but also becomes, through disembodiment, the abstract form able to be the 'normative backbone of western culture, making linear time itself into an agent of change, innovation and progress',[7] to which humans can adapt, but not really build. This is a 'false recognition', similar to the déjà vu used by Virno to describe the corresponding state of mind as a particular form of spectatorship, that of 'those who set on watching themselves live' and are inhabited by 'apathy, fatalism and indifference to a future that seems prescribed even down to the last detail [...] These people must renounce any influence on how the present plays out. As such they give up on action. Or better, they become spectators of their own actions, almost as if there were part of an already-known and unalterable script'.[8] Before a time without bodies that seems to be an agent of change itself, we become spectators of our own lives and of our own time, giving up on the agency that we actually have. 'How to use the time?' becomes a question that looks at the chances of temporal reappropriation, though often the answer to that question is reduced to the choice between pre-given options and animated by a continuous sense of scarcity. In this context, it appears almost impossible to use time differently, to build it while using it, and while using it, to build a position to act freely rather than a set of options to choose from.

II

This peculiar temporality affects the sphere of performance-making exactly at that knot between the conditions of production and the way in which we represent and possibly act on our future, as analysed by Bojana Kunst in *The Project Horizon: On the Temporality of Making*: 'Paradoxically, despite that so many creative people are preoccupied with imagining and creating proposals for the future, we are living in a time that is deeply characterised by the impotence and impossibility of imagining and creating modes of political and economic life different from the ones that we already know'.[9] Within projective temporality, art production suffers the mechanism of the modern time regime, characterised by the insistent breaking of time continuity and the emphasis on rupture that sets human action in

6 | Assmann, "Shapes of Time", 60.
7 | Ibid.
8 | Virno, *Déjà Vu*, 8.
9 | Bojana Kunst, "The Project Horizon: On the Temporality of Making", *Manifesta Journal* 16 (2012): 112.

a dynamic of constant change.[10] Yet, this constant change becomes, in the projective temporality of performance production, only valid on the level of the narrative that it nurtures, affecting both how we use the time and how we might produce it: 'In the continuity, one always has to begin again; however, the new start is not about differences but about another promise for the future; another indebted engagement to that which has yet to come'.[11] In this way, the present is reaffirmed as ephemeral and eternal, and the inherent link between time, value production and the difficulty of change emerges clearly, as every endeavour within projective temporality seems to corroborate this system of production. And while the contents of the projects may call this into question, they hardly pave the way for a structural change. The men performing the eclipse in Bela Tarr represent this mechanism of absorption and its temporal counterpart: an ephemeral variation of the orbit would not do much more than than reinforce the normal functioning of the system. Similarly, performance as a live art and as a live gathering is always thought as ephemeral in a context that is more and more perceived as natural, not far from the functioning of the solar system, and thus eternal. Possible interruptions of these mechanisms are to be found also in time, and more specifically in the present: 'only when we are able to simply be "alive" in the present will radical alternatives begin to bloom once again'.[12] How to build the time, then, for a performance that is and can stay alive and thus be able to deviate from the orbit?

Notwithstanding the link between the temporality of performance-making and the productive and reproductive processes of neoliberal capitalism, a lot of the perspectives on the temporal category of liveness seem to have focussed on the ephemeral, lining up with the state of mind of Virno's spectators watching themselves live, living a time that doesn't feel really as their own, being live rather than alive. Regardless of the different perspectives on the politicality of performance, ephemerality is a recurring element of a definition of the temporal character of liveness and it has been only seldom put into question. It is the temporality disclosed in Hanna Arendt's analysis of performing arts and politics that emerge as intertwined in the very ephemeral temporality of the *virtu* that characterises both as practices 'where the accomplishment lies in the performance itself and not in an end product which outlasts the activity that brought it into existence and becomes independent of it'.[13] Ephemerality becomes even the defining element of liveness in Peggy Phelan's *Unmarked: The Politics of Performance* and constitutes, as the title betrays, the basis for another politics of

10 | Assmann, "Shapes of Time".
11 | Kunst, "The Project Horizon", 113.
12 | Ibid., 115.
13 | Hanna Arendt, "What is freedom?" in iPeter Baher (Ed.), *The Portable Hanna Arendt* (London: Penguin 2003), 446.

performance, where the latter is political exactly because it 'plunges into visibility and disappears into memory'.[14] Here, liveness is reduced to immateriality and bestowed with political relevance on this basis. Almost thirty years after this text, thinking the temporality of performance as ephemeral means pushing it even closer to the current economic paradigm that revolves around immaterial value and corroborates the perception of time as ephemeral.

In more recent years, durational performance emerged as a possible answer to solve the questions raised by looking at live art only as ephemeral, not without posing questions of its own. Durational performance looked for its politicality by rightfully reclaiming the time spent at the theatre as a time contiguous to that spent outside of it. It often investigated slowness as a way of contrasting, at the aesthetic level, the accelerating pace of life by exposing the time experienced in performance as the time experienced in life, with the aim of using it as a ground to build agency and resistance to the dominant regime of time.[15]

Duration is another way of dealing with the questions that are at the base of this article – how to use the time and how to build it: durational performance often worked to create a temporal shelter where 'our ego *lets itself live*'.[16] Yet we are no longer in the time of industrial capitalism, where the distinction between work and leisure time was well defined and the abstract model of linear time could be contrasted by exposing time in its multiple nature. On the contrary, the time we're collectively constructing now seems to suffocate us in its exposed multiplicity. And the dominant paradigm of work is that of multitasking, as Lara Shalson rightfully notices: 'clock-time has not been overcome; it would seem it has multiplied'.[17] In this sense, it is possible to argue that instead of enacting and making possible a re-appropriation of time through a different way of using it, the durational approach sets performance back into confrontation with time as scarce resource, rather than using it as a ground of resistance as it strikingly proposes: 'ironically, by focusing on the time spent, rather than on what transpired during it, [that period] is transformed into a quantified representation of precisely that which escapes such measurement'.[18]

14 | Peggy Phelan, *Unmarked: The Politics of Performance* (London and New York: Routledge 2003), 148.
15 | See for instance Pamela Lee, *Chronophobia: On Time in the Art of the 1960s* (Cambridge: MIT Press 2004), 308: 'It is in slowness and the capacity to parse one's own present that one gains ground on what's coming up next, perhaps restores to the everyday some degree of agency, perhaps some degree of resistance'.
16 | Bergson, *Time and Free Will: An essay on the immediate data of consciousness,* (New York: Dover Publications 2001), quoted in Lara Shalson, "On Duration and Multiplicity", *Performance Research: A Journal of the Performing Arts* 17, no. 5 (2012): 98-106.
17 | Lara Shalson, "On Duration and Multiplicity", *Performance Research: A Journal of the Performing Arts* 17, no. 5 (2012): 103.
18 | Ibid, 105.

In asking how to use time, there is always the chance to ask how to build it, and these questions unfold on the level of representation and imagination as well as on that of performance-making as regards the temporal conditions of production.

There is an attempt, on the first level, to act on how we imagine and represent time but today, it has become clear that the chance to bring such imaginative experience out of the theatre has been substitute by its opposite: the temporality experienced in theatre is not extending outside of it but rather is the contrary.

Most importantly, we cannot avoid confronting the fact that durational performance most often remains on the level of aesthetics while articulating at the same time a conviction to act on the temporal conditions of production. In this sense, it runs the risk of confusing a stylistic instrument with a structural one: how we represent time on stage (as slow or fast) and how the production of this representation takes place.

Today, reflecting on the politicality of performance calls for an investigation of the temporality of liveness that cannot confine itself to the aesthetic level; rather, this investigation has to engage also with the conditions under which performance-making and attending takes place. The temporality that conjugates these two connected efforts emerges in my opinion *in the meantime*. Thinking performance in this very ordinary temporality might not only bring ourselves to a shift in perspective – from how to use the time to how to build it – but also shed a light on performance as an instrument for time building, to be used exactly at the knot between the temporality of performance-making and that of wider collective imagination.

III

'In the meantime: performance remains',[19] writes Rebecca Schneider, and the meantime might also be a fertile temporality to think of live performance as coexistence of production and consumption outside of the framework of the ephemeral, as a lived time that is not simply duration, a moment extended and yet isolated. Schneider's contribution is set in a different context because it regards the debate on performance's liveness, but her thoughts constitute a good ground on which to think of the meantime not only in relation to the temporality of live performance per se, but also to performance's politicality at large. Inspired by Gertrude Stein's

19 | Rebecca Schneider, *Performing Remains: Art and War in Times of Theatrical Reenactment* (London and New York: Routledge 2011), 87.

description of theatre's 'syncopated' time as 'one thing and another thing, simultaneously', Schneider looks at liveness as a complex time category and speaks of performance temporality as 'a syncopated doubleness' which '(re)occurs', 'travels *and* returns'.[20] According to her, 'if liveness must imply an immediacy or a "real time" devoid of other times [...] theatre can never be "live". Or never *only* live'.[21] Performance, indeed, is always a temporality next to others, and the meantime regards the coexistence of different times starting from its double meaning. On the one hand, the meantime refers to 'the intervening time' until something happens, on the other it means 'at the same time' that something else happens: it's simultaneous to the present and separates us from the future. It is a present hosting both the time of imagination and that of production. At the intersection between the two, in this meantime, performance might unfold its political potential within the current context.

In the intervening time separating us from the future, the politicality of performance grows in resonance with preenactment and prefiguration, sharing with them the desire of enacting the political in the present rather than enacting a specific or predictable event: its politicality doesn't lie in performance *per se* but could appear suddenly as a consequence of the artistic gesture in a live gathering. In the time simultaneous to the present, performance, as an instrument of time building, might disclose the possibilities of reappropriation of (art) production by challenging its conditions: performance's politicality on this level rests and grows on the ways these conditions are set, questioned and reproduced. However, given the ability of neoliberal capitalism to profit from the artistic lifestyle's peculiar temporality and the way it produces time – a disappearing present filled with the illusion of a future – thinking about the meantime means to enter a slippery territory. Within the post-Fordist mode of production, the meantime easily becomes the moment still usable to work, or generally, to contribute to the production and reproduction of the ways in which we work and live, but which we would like, at the same time, to change. It's not in spite of this but actually because of this that the meantime could be the temporal category for reappropriating as we think of performance's political relevance today and envision its temporality as a live gathering. The meantime emerges as time on our hands between the moments dedicated to specific activities, and in this way it lends itself to disguise: it is a time 'under cover'. It's a time that seems to be slipping away, and yet it is always there to imagine and practice a not yet imaginable autonomy of work in the meantime of the general rhythms of production. In a context where the blurring between work and life is being pushed to the

20 | Ibid, 94.
21 | Ibid, 92.

extreme, the meantime offers cover for working on a small scale, slowly but defiantly, for changing the ways we work and live as cultural labourers. In this meantime, performance is always political, as it builds the time to ground a liberated art production and might be politically relevant within society in its appearance as a persistent way of doing things differently, as an exercise and as a reminder of the possibility that work can always be thought otherwise. This chance of reappropriation is not limited to the sphere of performance. But at the same time it cannot be set aside in a field that is more and more engaged in thinking possible alternatives, as any effort of invention, any exercise of imagination, any instituting practice becomes empty if the people and institutions engaging in it do not look critically at what they are challenging or reproducing every day. The meantime challenges the opposition between the ordinary work of art production and the artistic grand political statement, finding a wider politicality in the link that it builds between being and becoming.

As a time under cover, the meantime offers a temporal shelter not only for working towards truly free and equal ways of producing and continuously instituting theatre, but also for attaining the space to act as if these conditions were already present. By doing *as if*, in the time that separates us from the future, performance practises both its instruments of critique of the existing, and its tools of imagination for that which has yet to exist. By doing as if things were already different in the time simultaneous to the present, performance contributes to the development of different conditions of art production and also exposes the unexpected consequences that an artistic gesture can have in the wider social context

In this movement – from the practice in the present as a time where different possibilities coexist and are directly experienced, to the exposure of the consequences that these possibilities have once they are enacted – the meantime appears as a time under cover as regards another point of view: as a suspension in disguise within the normal temporality of production and imagination. What the meantime disguises is exactly itself, as a time actually there and without a pre-given purpose, as a possible interruption of the orbits, opening up a present in which to be alive.

In this sense, the meantime hosts the chance of interrupting the dominant image and functioning of time. At the theoretical level, the interruption functions by exposing the current temporality exactly for what it is: a narrative constructed culturally and naturalised every day by a variety of elements that compose one single coherent temporal regime – linearity, flow, direction, multiplicity, etc. This idea of interruption resonates at the abstract level with Deleuze's thoughts on the temporality of the new, the time of beginning that can always and forever begin again and anew.[22] In this sense, an interruption doesn't only provide the distance from the time narrative, allowing its critique and deconstruction by emptying it out, by creating a gap and making room for imagining things otherwise; it is also a tool at the service of this imagination that operates by filling and re-filling the void it creates, by means of invention and excess.

The meantime as an interruption in disguise is not only an abstract concept. According to Virno, every moment we live is a time with a gap. Virno speaks of it as none other than the absence of a consistent and detailed environment and thus sets it in relation to our perception of time, not as an abstract void but rather as a 'biological' one that defines the temporality specific to humans – the time unfolding through their bodies, I would add – and springs from a continuous intersection between the void and the filled, between the potential and the actual, between the now and the not-now. In our perception, every moment in time has a gap, without it we wouldn't be able to connect to the past or the future – in a linear or any other way – and it would be sealed off and unavailable as a time to live and act.[23]

Reappropriating the meantime, embracing it as a suspension in disguise, then, is an instrument of time building that works on two different levels. The first regards once again the politicality inherent in the ways we work. The meantime is an interruption that shares little with the modern idea of a rupture in time and the anthropocentric vision of beginning that places in the hands of human beings – often even one single human being – the chance to start history anew. The latter is what in the current exacerbated version of the modern time regime became the backdrop of the projective temporality characterising art production and setting it in a dynamic of constant change that produces no change at all. In this context, the meantime brings forward the chance for a very ordinary beginning – which in its ordinariness can easily be multiplied – that is there to reappropriate, together with the possibility of a present time that again becomes inhabitable and would thus provide shelter for the possibility of change. Thinking the working process in the meantime represents also a counter-perspective to the endless processuality that has characterised performance production, maybe embodied best in the form of the 'work in progress', and that, besides running the risk of never turning into something different than the process itself, seems to rely on a division between products and processes which appears more and more outdated in terms of value production.

22 | Gilles Deleuze, *Difference and Repetition* (New York: Columbia University Press 1994).
23 | Virno, *Déjà Vu*, 59–146.

The second level regards the temporality of performance as a live art and as a live gathering. A temporality of liveness that is reduced to the ephemeral brings performance closer to the current economic paradigm that assigns to the transitoriness of continuous change the role of reproducing that which remains always the same. A temporality of liveness revolving around the aspect of duration alone confronts us with time as a scarce resource. A performance thought in these temporalities cannot become an instrument of time building; it cannot challenge the dominant image of time nor the other social dynamics connected to it. We would think of it as a performance that disappears, not so much from the equation of value production but rather as a work leaving no traces, having no consequences in a time that is isolated from the rest. Thinking performance as a live art in the meantime, on the other hand, opens the work to the past, the future and the elsewhere, it sustains the idea of a performance with consequences, although they cannot be predicted or planned beyond setting the conditions for their happening. It is then a temporality that grounds the single artwork in time, and at the same time challenges what we consider to be 'normal time', not by virtue of being a temporality outside of the ordinary, but rather by exposing the ordinariness of how that conception of normal time is built and could be built differently.

Performance as an instrument for time building unfolds in the creation of a temporal space for things to take another direction, things ranging from the nature of the work to that of the gathering it creates around it. In this sense, what it does is open up a present, exposing it in its inherent interplay of emptying and filling and keeping it incomplete. In the writings of Walter Benjamin and Paolo Virno, amongst others, the incomplete part of time is a productive force that connects and reconnects moments into history: it is thanks to this incompleteness that the present represents a centre of production as well as the temporal category where the generative capacity of human beings is truly at work. When thinking about performance as a live gathering, this present time, incomplete rather than ephemeral, expands; it is built and made inhabitable by the many individuals that make up the gathering. In the gathering, the meantime is the temporality where performance as instrument of time building becomes collective. It does so on a solid base, as a time that is always already shared: as much as it is hardly perceived as time at our disposal, it is the only time we have for living together with others – our time is in this sense always a 'meantime'. A live gathering thought in the meantime, is an incomplete present that emerges for individuals as a time porous to the time of others and for the gathering as a time always already shared and built together. As such, the meantime establishes an unexpected resonance with the time of revolt, which Furio Jesi distinguishes from both the time of revolution and 'normal time'. In his writings, what separates revolt and revolution is specifically the experience of time: 'Revolt suspends historical time, suddenly establishing a time in which everything that is done has a value in itself, independent of its consequences and of its relations with the transitory or perennial complex that constitutes history. Revolution would be instead wholly and deliberately immersed in historical time'.[24] In this suspension of historical time, Jesi sees also the chance of calling into question the dichotomy between the collective and the individual. One partakes in revolt by committing her individuality to an action whose consequences are unknown and unforeseeable, as the suspension of historical time provides a shelter for a possible form of collectivity: 'The concept of permanent revolution reveals – rather than an uninterrupted duration of revolt in historical time – the will to succeed, at each and every moment, in suspending historical time so as to find collective refuge in the symbolic space and time of revolt. The sleep before the revolt – presuming the revolt begins at dawn! – may even be as tranquil as that of the Prince of Condé, but it does not possess the paradoxical tranquillity of the moment of the clash. In the best of cases, it is an hour of truce for the individual who has gone to sleep without ceasing to feel like an individual'.[25] Yet, this process is not inherent to revolt and Jesi has no romantic views on the outcome of this temporality, which he intends more as an isolated suspension of historical time rather than a gap interwoven inside it: in the end, 'everyone goes back to being an individual in a society that is better than, worse than or the same as before'.[26] After the revolt, a normalising force comes into play, thriving on the dichotomies that continuously corroborate the dominant image of time, life and politics, and not least the opposition separating the temporality of revolt from that of normal time.

Questioning this opposition is particularly interesting for thinking the temporality of performance's live gathering as a meantime. Jesi sees in revolt the refuge that a collectivity can find from 'normal time' and then proceeds to question it. This refuge is not connoted as a comfortable space where a plurality of different individuals easily becomes a collective body – an idea that sometimes romanticises the live gathering of performance. It is instead a process of destruction of the self. What needs to be destroyed is not the life of the self, rather its naturalised components in collaboration with keeping the revolt outside of history: the individuals that succeed in this effort are those able to place themselves at the intersection between their bodies and the collective, between the time of revolt and that of history.

24 | Furio Jesi and Andrea Cavalletti, "The Suspension of Historical Time", in *The Book of Books, 100 Notes – 100 Thoughts*, dOCUMENTA(13) (Berlin: Hatje Cantz 2012), 433.
25 | Ibid, 435.
26 | Ibid.

At the collective level, in the gathering, individuals are both subjected to a suspension of time and to its passing – a meantime in the end – they are in a temporal spot that allows them to suspend the spell of what has imposed itself as normal time and to destroy the conditions that sustain its continuous reinforcement and normalisation: they are in a position of time-building rather than time using.

IV

The time of performance is not that of revolt. Like the latter, performance is a time shared amongst and produced by individuals who do not expect to know the consequences of their gathering, a time in which 'every act is valuable in and of itself'.[27] On the other hand, embracing this similarity thoroughly would mean to bind performance to a limited notion of autonomy that prevents, rightfully, any inquiry into its direct impacts, but also wrongly empties performance of its sense and possible roles within today's society.

What a performance and revolt share is a temporality of the meantime, the power of suddenly instituting a time: the possibility of failure is always also accompanied by the chance for things to deviate and take a direction different from the expected. The political consequences of performance as a live gathering – as those of revolt – are not to be underestimated. They simply cannot be planned, controlled or directed; they can be assessed only afterwards. In this sense, Jesi's thoughts do not stand here as an attempt to draw a simplistic parallel between performing and political practices, or between the temporality of liveness and that of revolt. Rather, they expose the central role of temporality and of relation between the individual and the collective while thinking about the politicality of performance today, especially as regards the chance of looking at time as something to build collectively rather than to save individually.

Thinking the temporality of performance – both as a live art and gathering – as a meantime opens in this context the chance for it to be an instrument: if the political consequences of an artistic gesture can be assessed only in the aftermath of the gathering it creates, the conditions that support and multiply these consequences are to be built ahead. Performance is hosted in, and simultaneously builds, a meantime, operating as an instrument that works for deconstruction (and destruction) as well as for construction. In this movement between the void and the filled, between building and destroying, across art production, its conditions and the imaginative effort

27 | Ibid, 433.

for a future, performance as an instrument creates a suspension and sets it again in historical time, an incomplete present that is intertwined with the past and the future and with the temporalities lived by the individuals gathering around it.

In the meantime simultaneous to the present, performance politicality unfolds if the conceptual and aesthetic effort deconstructing the dominant image of time is sustained by an incessant work on the conditions that sustain this image and affect the ways performance is produced and attended on a very material level: an aesthetic and conceptual work of deconstruction is politically relevant when matched with a material work of destruction. In the meantime that separates us from the future, performance's politicality unfolds in the ordinariness of the new beginnings it brings as it re-appropriates, constructs and practises different temporal conditions of production and imagination as if they were already present.

In this meantime, the gathering brings to liveness the chance to be really alive, that is, to be always able to deviate and take another direction. This chance is built into time not as an eclipse deviating temporarily from its orbit and bound to reenter it, not aiming at the ephemeral encounter between the performative and the political but rather at the building of an inclined plane between the two: the condition for an artistic gesture to bounce, appear and have consequences in the sphere of the political.

VALERIA GRAZIANO

Coming together
it is easier to work
after our bodies
meet
paper and pen
neither care nor profit
whether we write or not

from 'Recreation', Audre Lorde

Audre Lorde's poem 'Recreation'[1] is a parallel exploration of writing and of making love, a queering of *ars poetica*, that simultaneously becomes a resignification of what this genre stands for: a poem that speaks of the art of poetry itself, thus mobilising both content and form to perform its meditation. 'Recreation' instead sets up the two activities of lovemaking and composing as compenetrating and reciprocal: sex and poetry contour each other as intertwined acts of co-creation, making each other possible in specific ways. Crucially, the living body is implicated in both, equally making and taking in the world its love object and the poem itself. The temporality evoked in Lorde's poem presents us these two activities not as isolated events, however, but as inserted in a sustained, continuous and fluid temporality in which they exist and return as ongoing activities, one flowing into the other and vice versa, in over-spilling cycles that contribute to the making of a bibliography and of a biography. In the joy of repetition, creation is transmuted, it sheds its messianic quality and becomes *recreation*: repeated, the act of creating becomes more akin to *playing* than to labouring: *It is easier to work / after our bodies meet.* The prefix re- opens up creation, allowing it to ripen into its full potential: beyond the single deed that marks the messianic event, the intricate interlacing of gestures and conditions practices that, and, in their diverging unfolding, brings history into being.

1 | Audre Lorde, "Recreation", in *The Collected Poems of Audre Lorde* (New York: W.W. Norton and Company 1997).

I start from Audre Lorde's intuition around the polysemy of *recreation* to put forward this concept as an organisational principle. Via the framework of recreation, I want to think about some of the main political stakes of the forms used by collectivities able to act politically in the present. In what follows, I intend to play with the capacity of *recreation* to hold together multiple meanings and to modulate them from contiguous fields of practice in order to transgress some received ideas around the organisation of cultural production, the locus of creativity and the politics of use of collective pleasures. In other words, I want to transpose the double binding that Lorde ascribed to *recreation*, with its connotations of play, reciprocity, repetition and regeneration, from the realm of intimate, one-to-one relationships – with one's lover, with the blank page – to bear consequence upon the organisation of collective endeavours. I wish to ask how recreation can sustain us in becoming capable of an art and culture measuring up to our epochal conditions (expanding upon the art of writing on offer in her poem) and in generating plural relationships and political love (over-spilling from the original ode to her partner).

The importance of recreation shall become sharper as I move from this notion to what I named, with an admittedly less poetic, yet hopefully effective, play of words: the *recreative industries*.[2] By this term, I name a type of organisation, which has existed in various forms throughout modernity, dedicated to regenerating living labour and sustaining the free time of the oppressed and the exploited against capitalist temporal structuring and valuation – and in opposition to the limitation of an experience of public pleasure as solely organised around work or consumption.

The necessary background for grasping the urgent need for such a project has been largely debated and I will suffice to quickly recall it here. The restructuring of economic production into its financialised and post-Fordist mode has de facto reframed all industries as immediately cultural per se.[3] Already twenty years ago, Paolo Virno noted how the most successful techniques for the management of labour (such as soft powers or informal networking, for instance), as well as the techniques of subjectivation of workers (flexible, invested, ambitious, mobile, opportunist etc.) that prevail in contemporary business are traceable to the arts and were first experimented with within the cultural industries. Moreover, as Stefano Harney articulated, the contemporary commodity has itself taken on the qualities previously ascribed to the work of art, such as incompleteness, authoriality and performativity.[4]

2 | As first explored in the context of the II Radical Open Access conference, "The Ethics of Care", Coventry University, June 2018. The presentation was published with the title 'Towards a Grammar of the Recreative Industries' in *Competition and Cooperation* (Berkeley: Crossing Press [1984] 2007), 110–114.
3 | Paolo Virno *A Grammar of the Multitude* (New York: Semiotext(e) 2003).
4 | Stephen Matthias Harney, "Unfinished business: Labour, management, and the creative industries", *Cultural*

The last thirty years saw a related burgeoning of the investment policy known as the 'creative economy', a framework as rhetorically seductive as it has been untenable. Countless scholars produced arguments and data to confirm the unabashed faulty claims such as those ascribed to the 'creative industries', the 'creative city' or the 'creative class'.[5] Nonetheless, these notions have sequestered 'creativity' and 'innovation' as cornerstones of the contemporary neoliberal imaginaries, and not as tools to dismantle them,[6] leaving us with a possibly historically unprecedented depletion of imaginal resources able to sprawl political consequences for the present.

The notion of the *recreative industries* that I put forward here is thus an effort to name some slighted organising efforts punctuating both neglected histories of class struggles as well as contemporary counter-cultural productions, in order to call to attention and strengthen certain tendencies within them.

PREFIGURATION TAKING PLACE

Before I turn to the recreative industries proper, a preamble is necessary to contrast them with the dominant framework they seek to shatter – that of the 'creative economy', together with its 'cities' 'districts', 'classes' and 'industries' – and link this kind of organisation to the specific form of cultural action that it can host.

Mark Bank and Justin O'Connor recently surveyed twenty years of research around the creative industries highlighting how even some of their old proponents are now publicly distancing themselves from previously held beliefs around their viability and capacity to generate positive societal change.[7] The title they chose for their article was 'Inside the Whale', an homage to George Orwell's critical review of Henry Miller's *Tropic of Cancer* of the same title. While the authors did not explore the juxtaposition of Orwell's piece in their own article, its urgent, lucid and yet disconsolate

Studies 24, no. 3 (2010): 431–44.

5 | For some early, seminal critiques of the creative industries, see for instance: Toni Bennett, *Culture: A Reformer's Science* (London: Sage 1998); Stuart D. Cunningham, "Trojan horse or Rorschach blot? Creative industries discourse around the world", *International Journal of Cultural Policy* 15, no. 4 (2009): 375–86; Justin Lewis and Toby Miller (Eds.), *Critical Cultural Policy Studies: A Reader* (Oxford: Wiley-Blackwell 2002); Geert Lovink and Ned Rossiter, *MyCreativity Reader: A critique of creative industries* (Amsterdam: Institute of Network Cultures 2007); Rosalind Gill and Andy Pratt, "In the Social Factory?: Immaterial Labour, Precariousness and Cultural Work", *Theory, Culture & Society* 25, no. 7–8 (2008): 1–30; Angela McRobbie, "Clubs to companies: Notes on the decline of political culture in speeded up creative worlds", *Cultural Studies* 16, no. 4 (2002): 516–31; Andrew Ross "The mental labor problem", *Social Text* 18, no. 2 (2000): 1–31.

6 | Audre Lorde, "The Master's Tools Will Never Dismantle the Master's House" in *Sister Outsider: Essays and Speeches* (Berkeley: Crossing Press [1984] 2007), 110–14

7 | Mark Bank and Justin O'Connor, "Inside the whale (and how to get out of there): Moving on from two decades of creative industries research", *European Journal of Cultural Studies* 20, no. 6 (2017) 637-54.

overview matches closely the affective politics of my recreative industries proposal. Orwell's essay was a complex meditation on the politics of art, and specifically literature and poetry, written amidst the turmoil of the war in 1940. Looking back at the previous two decades of literary production in the English language, Orwell sought to lay out the nexus between historical conditions, art and politics. He insisted that conformity comes in many forms, not only in the guise of an avoidance of overtly political subject matters, as had happened throughout the 1920s, but also in an obstinacy to produce 'constructive', positive and activist outlooks while the world faced the incommensurable challenges of mass murder and totalitarism, a vice he insisted characterised the Marxist (yet bourgeois in experience) British writers of the 1930s. For Orwell, the crux of the matter is that the liberal sphere of free speech that allowed for literature was no longer, and that:

> *'The all-important fact for the creative writer is going to be that this is not a writer's world. That does not mean that he cannot help to bring the new society into being, but he can take no part in the process as a writer. For as a writer he is a liberal, and what is happening is the destruction of liberalism. [...] Progress and reaction have both turned out to be swindles. Seemingly there is nothing left but quietism — robbing reality of its terrors by simply submitting to it. Get inside the whale — or rather, admit you are inside the whale (for you are, of course)'.*[8]

In praising Miller for his outlook in *Tropic of Cancer*, he simultaneously and ironically decrees the fate of this book: the impossibility of bearing any kind of historical consequence rather than confirming the impossibility of getting out of this comfortable 'womb big enough for an adult'. For Orwell, it is the very attempt to intervene in the politics of the present *as a writer* that is doomed and delusional, as the world requires a different regime of interventions before writing, creating and free thinking can be relevant again.

The creative industries discourse was first generated in the 1990s in Australia and became internationally popular shortly after the New Labour government launched its agenda for a Creative Britain. Unlike the notion of the 'cultural industries', which the scholars of the Frankfurt School invented to critically address the conditions of cultural production in the era of mass industrialisation, the creative industries discourse was not born as a critique of capital, but was conceived from the start as an instrument of direct intervention in the governance of cities during a profound shift to post-industrial economies. For a short season, the creative agenda provided a convincing rhetoric, a perfect 'inside the whale': a political imaginary where economic prosperity was coupled with increased democratic participation. Depleted neighbourhoods were to be regenerated

8 | George Orwell, "Inside the Whale", in *A Collection of Essays* (Orlando: Houghton Mifflin Harcourt 1970), 250.

and jobs were going to be fulfilling endeavours. Education, culture, sports, leisure and tourism were going to be financially supported and become the cornerstones of consumption. However, in reality, the creative economy quickly proved to be just one of the many tricks by which capital performs what Marx called its 'necromancy'.[9] On the one hand, the notion of 'creativity' allowed governmental accountants to cluster together various sources of wealth generation,[10] combining profits from intellectual property (such as those of the IT sector), with more traditional, craft-based services (such as hairdressers or florists' shops) and artistic or cultural productions proper. On the other hand, it normalised the ideology of micro entrepreneurship, introduced metrics for the evaluation of culture via its economic impact, and promoted a new kind of subjectivation, more compatible with the needs of a post-industrial social norm: the self as a hard-working 'self-facilitating media node', to borrow an iconic line from the sitcom *Nathan Barley*.[11]

This paradigm never delved into the philosophical complexities of the term 'creativity', yet it weaponised it to render the regime of private property central to cultural processes. While the generic vocabulary of the 'new' – innovation, disruption, change – coloured the language of the rise of neoliberalism to a global paradigm, its political philosophy could be summarised, as Melinda Cooper suggested, as 'pre-emptive':[12] '[i]f neoliberalism is prepared to accommodate the new of "uncontrolled social forces," then, it is only in order to channel them into the constantly reinvented form of private wealth and familial inheritance'.[13] By the same token, the networks and communities of practice who made up the fabric of countercultural scenes and minoritarian aesthetics were de facto recast as resources made available in the city-factory, or bulldozed out from urban life. This, in short, is the state of affairs that the recreative industries wants to intervene into and crack open to reveal its necromancy.

By switching to recreation, I want to perform a counter-sorcery, cut the belly of creativity open. The first way to do so is to refuse a grand gesture, so I have simply added the *re-* and avoided the temptations of an ex nihilo creation. This would have meant contradicting the message by virtue of performance. Turning now to what the recreative industries stand *for*, rather than against, I return to a regime of cultural practices that I named

9 | Karl Marx, *Capital, Volume One* (1867), *Marx/Engels Internet Archive*, http://www.marxists.org/archive/marx/works/1867-c1/index.htm (last accessed May 25, 2019).

10 | See for instance Nicholas Garnham, "From cultural to creative industries: An analysis of the implications of the 'creative industries' approach to arts and media policy making in the United Kingdom", *International Journal of Cultural Policy* 11 (2005): 15–29.

11 | Written by Chris Morris and Charlie Brooker, produced by Channel 4, 2005.

12 | Melinda Cooper, *Family values: Between neoliberalism and the new social conservatism* (Cambridge: MIT Press 2017), 312.

13 | Ibid.

'prefigurative', after a recent polemical debate that took place in the mid-2000s around the politics of prefiguration within social movements.[14] In political theory, prefiguration emerged as a framework of analysis in the 1960s, to make sense of the new modes of performing the political generated within social movements. It has recently been picked up again to assess the import of experiences such as the Arab Spring, Occupy, Gezi Park and M15, just to mention a few of the most readily recognisable examples. In proposing that prefiguration has much to offer for a contemporary possibility for formulating a political outlook on the artistic practices of our time, I also saw them as an antidote to the pitfalls of both understandings of art as 'contemporary' or 'avant-garde', in a vein that might not be that distant from Orwell's. I wished to call attention to the characteristics of cultural practices that perform their political struggles against the conditions of their own taking place, and in ways that make them politically available for other experiences beyond themselves.

The work around prefigurative practices, in the midst of so many *post*-designations that qualify our present, articulated a materialist approach to collective imaginal activities that sought to challenge capitalism on the very ground of the re-appropriation of the conditions of its libidinal production. What is therefore needed now is an articulation of the organisational forms where such figurations can, literally, take place, claiming space and time, in ambiences where it can become possible, literally, to figure things out. How can we conceptualise the techniques of counter-organisation at our disposal, how do we ensure the continuity of prefigurative practices beyond the waves generated through social movements and mass mobilisations? At stake is not only how to find viable forms of resistance – and to constantly renew them against the perpetual mutations of capital – but how to make them politically available beyond the particular experiences that generated them, giving them conditions in which they can *take root*. While prefigurative practices appear ubiquitously across the social body, in unruly ways, perhaps undetected or unwelcomed, they can also give rise, sometimes, to unexpected organisational forms.

JUNKOLOGY: THE PLAY OF REFUSE

In order to introduce the stakes of *recreative industries*, I will start from a playground that is also so much more, that appeared in Denmark in the early 1940s, amidst the drama of the war and the Nazi occupation of the country.

14 | Valeria, Graziano, "Prefigurative Practices. Raw Materials for a Political Positioning of Art, Leaving the Avant-Garde", in Lilia Mestre and Elke Van Campenhout (Eds.), *Turn Turtle, Turn! Reenacting the Institute* (Berlin: House on Fire Publications, Alexander Verlag and Live Art Development Agency 2016).

In 1943, in the periphery of Emdrup, in the northern outskirts of Copenhagen, a landscape architect named Carl Theodor Sørensen and a pedagogue named Hans Dragehjelm, inaugurated a shared project they had been gestating since the mid-1930s: it was the first 'Skrammellegepladsen', a made-up word which in Danish means 'Junk Playground'.[15] This is not just a recreation area where parents can bring their children for some exercise, but a new kind of urban space dedicated to free play, a new kind of pedagogy and a new type of pedagogical organisation. The area is quite ample, surrounded by greenery. Here, children can find a vast variety of waste and scrap materials with which to play and build their own landscapes. In 1935 Sørensen described his vision for the junk playground as:

> *'An area [...] where we should gather, for the amusement of bigger children, all sorts of old scrap that the children from the apartment blocks could be allowed to work with, as the children in the countryside and in the suburbs already have. There could be branches and waste from tree polling and bushes, old cardboard boxes, planks and boards, 'dead' cars, old tyres and lots of other things, which would be a joy for healthy boys to use for something. Of course it would look terrible, and of course some kind of order would have to be maintained; but I believe that things would not need to go radically wrong with that sort of situation'.[16]*

Sørensen had been already working as a landscape architect for the *Workers' Cooperative Housing Association* since the mid-1920s. It was in this context that he came to the realisation that playgrounds could provide an opportunity to re-create intergenerational and neighbourly relations in a different mode. They can be a place where the environment is shaped by play rather than toil, and where humans young and small congregate around the potentiality of materials in the absence of predetermined rules or purposes beyond creating a commonly enjoyable ambience. The junk playground project yielded profound implications for Sørensen's own role as an urban planner, questioning the authority of specialist knowledge as it encounters others, as he found himself now planning for disorder, carving out a space where things could happen in another way. In the words of Robert Dighton, Sørensen's position went from that of an 'architect' (who held the power and control regarding what play opportunities were made available to children) to facilitator (who passed his power and control to children in order that they themselves could create their own play environments)'.[17]

15 | The Adventure Playground website reports that: The Danish word '*Skrammel*' means junk, reusable rubbish etc. and '*Legepladsen*' means playground. It is noteworthy that the term '*Skrammel*' has a positive connotation in Danish, whereas the term 'junk' has a more negative value in the English language. Over the years, Emdrup has also used the term 'building playground' – Robert Dighton, "The History of Adventure Play", http://www. adventureplay.org.uk/history2.htm (last accessed May 1 2017).

16 | Carl Theodor Sørensen, "Etagehusets Have", *Arkitektens Månedshæfte* (1935), 61. Quoted in Ning de Coninck-Smith, *Natural Play in Natural Surroundings. Urban Childhood and Playground Planning in Denmark, c. 1930 – 1950, Working Paper 6* (Odense: Odense University Printing Office 1999).

17 | Robert Dighton, "The History of Adventure Play".

This was a time when pedagogy too was an effervescent discipline intersecting with many other political concerns. Sørensen's collaborator, the educator Hans Dragehjelm, was well known for being the inventor of the sand-box and also for co-founding the Danish chapter of the Froebel Society, a pioneering initiative to promote progressive education for young children. The society had been initiated some thirty years earlier in England by a cohort of German and British women inspired by Friedrich Froebel's ideas about education. Froebel was among the first advocates demanding 'the provision of special centres for the care and development of children outside the home'.[18] His proposal of the 'kindergarten system' was radical at the time. It emphasised free play with different materials or 'gifts'. It understood human development as being intrinsically linked with interaction with the environment, which should be as meaningful, varied and pleasurable as possible for young humans.

Significantly, Froebel's pedagogical philosophy also influenced landscape architecture during the 1930s, as architects were expected to play a progressive social role by producing the best settings for a comfortable living affordable by all. This sense of shared social responsibility extended, of course, also to children, who were thought to benefit from free play in natural environments. The return to nature as a site of learning and self-realisation constituted a break from earlier educational beliefs that saw free play in children as a source of concern, as a destructive impulse to be disciplined, suppressed – in one key world, civilised. The dominant views in the 1930s pushed for educational reforms in the name of the right of children to develop 'naturally' and in nature, away from the negative environment of cities and urban infrastructures perceived as polluted and corrupting. This was a vision of childhood close to the conception of man as 'naturally good' as first theorised by Jean-Jacques Rousseau almost two centuries earlier. In contrast, Dragehjelm and Sørensen's junk playground broke off from such sentimental views of the natural state: rather than Nature, the experience of human freedom to be passed on to children is realised in an environment that is both *artificial* and *political*.

Another key figure in the new organisational experiment of Sørensen and Dragehjelm was the 'playleader', an adult presence employed to offer minimal, non-intrusive supervision and support to the children at play.[19] John Bertelsen, who was appointed as the first 'playleader' at Emdrup also contributed to the history of the junk playground by inventing the world

18 | Mark K. Smith, "Friedrich Froebel (Fröbel)", *Informal Education Encyclopaedia* (London: YMCA George Williams College 1997), http://infed.org/mobi/fredrich-froebel-frobel/ (last accessed May 25, 2019).
19 | In his first proposals, Sørensen did not seem convinced of the necessity of an adult supervisor, but it was the Workers' Co-operative Housing Association who wanted to hire one, in compliance with its policies. Cfr. Carl Theodor Sørensen, "Etagehusets Have".

'skrammologi' ('junkology') to describe the kind of activities that became possible in such spaces. In the words of Bertelsen, junkology corresponded to an inversion of accepted social norms, whereby 'all pedagogical and occupational ideas were quickly turned upside down'.[20] He understood his role of supervising children in such a way as to be as unobtrusive as possible, so as not to conflate the adult figure with a figure of authority. He insisted, 'the initiative must come from the children themselves [...] I cannot, and indeed will not, teach the children anything'.[21] In his diary of his time at Emdrup, he described the junk playground as an expression of the conflict between children and the over-regulated urban environment, a context increasingly hostile to the free exercise of the faculty of imagination, so crucial to human development:

> *'The city has become a place where there is no space for the child's imagination and play. Access to all building sites is forbidden to unauthorized persons, there are no trees where the children can climb and play Tarzan. The railway station grounds and the common, where they used to be able to fight great battles and have strange adventures, do not exist any more'.*[22]

Significantly, Bertelsen was also an active member of the Danish Resistance Movement against the Nazi occupation, spending several months in prison for his partisan activities. This was a renowned fact in the neighbourhood of Emdrup, contributing to his reputation and in shaping activities at the playground. It can be said that his commitment to an anti-authoritarian view of society, 'the culture of bourgeois society',[23] continued in his work as educator. Bertelsen's pedagogy also contributed to progressive pedagogical discussions of the time that insisted on the importance of teaching children the values of the Resistance without conflating its meaning with a vision of violence or disregard for social rules. His writing and biography grappled with the question of how to lead – and foster, as a facilitator – a non-fascist form of life, articulating the crux of the matter of junkology as a praxis: it is not the city that is an enemy of the child, but the rules and protocols that govern the access to it. What emerges from Bertelsen's writings is also a class analysis of the function of the playground as an emotionally nurturing shelter for working class children, who he described as lacking

20 | John Bertelsen, "The Daily Round on a Junk Playground", *Danish Outlook* 6.6 (1953), p. 688. Quoted in Roy Kozlovsky, "Adventure Playgrounds and Postwar Reconstruction", in Gutman, Marta and Ning de Coninck-Smith (Eds.), *Designing Modern Childhoods: History, Space, and the Material Culture of Children; An International Reader* (New Jersey: Rutgers University Press 2007).
21 | John Bertelsen, "Early Experience from Emdrup", in Bengtsson, Arvid (Eds.), *Adventure Playground* (New York: Praeger 1972), 20.
22 | John Bertelsen, Personal diary (1946). Quoted in Arvid Bengtsson, *Adventure Playgrounds* (London: Crosby Lockwood Staples 1973).
23 | John Bertelsen, quoted in Stephen Gadd, "The Junk Playground – Denmark's Eco-Contribution to Outdoor School Education", *The Copenhagen Post*, March 19, 2017, http://cphpost.dk/history/the-junk-playground-denmarks-eco-contribution-to-outdoor-school-education.html (last accessed May 24, 2019).

not so much material goods, but interactions with their parents, often busy with work for long hours.

The philosophy of the junk playground as introduced by its first three organisers therefore articulated a vision of society predicated upon a not-at-all naive concept of self-determination as relational and technologically-enabled, while items de-classified as ruins, garbage, scraps and leftovers embodied a complex position between the natural and artificial condition. What the proposal of the new organisation articulated in practice is that a healthy and joyful childhood must be organised as the experience of one's capacity of *autonomy* within a *collectivity*. The junk playgrounds enabled an original organisational form whereby children could experience and learn the skills to bring their singular and collective fantasies into being, not as an act of creation, but of re-creation with previously discarded items and materials; they were given the tools to produce their own worlds and each other.

Finally, recreation can be convoked in this story in one last sense. Despite being a large experiment – hosting around 200-400 children per day – Emdrup would have perhaps been an isolated and less known experience if it weren't for the efforts of Marjory Allen, a British landscape architect, to recreate it elsewhere. After a visit, she wrote about the Danish experience for a UK journal and started a movement dedicated to grassroots democratic planning and collective administration of 'adventure playgrounds', which grew to over 75 sites across the country. Allen was an aristocrat and her network held a more conservative vision of the social function of the playgrounds: she promoted their role in preventing juvenile delinquency amongst the urban poor and highlighted their usefulness for the acquisition of employable skills, a utilitarian view that contradicted the spirit of the Danish initiative. Yet, her initial gesture of retelling the story of Emdrup, insisting it to be an excellent form of reuse of bombed sites, led to a re-creation movement and the spread of a highly influential idea that impacted the politics of informal pedagogy, especially during the 1960s.

RECREATIVE INDUSTRIES

I departed from the junk playground – not only a space, but foremost a new civic organisation – as it agglutinates the characteristics of the object of knowledge that the speculative expression 'recreative industries' attempts to hold together. What follows is not the theory of all of this, which belongs to a larger project, but it is a prolegomenon to where the concept of the recreative industries can lead to: not an alternative to the creative industries, but an alternative to the capitalist economy hiding within that sector.

RE-

The polysemic potency of the prefix *re-* in recreation goes beyond those activities of recycling and reuse that are key to ecological reparation as in Serge Latouche's '8 R's'[24] (Re-evaluate, Reconceptualise, Restructure, Redistribute, Relocalise, Reduce, Re-use, Recycle), but it simultaneously opens the question of 're-appropriation, revolt and revolution',[25] In the most immediate sense, recreation is a repetitive act, as is any form of organising. But as in the case of the junk playgrounds, recreation also connotes an act of beginning again. In the case of the spread of the playgrounds, this can be immediately linked to the necessity of dealing with the ruins of what was there before and is now only perceivable as a by-product (the bombed houses of the war, the waste materials of consumerism). Similarly, recreating the possibility of use value in the context of the junk playgrounds referred both to the organising taking place in a context of material scarcity (economic crisis), but also a scarcity that was felt in terms of a lack of room for political action (amidst rising fascism).

-CREATIVITY

At the same time, recreation points to the need to confront the question of creativity on a more sophisticated philosophical ground than the one afforded by the creative industries. Out of junk, it is possible to conjure up something different, to restore use value in unexpected ways. Despite the crisis of credibility, the ideology of the creative industries lingers on: as a toxicity tainting the imaginal and what is at stake in the possibility of creation itself, here limited to a productivist proprietary model. If Fordism enticed people to believe that satisfaction in life could be obtained via affluent consumption, Post-Fordism, and especially the discourse of the Creative Industries exhortation is to seek happiness in relentless productivity. The relentless invocation of 'creativity' as an unsurpassable modern value perhaps chokes its revolutionary potential beyond recuperation. And yet, a political critique and affective re-appropriation of the ground this term corresponds to could be staged as a seizing of control of the means of cultural production that in turn shape our subjectivities, as an act of autonomy and relationality. Recreation is a way of naming current tendencies prefiguring what could grow as a discourse of creativity from the ruins of two visions,

---

24 | Serge Latouche, *Farewell to Growth* (Cambridge: Policy Press 2009).

25 | This expression is borrowed from RiMaflow, a workers-run, occupied factory in Trezzano sul Naviglio (Milan, Italy) that has been also hatching itself as a recreative industry, out of the empty shell of an automobile components' firm. The slogan written at the entrance of RiMaflow's plant reads: 'Ri' for *rinascita* (rebirth), *riuso* (reuse), *riciclo* (recycling), *riappropriazione* (reappropriation), *reddito* (income), *rivolta* (revolt), *rivoluzione* (revolution)'.

that of the democratisation of affluent consumption of the industrial phase and the democratisation of creative production of the post-industrial era. Pragmatically, a re-politisation of creativity needs an active opposition to regimes of private property as they are applied to the realm of knowledge production via patents and copyrights, and inventing counter-conduct to the mandatory regime of authorial self-branding.

INDUSTRIES

The notion of industries in the context of recreation serves as a marker for re-appropriating what our possibility of discussing collective deeds and the organisation of social cooperation might entail. Michael Hardt and Antonio Negri recently sought, in a similar vein, to re-appropriate 'entrepreneurship' away from an idea of individual talent thriving in a hierarchical social order and capital-driven chain of causations. In the section of their book *Assembly* concerned with the 'Entrepreneurship of the Multitudes', Hardt and Negri revisited this key figure of capitalist's cultural imaginary via its most renowned theorist, Joseph Schumpeter. According to the latter, the virtue of entrepreneurship boils down to 'to create new combinations among already existing workers, ideas, technologies, resources, and machines' and to a number of operations geared towards the 'continuous expropriation of the cooperative power of the multitude'.[26]

As Schumpeter explained, the essential quality of entrepreneurship is not to really foster or care for something that is new in a progressive sense of the term, but to master the rules underpinning the possibility of an endless recombination of already existing factors, including machines, resources and affects, optimised to extract capital value both from them directly and from the very operation of reshuffling them (Schumpeter's 'creative destruction'). What entrepreneurialism does is to go only for what is profitable or rentable within the new – hence the creative destruction of the old and the backgrounding of social reproduction.

If anyone were to object that the junk playgrounds or an occupied space would not strictly speaking qualify as an 'industry', then it would be easy in turn, following Hardt and Negri's re-appropriation of entrepreneurship as a collective capacity, to argue that indeed this critique would not allow any understanding of the crucial role for the economic cycle of creating different combinations across subjects, tools and infrastructures.

26 | Michael Hardt and Antonio Negri, *Assembly* (Oxford: Oxford University Press 2017), 143-44.

By shifting the discursive terrain from *enterprise* to *industry* however, I want to introduce a crucial aspect of the kinds of operations needed to oppose the culture of capitalist entrepreneurship. There is an interesting gap in the etymology of *industry* and *enterprise* that might support this view. While the root of *industry* connotes an outward movement towards its object, an act of diligence and zealous care, *enterprise* is an action that takes, appropriates. One is about the giving of attention and dedication; the other is about laying claim to something as part of an activity. Raymond Williams, who in his work on cultural keywords also addressed how the use of the adjective 'creative' masks the political difference between innovation and novelty,[27] noticed that the idea of industry went from connoting a certain 'human quality of sustained application' to becoming a 'set of institutions for production'.[28] Moreover, as Franco Moretti usefully summarised, in the 16th century the initial meaning of 'industry'

> *'Was that of "intelligent or clever working; skill, ingenuity, dexterity, or cleverness". Then, in the mid-sixteenth century, a second meaning emerges – "diligence or assiduity ... close and steady application ... exertion, effort", that soon crystallizes as "systematic work or labour; habitual employment in some useful work". From skill and ingenuity, to systematic exertion; this is how "industry"contributes to bourgeois culture: hard work, replacing the clever variety'.*[29]

Both processes, the move from the quality of action to the form of organisation, and from skill to toil, highlight how the current debates around post-work would benefit from a more granular description of what anti-work activities and ways of organising might consist of, what their subjects, procedures and objects (in Marxian terms, their political and technical composition) could be. As artists, as producers, as carers, as lovers, even as patients or the unemployed, we have been told it is of utmost importance that our self-worth and biographical gestures carry an enterprising responsibility. The recreative industries thus find themselves fighting the pressure of managerial rationality. In contrast to this, it would be possible to play with the notion of recreative industrialists as a subjectivity striving precisely for the opposite reason of preventing all of the above-mentioned heterogeneous elements of interest to the entrepreneur from being put to work by capital. Echoing the words of Mariarosa dalla Costa and Selma James in the introduction to their seminal work on social reproduction:

27 | Raymond Williams, *Keywords: A Vocabulary of Culture and Society* (Oxford: Oxford University Press 2014), 46.
28 | Ibid, 118.
29 | Franco Moretti, *The Bourgeois: Between History and Literature* (London and New York: Verso 2013), 31.

"We inherited a distorted and reformist concept of capital itself, as a series of things which we struggle to plan, control or manage, rather than as a social relation which we struggle to destroy".[30]

Opposing such managerial rationality means, crucially, to challenge the normalised approaches to the division of labour within organisations and to replace the rampant managerial culture with contra regimes of practice. One suggestion on how to move away from the processes of subjectivation associated with entrepreneurship comes from Pierre Dardot and Christian Laval in their treatise on the philosophical history of the Common. They returned to the philosophies of Rousseau and Saint-Simon to propose the art of *administration* against that of *management.* While administrative functions might be inevitable functions of any collectivity, capacity of action and creation, they should be organised in manners that counter the power principles of bureaucratic governmentality.[31]

CREATIVE REPRODUCTION

The recreative hypothesis is moreover a political framework for reclaiming the organisation of those semiotic, affective or relational productions that, under capital, stand severed from the other kinds. Crucially, in refusing to confine creativity solely to the realm of production and insisting instead on its import for the realm of social reproduction, the recreative industries undo one of the founding, and most persistent, cultural techniques (of the so-called western canon at least), which predicates the separation of the cultural event from the conditions of its own production, in order to produce a spectacular effect. In this respect, recreative industries are those organisations that refuse to present the cultural value they generate as content for the belly of the whale. The junk playground, by admission of one of its creators, is not an aesthetically resolved piece of architecture. It is ugly, messy, chaotic. Instead, its founders got creative with the organisation of social reproduction in a quotidian and intergenerational sense. How can we bring up our children differently? How do we experiment with the space of everyday community life, how do we set them up differently as spaces of autonomy? Ultimately, how do we redistribute the burden of keeping ourselves alive in this world in the best possible way?

30 | Mariarosa Dalla Costa and James Selma, *The Power of Women and the Subversion of the Community* (Bristol: Falling Wall Press 1973), 5.
31 | Pierre Dardot and Christian Laval, *Del Comune, O Della Rivoluzione Nel 21. Secolo* (Rome: DeriveApprodi 2015), 213–15, translation VG.

RECREATION

Finally, we must turn to *recreation* properly understood as referring to leisurely activities and a time for enjoyment, amusement, fun and pleasure, such as that experienced by the children at play at Emdrup. In Romance languages, recreation is also the name given to school breaks, the pause from mandated classroom activities when children can engage in free play. Recreation at school has been deemed so important by education specialists that these leisurely breaks have been included in the Charter of Human Rights as providing essential relief from the disciplined toiling of school work.

By pointing to the political potential of the space that is opened in recreation, I mean to more broadly foreground the unique politics that becomes possible in this interval. The leisurely and playful activities it hosts are not, however, extraneous to the structuring of productive cooperation under capital. Rather than being freely arranged, their form and tempo directly relate and grapple with the bulk of other social relations, their hierarchies and exclusions. How then to conceive of recreation as a politics for free play? In the same way as the junk playground did not need to rely upon a fantasy of return to a separate state of nature, but to the contrary were conceived as part of a cooperative organisation of housing and neighbourhoods, so recreative industries can be thought of as exercises in sustaining 'the relative autonomy' that emerged historically for cultural workers, or as Paolo Virno puts it, in the growing gap between what the labour force becomes capable of during time spent in 'the acquisition and the enrichment of its linguistic-cognitive competences',[32] that is, in formal and informal education, and the actual drudgery of the tasks they will be hired to perform by capitalist enterprises. Virno identified that this 'divergence between training and contingent execution is a distinctive trait of contemporary forms of life' and 'a seismograph of future conflicts'.[33] In other words, the politics of recreation beyond the liminal status of children who are not yet fully part of the workforce consists of what becomes possible in the interval between the wealth of experiences of preparation and the paucity of conditions for execution.

And finally, to add one last point to this exploration of recreation, it must be considered also in its meaning as regeneration, a replenishing of the body. When the concept of recreation first appeared in the English language by way of French during the 14th century, it carried precisely this meaning of

32 | Paolo Virno, *L'idea di Mondo: Intelletto Pubblico e Uso della Vita* (Rome: Quodlibet 2015), 178.
33 | Ibid.

'refreshment or curing of a sick person':[34] One only has to think of the bursts of energy accompanying children's break time in schools everywhere to see how ceasing to work can be, in its own right, a healing experience. Yet, the realm of the *recreational* as an area of activities organised and enjoyed away from work (including the shadow work of consumption) and from the relentless duties of social regeneration proper is still under-theorised in discourses that grapple with post-work scenarios. The recreative industries open up this line of investigation by helping to name those organisations that, both today and in the past, have been reclaiming the role of non-productive activities as central to prefiguration, in which another kind of social cooperation is allowed to temporarily become the predominant logic: to experience of the presence of others as a source of pleasure.

It is worth trying to discover just what the organisational mechanisms are that can make the time – and crucially, also the spaces and tools – of recreation available as a political resource for the oppressed and the exploited. Throughout modernity, this is a minoritarian history in comparison to political life understood as participation in a reading public, political meetings and more violent forms of class struggles, one that took root in unexpected contexts, such as an international movement of playgrounds made of junk. In order to grasp what this constellation of recreational mechanisms can generate in the present, we must turn now to a contemporary experience that rather than playing with the debris left over by the bombs of the second world war, took root since the last financial crisis amongst the carcasses of empty buildings left behind by deindustrialisation and within the imaginal void peeping through the cracked horizon of the creative city.

FROM THE CASE DEL POPOLO TO OCCUPYING THEATRES: AN ITALIAN CHRONICLE

In the period 2011-2013, Italy, like many other countries, was affected by the financial crisis that triggered – and ideologically justified – a ripple of austerity reforms that cut public spending for welfare provisions. Many Italian cities saw a parallel disinvestment of both capital and state interests, which made a number of empty properties in urban areas available for squatting by other constituencies such as migrants and homeless populations. The same years, however, also saw a peculiar wave of occupations carried out in the name of a different cultural production. Italian activists and cultural workers organised themselves in collectives that entered and reclaimed a number of abandoned buildings, many of

---

34 | "Recreation", Online Etymology Dictionary, https://www.etymonline.com/.

which were former infrastructures of welfare, such as schools and theatres, to claim them as 'commons' and in the name of 'civic uses'.[35] A non-comprehensive list of the spaces reclaimed as part of that wave of cultural occupations includes (in rough chronological order): Nuovo Cinema Palazzo, Rome (April 2011); Teatro Valle, Rome (June 2011); Teatro Coppola, Catania (December 2011); Ex Asilo Filangeri, Naples (March 2012); Teatro Garibaldi, Palermo (April 2012); MACAO, Milan (May 2012); Teatro Rossi, Pisa (September 2012); Cinema America Occupato, Rome (November 2012); Teatro Meditteraneo Occupato, Palermo (December 2013); Cavallerizza Irreale, Turin (May 2014); Spin Time Labs, Rome (2014). To these, a couple of other notable examples must also be added: S.a.l.e Docks, active in Venice since 2002, and Angelo Mai, opened in Rome in 2004; while these last two experiences began almost a decade earlier, they have been important nodes of the network and were also early instances of occupations made in the name of opening up spaces for a different cultural and artistic production.[36] These squatted cultural centres have, for about a decade now, constituted one of the few living political horizons in the Italian context – which is one where the ruling classes have been extremely hostile towards any cultural practice that is minoritarian, erotic or opaque (or new, innovative and creative, to put it in neoliberal terms). Italy is not, however, particularly exceptional in this respect; the recreative capacities of the network of occupations have also connected them with other international cultural circuits, maintaining a transnational space for the circulation of artistic practices and discourses that is of a different register than those currently made available via the official infrastructures for cultural cooperation. Indeed, the emphasis of the re-politicisation of cultural production, not in the name of art but as a creative reconfiguration of political praxis, and the idea that political struggles are necessarily inserted in different cultures of production, have been one of the cornerstones of the discourse produced by the cultural occupations.

A genealogy of these occupations looking into the historical conditions of their coming into being could go back as far as the second half of the 1800s,

---

35 | Cf. Teatro Valle Occupato, "Lo Statuto della Fondazione Teatro Valle Bene Comune", June 14, 2014, http://www.teatrovalleoccupato.it/statuto-fondazione-teatro-valle-bene-comune, and L'Asilo (Ex Asilo Filangieri), "Dichiarazione d'uso civico dell'Asilo", January, 2nd, 2016, http://www.exasilofilangieri.it/regolamento-duso-civico (last accessed May 25, 2019).

36 | On 2nd September 2011, two of the cultural centres mentioned above, Teatro Valle and S.a.l.e. Dock, jointly occupied a liberty theatre building in Venice that goes under the name of *Ricreatorio Marinoni*. Its name comes from the original use of the building that, before being turned into a theatre, was created in 1921 to host the play of convalescent children being treated in the nearby Marine Hospice, a sort of proto-institution for art-therapy. Such *ricreatori*, or recreation centres, are a peculiar public institution that only exists in the northeast of Italy, particularly around Trieste, a locality with a strong tradition of radical experimentations with social service provisions (for instance, the anti-asylum movement headed by Franco Basaglia also took root in this area). The *ricreatori* are worth mentioning here as they constitute an early example of a public and laic effort to support and yet, simultaneously govern, the free time of children and youth through informal pedagogical settings.

when nascent international working-class movements were beginning to make the need for a different society felt across Europe. From meeting in taverns, workers clubs and cafes, the workers movement in countries such as Belgium, Austria, and particularly Italy began to create their own people's houses, a new kind of organisation dedicated specifically to the 'intertwining' of 'political and recreational activities'[37] that characterised socialist gatherings. While they had different characteristics in different contexts, people's houses were often founded with great sacrifice by groups of workers who donated money and time to build them from scratch, also because they were often denied the possibility of renting other kinds of rooms as their meetings were considered subversive. They were often set up to host in proximity the coexistence of a varied range of activities, from political assemblies to evening classes, from card playing and boxing to dancing events and concerts. Many also became a node of a different economy by becoming consumer cooperatives, offering basic necessities at discounted rates for members.

Later on, during the 1970s, the Italian context would become renowned internationally for another form of organisation that reunited political and recreational activities: the *centri sociali occupati autogestiti* (or *csoa*, or 'occupied, self-managed social centres' in English). These first emerged as part of the Movement of '77, out of the model of the *centri di proletariato giovanile* (Proletarian Youth Clubs), a slightly different form of association that lasted for a brief season in the mid-seventies. Both experiences – *centri di proletariato giovanile* first and *csoa* – marked a continuity but also a crucial point of break with the legacy of the people's houses, more linked by then to the Communist Party. The aim of the latter had veered more and more towards an educational or leisurely agenda for the working classes,[38] the *csoa* emerged as spaces for the militant re-appropriation of that intermingling of the political and the recreational. As the Leoncavallo collective (Milan) put it in a co-investigation on the history of *csoa*:

> *'We are also far from the vision of csoa as a ritualisation of the "case del popolo" […] The **case del popolo**, in fact, despite having played an extraordinary role in the history of the labour movement as places of sociality and territorial points of reference and of "capture" of the class, delegated the most strictly political functions to the party or the trade union'.[39]*

The novel organisational form of *centri sociali* can further be contrasted with the *centri di proletariato giovanile*, with which they briefly coexisted,

---

37 | Maurizio Degl'Innocenti, *Le Case Del Popolo In Europa: Dalle Origini Alla Seconda Guerra Mondiale.* (Florence: Sansoni 1984), 6.
38 | Degl'Innocenti, *Le Case Del Popolo In Europa.*
39 | Piero Moroni, ed., *Centri Sociali: Geografie del Desiderio* (Milan: ShaKe Underground 1996), p. 99, translation VG.

but that quickly folded.[40] For Primo Moroni, the latter were the last expression of a 20th century relation between plebeian sociability and the accumulation of capital in the city. As long as the elites had their territory clearly demarcated in the prestigious locations of the city centre, they took an active disinterest in the manifestations of other kinds of social productivity in the peripheries, which led to the opening of *centri di proletariato giovanile*. But the imaginal ambition of the *centri di proletariato giovanile* was still the city centre, the conquest of this symbolic space of power. Instead, the passage to the *csoa* model of organisation marked a shift in the spatialisation of desire and the dissolution of the familiar duality of city centre/periphery. The city centre simultaneously ceased to be the symbolic locus of power and it was no longer approachable for the proletarian youth, who used to access it via 'a path that is for a large part 'amicable' and convivial [...] ensured by a concatenation of shops [...and] of spaces for gathering and entertainment (pubs, taverns, bars, bowls clubs, etc.)'.[41] While the city began its mutation into a polycentric social factory, *centri sociali* resisted such reconfiguration of the material and existential spaces of metropolitan creativity, understanding the need for self-organised cultural and convivial activities as immediately political and not simply propaedeutic. As for the people's houses, an important aspect was the invention of different modes of cohabitation in the same space, rather than the achievement of an overall coherent aesthetic. One last point to note: the subjectivity of the youth involved in *csoa* introduced a mutation from the previous generations who set up the *case del popolo*. They were, as Moroni portrayed them,

> '*for the vast majority children of proletarians; many of them were initiated to work at a very early age (14-15 years old). The neighbourhood recognises them as part of itself. Spontaneously they feel that something has ended. Their fathers and their older brothers have memories of struggles and imaginaries of distant utopias to be implemented at an undefined, later moment. But to them, it seems that the immediate memory of the previous cycle of struggle has not changed their future prospects and their need for happiness that much. They do not have and do not believe in future horizons: they desire almost spasmodically the "here-and-now" realisation of "spaces"of happiness and full, direct, conscious communication. It can be said that the "invention of the present" starts with them and will be prolonged in time throughout the Eighties'.*[42]

Firmly situated in this genealogy, the Italian cultural occupations of the 2010s have been described in terms of 'new cultural institutions'

---

40 | To give an example of the short-lived exuberance of the phenomenon, Primo Moroni reports that 52 of them were opened in Milan alone between 1975 and 1976. – Cf. Piero Moroni, "Un certo uso sociale dello spazio urbano", in Moroni (Ed.), *Centri Sociali*, 172, translation VG.

41 | Ibid, 165.

42 | Ibid, 170.

or 'autonomous alterinstitutions'.[43] Yet I want to argue that in fact their organisational specificity can be best grasped from the perspective of the recreative industries. The need to repair abandoned buildings, organise their maintenance and equip them by making do with often recycled materials; the refusal to be cast as centres for the production of 'political' art and the insistence instead on generating new cultures of political action; the interest in experimental solutions for the collective care of social reproductive needs; the organisation of tools to allow the maximum free play of the constituencies involved; their investment in practices of collective joy are all characteristics that would contribute to this narration. Those involved in the occupations, both activists and cultural workers, had to confront the problem of how to make a living while dedicating themselves to maintaining these open and lively spaces, how to generate some kind of economy that could enable a diverse participation, while at the same time refusing to turn the occupations into commercial venues. Doing so would have meant giving in to the very self-entrepreneurial logic they wished to dismantle. Moreover, in the Italian context, such as many other cultural institutions dedicated to the production and transmission of living, contemporary cultures, they do not, and never did, enjoy full support from the State apparatus. Through engaging in the struggle to reorganise the processes of cultural production, these occupations both perform a materialist critique of the capitalist economic environment in which they operate, and actively expose the creative industries' mythologies as bogus. And this is where the example of one of the occupations, MACAO, becomes particularly relevant to examine from the perspective of a politics of recreation.

TO SHELTER AND TO REPAIR: MACAO

Whereas the ideology of the creative industries focused on ideas of virtuosity, productivity, excellence and disruption, all practices that are the handmaiden of 'corporatisation, flexibilisation and militarisation',[44] the recreative industries as we have seen are characterised by amateurisation, gestation, eroticism and regeneration, all terms that hint at the centrality of pleasure for a politics of the common. It this respect, it is both funny and sad that, despite the obsession of business and management studies with metaphorical language, we still lack an image in that discourse capable of describing organisations as sites of production of the possibility of common

43 | Marco Baravalle, "Tra Governamentalità e Autonomia", *Opera Viva Magazine*, August 3, 2018, http://www.operavivamagazine.org/alteristituzioni-e-arte/ (last accessed May 25, 2019).
44 | Brian Holmes, "Disconnecting the dots of the research triangle: Corporatisation, Flexibilisation and Militarisation in the Creative Industries", in Geert Lovink and Ned Rossiter, (Eds.), *My Creativity Reader: A Critique of the Creative Industries* (Amsterdam: Institute of Network Cultures 2007), 177.

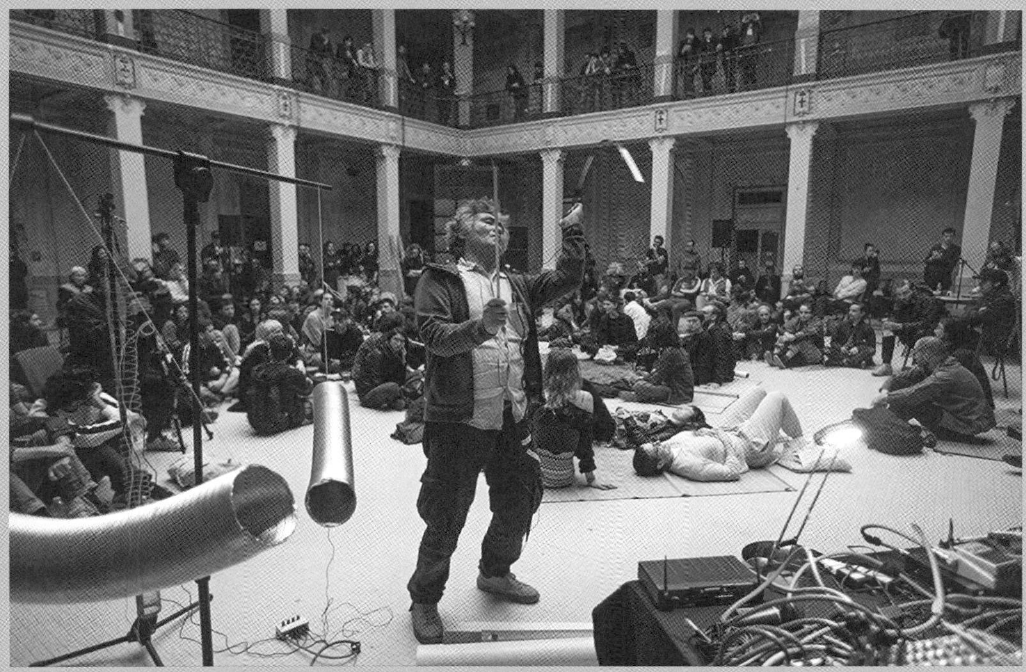

Figure 9.1. Guida Galattica per Nuove Istituzioni at Macao, Milan, 2018. Photo: Luca Chiaudano. CC BY-NC-SA 4.0

pleasure for all those involved. For instance, in the classic book *Images of Organization*,[45] organisations are presented as machines, organisms, brains, cultures, political systems, psychic prisons, flux and transformations, instruments of domination, but offer no hints to the possibility of recreation. In a recent text, MACAO, a squatted cultural centre opened in Milan in 2012, offered itself up as a *'rifugio'*,[46] a refuge or a shelter. In Italian, another meaning of this word, used to denote temporary shelter, is a 'repair'. This double semantic meaning of *rifugio* – a shelter and place of repair – establishes a rich and significant connection between a site of respite and rest, and one of mending and regeneration. It also connotes an awareness of the fragility of those structures that are able to offer repair (in both senses of the term), from the underlying violence embedded in most institutional and infrastructural systems under capitalism. To echo Stephen Jackson's notion of 'broken world thinking',[47] to offer itself up as a space of repair is to stand in the ruins of capitalist destruction and coalesce despite the conditions that one occupies would make seem possible in forming a harmonious community, achieving economic prosperity or obtaining artistic excellence.

45 | Morgan Gareth, *Images of Organization* (London: Sage Publications 1986).
46 | MACAO, Desire Week, http://www.macaomilano.org/spip.php?rubrique146 (last accessed May 1, 2018).
47 | Steven J. Jackson, "Rethinking Repair", in *Media Technologies: Essays on Communication, Materiality, and Society* (Cambridge: MIT Press 2014), 221-39.

I want to turn next to the experience of MACAO in more detail precisely to conclude the genealogy of recreation in the Italian context outlined above with a zooming in onto a more granular description of its principal organisational dispositives, which incidentally are also those elements that are consistently omitted by the dominant narrations around the creative industries. As I'm a part of the Italian diaspora, my interest in MACAO and the Italian Cultural Occupations goes beyond any disinterested scholarly inquisitiveness. Instead, I see such concern as implicating me in a form of thinking as care.[48]

Currently occupying the buildings of a dismissed slaughterhouse (from which it is menaced to be displaced again), MACAO presents itself as 'an independent centre for art, culture and research that considers artistic production as a vital process for rethinking social change and for elaborating independent political critique'.[49] MACAO began in 2012 with the occupation of a different building, an empty skyscraper in the centre of Milan. A crowd of cultural and creative workers entered Torre Gualfa to protest the systemic negligence of public support to cultural provisions in the city and across the country, the unbearable levels of precarisation faced by those who make a living in the cultural and creative sectors, and the lack of future awaiting students in these areas. In denouncing the endemic corruption of the Italian political system and the embarrassing levels of ignorance of decision makers ruling over the country's culture industries, the activists reclaimed a space to put forward a different vision of society. Maddalena Fragnito, one of MACAO's activists whose words I will rely on for this description, summarised some of the key concerns that inspire this collective's experimentation with organisational forms:

> *'What desires define a new institution? How is an institution designed and how is it used? Who decides? How does a changeable community relate to organisational forms? What is the relationship between a collective that transits through such a space and the technology that is used for its organisation?'*[50]

The self-management of MACAO is organised around a number of techniques and devices. There are weekly political meetings and a quarterly scheduling meeting that represent 'the principal means through which a changing community of a hundred people governs itself'[51] and the place where decisions around the application of different workflows and

48 | Maria Puig de la Bellacasa, "'Nothing comes without its world': thinking with care", *The Sociological Review* 60, no. 2 (Thousand Oaks: Sage journals 2012): 197-216.
49 | Maddalena Fragnito, "Key Concepts for a New Cultural Institution", in *Competition and Cooperation* (Coventry: Post Office Press, Rope Press and Open Humanities Press 2018), 16.
50 | Ibid, 17.
51 | Ibid, 16.

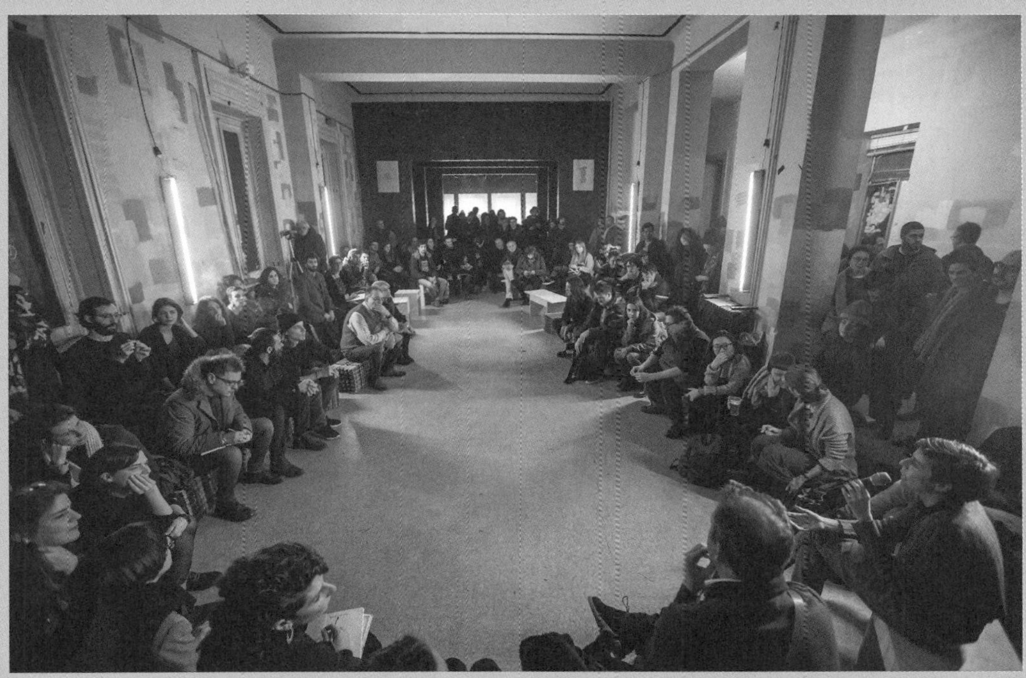

Figure 9.2
Marginal Consort
at Macao, Milan,
2017. Photo: Luca
Chiaudano. CC
BY-NC-SA 4.0

activities are discussed and renegotiated over time. Beyond these two recurring appointments, the collective invented names for a number of 'continuous functions' that are necessarily undertaken for securing the quotidian existence of MACAO both as a physical space and as a collectivity. These include: communication with the press, office work and accounting, technical operations linked to the production of specific performances and live events and the logistical management of the storage facilities. A number of open working groups autonomously coordinate the labour of participants around the tasks that require addressing in each area.

There is the function called *Curami*, an imperative reflexive verb that in Italian plays with the double meaning of 'Look after me' and 'Heal me'. This is the administrative tool by which the MACAO community takes care of its collective maintenance as a physical space in need of cyclical acts of cleaning, tidying up, restocking and refurbishing. Each week, a spreadsheet with the list of necessary activities is thus circulated via MACAO's main chat room, to which people respond by filling in their availability for certain tasks. 'In this way the activity of "looking after" is transferred to a public space, named and paid for',[52] landing a different status to the role of reproductive labour and collectivising the responsibility to attend to it. Morever,

52 | Ibid, 18.

'This shared maintenance is understood as an attempt to overcome the barriers between what is intended as work and what is defined as artwork (Ukeles 1969). Here, the physical nature of the space is seen as an opportunity to stay together, its maintenance as a demand for acceptable living conditions, and the resulting relationships that emerge as an area of artistic and political production. Indeed, the maintenance of MACAO's physical space has a lot to do with the care for the relationships that inhabit it.

Before the procedure was prototyped, maintenance work was invisible and exploitative (Federici 2012, 28), while the inability to overcome personal settings and comfort zones was producing a sharp divide between those who write and those who fix cables, between those who speak and those others who line up the chairs. As a consequence, it was hard to grasp the complexity of what was happening within such compartmentalised dimensions, and the competitiveness between different groups was taking time away from more important aspects of MACAO as a cultural institution. The introduction of a procedure for the shared and explicit maintenance of the place, however, has brought a more profound understanding of the workings of the machine/institution, and has made it possible to collocate every action within a dimension of co-dependency with all the other activities that surround it and give it substance. Those who do not wish to contribute to the maintenance of the place do not access the tools of mutualism that the community has given itself, but take part in the activities and scheduling of the place. Curami, as a tool, has not deprived people of their inclinations; on the contrary, they have benefitted from this instrument in relational terms'.[53]

The work of artist Mierle Laderman Ukeles that is cited here as an inspiration was amongst the first to broach the problematic and systematic invisibilisation of maintenance work not only in the cultural sector, but in virtually all relationships that underpin infrastructural functionality within capitalism. In one of her seminal performances for instance, Ukeles washed the staircase of the Wadsworth Atheneum's entrance.[54] MACAO's attention to the socio-political affordances of the physical proximity necessary for the social maintenance of a space in good workable conditions goes beyond Ukeles' interventions, which remained limited to a regime of symbolic representation. MACAO is about redefining the *conditions* of production of that very symbolic regime.

Another of the continuous functions involves the participation, on behalf of MACAO's collectivity, in broader struggles, militant networks and campaigns, such as *Non Una di Meno* (the Italian chapter of the recent international feminist mobilisations), FairCoop and No One Is Illegal, as well as other institutions. This function names the necessity for MACAO to exist as part of a broader ecology of practices, and also its political

53 | Ibid, 18-19.
54 | Mierle Laderman Ukeles, *Hartford Wash: Washing, Tracks, Maintenance – Outside* and *Inside*, live performance, July 1973.

responsibility for contributing to the broader political struggles and in solidarity with constituencies beyond its immediate locality.

The *Take Care!* function names the labour involved to undo and prevent sexism and other forms of violence in MACAO, striving to denaturalise certain entrenched machist forms of abuse that pass as cultural norms of behaviour and stimulate an ongoing reflection within the broader MACAO community. Recent initiatives in this sense included the use of antisexist and antiracist messages as entrance stamps for events and the presence of an identifiable care team during large events like concerts and parties.

Yet another continuous function active at the time of writing is '*Come In!*', the open meeting to welcome newcomers, introduce them to MACAO's principal mechanisms of self-management and gather proposals for new initiatives to be organised in the space. 'This is possibly the most delicate moment of the relation between the cultural centre and the city,' – explains Fragnito – 'in that it represents the main access point for a different way of production. The hardest issue to manage, which is the question of "who's in charge," comes into play precisely at this moment'.[55]

The participation in MACAO's maintenance via the 'continuous functions' is remunerated in Common Coin, the community's currency, and it also allows participants to access MACAO's own Basic Income system. Taking care of 'continuous functions' is compensated according to tasks and not by calculating the time invested in them. This was a decision the collective took to experiment with measures able to discourage mechanisms of over-investment in working ethics and sacrificial approaches to political activism, in an effort to articulate a possible politics supporting the experience of collectivity as pleasure.

MACAO has been experimenting with its own system of alternative currency and distribution of basic income, generated via a percentage taken from tickets to events, bar sales, venue hires and projects financed via institutional collaborations and other grants. The mechanisms that regulate the redistribution of collectively-generated wealth is one of the most interesting aspects of MACAO's political experience, even more than the technology it uses (Common Coin is a virtual currency inserted in the broader network of FairCoin, the virtual money experiment of the international cooperative FairCoop). Rather than relying on a techno-solutionist approach that confers a thaumaturgical power to cryptocurrencies, MACAO's basic income mechanism is grounded in the refusal of both 'political and cultural volunteering and the idea of the wage'.[56] The basic income (currently oscillating between 200-400 Euros) can be claimed only by those who are active in a set number of different continuous functions during any given month (at least two assemblies, one Continuous Functions, one *Curami* action and one networking group per month – although this number can also be negotiated for individual participants to accommodate specific needs). If someone fails to or is not interested in meeting the requirements to access the basic income, this person will still be remunerated via a proportionate sum of Common Coins. The measure of paying for tasks rather than per hour is meant to be a dispositive to discourage overwork and burnouts, as over-commitment does not increase the total sum received during any given month. As Fragnito puts it '*it is not the quantity of work that is rewarded but rather the intensity of cooperation*', in an attempt to move away from '*the prevailing ethics of work*'.[57] While this measure remains experimental and partial, as it could allow for different kinds of de-valuation of labour to remain undetected, it can nonetheless become a powerful tool to reflect on the very problem of value attributed to different activities while these tools remain open to modifications by the collectivity.

Through the creation of these new administrative devices and the effort of naming its constitutive relations, MACAO went much beyond the simple games of metaphors often played by those contemporary cultural institutions that call themselves 'lab' or 'school' or perhaps 'assembly', without really engaging with different models of organisation. MACAO is a relevant instance of the politics of recreation as it has been able to host different kinds of cultural production, research and experimentation, spanning across a broad range of media and levels of expertise, while organising its relations and functions along the principle of achieving maximum intrinsic pleasure out of the experience of caring for an institution and constructing common rather than just sharing resources.

CODA

At the time of writing, MACAO is under thread of eviction. Many of the other cultural occupations in Italy have already lost their spaces and disbanded. The future of *csoa* appears similarly bleak in the current political climate. Junk playgrounds and people's houses have long lost much of their former political energy. Yet to keep these stories alive might be a way of contributing to a politics of recreation opening onto the future. As Anna Tsing and her co-authors wrote in *The Arts of Living on a Damaged Planet*, 'we

---

56 | Ibid, 21.
57 | Ibid.

can't shelter anything we don't notice'.[58] If the creative economy has been the dominant ideology of the neoliberal *pax*, the recreative industries could be picked up as a conceptual tool to notice the possibilities of organising otherwise.

This will be a large project, which in this text I have just touched upon, situated along two axes. The first is an historic line of argument. The tracing of a lineage, within capitalist modernity, of organisational forms that considered social reproduction as entangled with conditions of cultural production. The recreative industries encapsulates a genealogy that spans across a broad temporality, as well as diverse spaces, whenever and wherever modernisation has intervened in the production of culture, mutating its core processes of gestation, evolution, propagation and preservation. The second axis is a political discussion of how the recreative industries can intervene within existing cultures of production. These are just two avenues that this concept opens to. One is a subaltern history of economic relations where reproduction is not invisibilised – the other is an opening towards the question of what transforms libidinal economies, where this agency is and how we name it.

The recreative industries always corresponded to exercises in the fragile temporality of sheltering both our labour force, allowing us to experience its potency as it disentangles itself away from capitalist forms of relation, but also to experience our constitutive difference not as something to be merely managed, but as the true source of the pleasure found in the 'creative function'[59] of the body politics. Such are the stakes of recreation.

58 | Anna Lowenhaupt Tsing, Nils Bubandt, Elaine Gan and Heather Anne Swanson (Eds.), *Arts of Living on a Damaged Planet: Ghosts and Monsters of the Anthropocene* (Minneapolis: University of Minnesota Press 2017), 43.
59 | Audre Lorde, "The Master's Tools Will Never Dismantle the Master's House", 110.

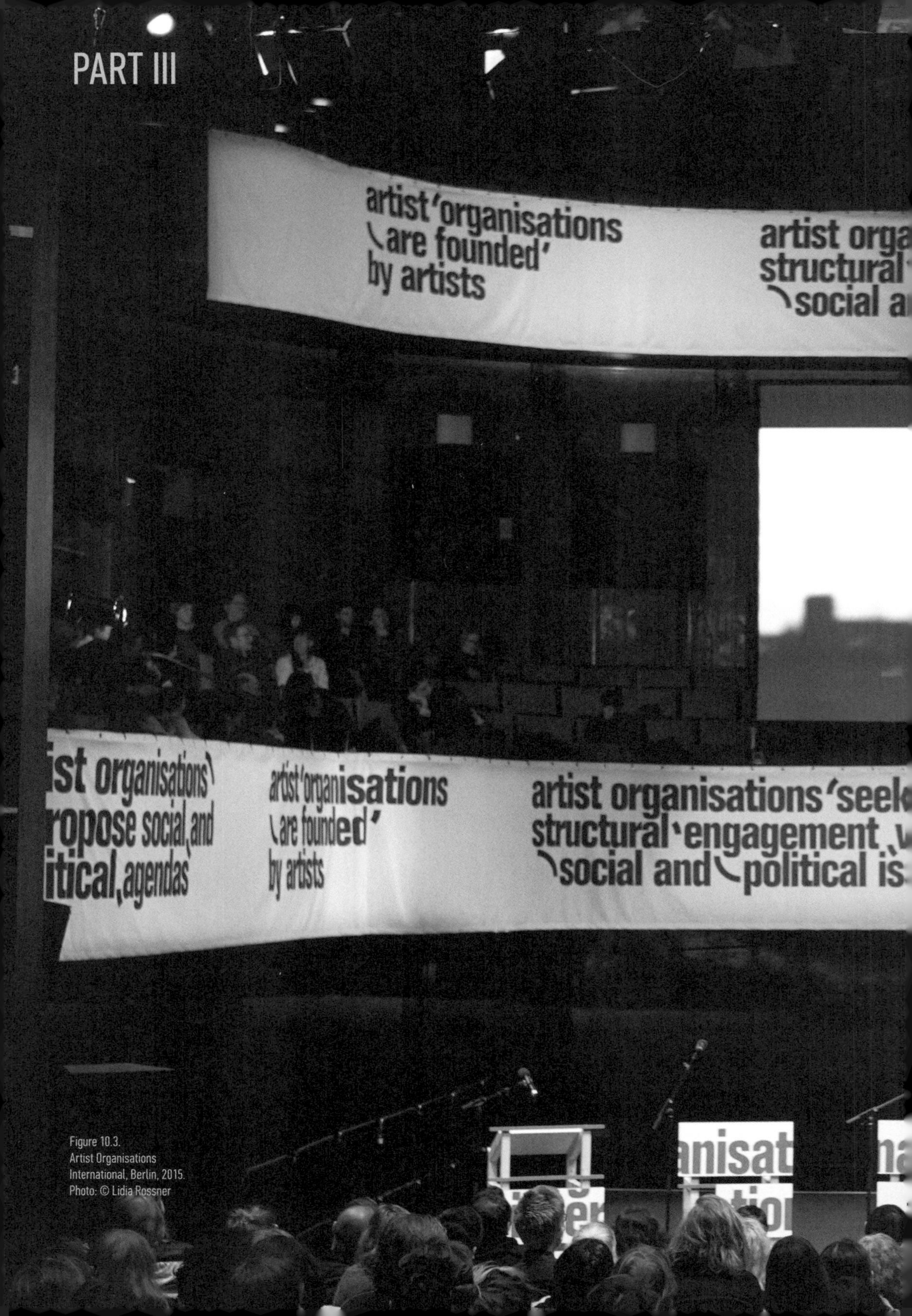

PART III

Figure 10.3.
Artist Organisations
International, Berlin, 2015.
Photo: © Lidia Rossner

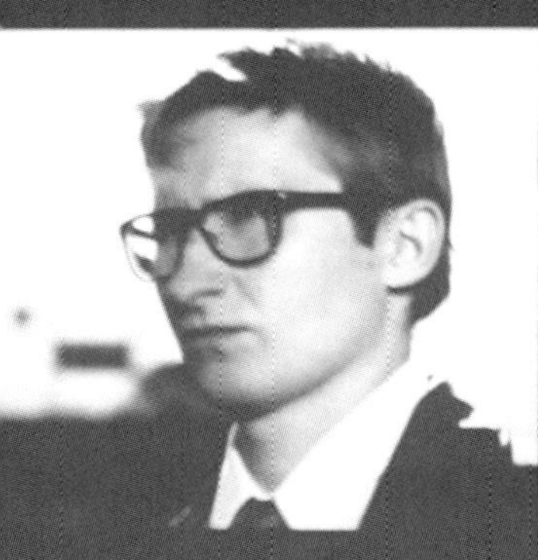

ations 'seek for
gagement with
political issues

artist organisations
choose the 'form
of the 'organisation

artist organisations
choose the 'form
of the 'organisation

artist organisations
'propose social and
political ,agends

artist organis
'are founde
by artists

FLORIAN MALZACHER — THEATRE AS ASSEMBLY:

It is a moment of truth when theatre director Milo Rau is called onto stage on the third day of his *General Assembly* at Schaubühne Berlin.[1] Sixty delegates from all over the world have gathered 'to debate on where we stand as a global community and what needs to be done – socially, ecologically, technologically, politically'[2] with the aim to create a *Charter for the 21ˢᵗ Century* – till one of them, a German-Turkish Erdoğan supporter, outright denies the Armenian genocide. Emotions run high; the game has reached its limit. Some participants demand the speaker be expelled, others argue that a true democratic discussion has to endure such opinions. Finally, Milo Rau decides to throw out the delinquent – just to call him back in a little later after further discussion.

This episode towards the end of an equally artistically and politically ambitious endeavour reveals much more than only the classic democratic conflicts around the limits of freedom of speech. Suddenly the thin line becomes tangible that marks the proximity as well as the distance between theatre and politics. A line that can be crossed, hidden, played with or be made porous – but not ignored. It is this at times almost invisible gap that for me marks the most productive challenge in recent years in the performing arts. The renewed interest in theatre as public sphere has shed light on the

1 | Milo Rau, *General Assembly*, live performance at Schaubühne am Lehniner Platz Berlin, November 3-5, 2017.
2 | "General Assembly", November 2017, http://www.general-assembly.net/en/.

specific potential of performing arts as a medium whose unique selling point is the creation of temporary communities defined by time, space and a changing set of theatrical rules. Such a theatre not only mirrors society but offers possibilities of trying out and challenging social and political procedures, of analysing, performing, enacting, testing or even inventing concrete aspects of society.

The assembly – in the way Occupy Wall Street for example used this term – is a core feature of an activism influenced by the traditions of Anarchism. It marks a zone of gathering, of building community, of making decisions – and by this, of experimenting with the way democracy can function. This very well relates to many aspects of what theatre as assembly – a theatre that puts its focus on creating public spheres – is trying to achieve. But there is a crucial difference: the activist/anarchist assembly is generally considered a space of authentic negotiation, a space for trying to abolish established hierarchies, for not only trying out but living a different way of decision making, usually based on the concept of consensus. At the same time, these assemblies are of a performative nature – and of a physical one, as Judith Butler points out in her speech at Occupy Wall Street (2011):

> *'It matters that as bodies we arrive together in public. As bodies we suffer, we require food and shelter, and as bodies we require one another in dependency and desire. So this is a politics of the public body, the requirements of the body, its movement and its voice. [...] We sit and stand and move as the popular will, the one that electoral politics has forgotten and abandoned. But we are here, time and again, persisting, imagining the phrase, "we the people"'.*[3]

Theatre as assembly might sympathise strongly with these ideas, but I would argue that at the end it has an essentially different take. Theatre is not only a social but also always a self-reflexive practice, despite the fact that conventional approaches have been neglecting this. Theatre is a paradoxical machine that marks a sphere where things are real and not real at the same time and proposes situations and practices that are symbolic and actual at once. It does not enable an artificial outside of pure criticality, nor is it able to lure its audience into mere immersive identification. The social spheres, the assemblies it can create offer the possibility of partaking and at the same time watching oneself from the outside. Brecht's alienation effect is not an invention; it is a discovery of what constitutes all theatre. Just not all theatre admits it – or even tries to make consistent use of it. The ways theatre is conceived as a public space that gives room for radical

---

3 | Judith Butler, speech at Occupy Wall Street at Washington Square Park, October 2013, Youtube video, 4:58, https://www.youtube.com/watch?v=rYfLZsb9by4 (last accessed May 24, 2019). In her new book *Towards a Theory of Performative Assembly* Butler further explains the theatrical and performative dimension of assemblies in popular movements, of course without claiming that the assembly itself is theatre.

imagination as well as pragmatic utopias are manifold and not seldom contradictory in their aesthetical as well as their political positions. But what unites them is the aim to expand the field of theatre, to push its very means and possibilities, to find ways of engaging with the social and political issues of our time and by this also giving inspiration to activism and political thinking beyond the artistic realm.

Dutch theatre director Lotte van den Berg's ongoing project (since 2014) *Building Conversation* aims at reducing theatre to its core. For her, theatre is first and foremost a place of communication, of meeting each other, a sphere where conflicts can be shown and experienced. An agreement to communicate by obeying a set of rules that might be very different at each occasion.

So *Building Conversation* is indeed just this: talking with each other. Inspired by communication techniques from all over the world, models and frames for dialogues are developed. There are no actors, no audience. Just the invitation to participate in a conversation without words, inspired by Inuit assemblies, or alternating between reflection, retreat and dialogue, following a method invented by Jesuits. Another conversation happens completely without a moderator, topic or goal – a method developed by quantum physicist David Bohm, exploring the patterns of our collective thinking. *Building Conversation* is directly influenced by Belgium political philosopher Chantal Mouffe and her concept of 'agonistic pluralism', and one of the talks is devoted to her theory. What makes these conversations theatre is their very framing as theatre, which enables us to engage and keep an analytic distance at the same time. Sometimes it just needs very few but precise decisions, gestures, rules to mark the space of art and opening up a wide field of experience.

PARTICIPATION AND THE FIELD OF AGONISM

Lotte van den Berg's work is one approach to answering a problem that Brecht had already analysed in his *Short Organum for the Theatre* (1949): 'The theatre as we know it shows the structure of society (represented on the stage) as incapable of being influenced by society (in the auditorium).'[4] Not only the play onstage but the whole theatrical set up (not to speak of the hierarchies within the institution itself) merely reproduces the system they aim to criticise. For a theatre that takes the form of an assembly, this question of real participation is obviously crucial: the rules of the involvement might differ as well as the means and degrees of possible

4 | John Willett (Ed.), *Brecht on Theatre: The Development of an Aesthetic* (London: Eyre Methuen 1964), 189.

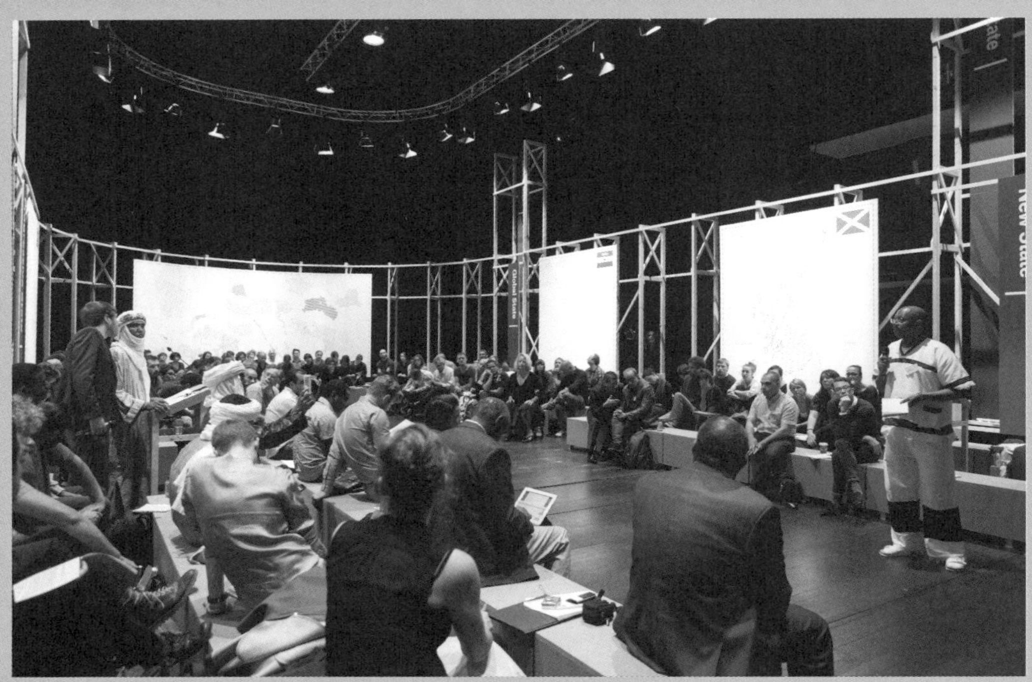

Figure 10.4.b. Jonas Staal, *New World Summit*, Brussels, 2014. Photo: © Ernie Buts

influence. But without the will to allow and use participation, there is no assembly. And yet: what does that even mean in a time where we are permanently forced into putative participation within an all-inclusive capitalist system that has rendered the term almost useless? A pacifier which perversely delegates the responsibility for what is happening to citizens that cannot influence it and thus enables the system to continue more or less undisturbed in its task of self-maintenance.

So-called participatory theatre all too often simply mimics such placebo-involvement; not just offering only stipulated choices but also forcing the audience to engage in this transparent setup where the main problem is not being forced into participation but being forced into fake participation. A permanent involvement (which basically means we are active only in the sense that we are consumers) that we can't escape and that only prevents us from participating in the powers that be. Passivity disguised as activity. Any theatre that understands itself as a space of assembly is inevitably confronted with the task of having to avoid false participation and at the same time reclaim the idea of participation as such. A participation that aims for more than merely replacing one mode of tutelage with another.

Among the most demanding artistic projects thriving for participation and diversity are some of the works by Dutch artist Jonas Staal. The *New World*

Summit (2012 onwards) opens up alternative political spaces in the form of quasi-parliamentarian conventions of representatives of organisations that are excluded from democratic discourse for being categorised as terrorists. These summits offer intense and touching moments where voices can be heard that are elsewhere silenced, and where a radical idea of democracy appears at the horizon. However, they also produce moments of a strong sense of unease, disagreement or even anger since these organisations are obviously not chosen on criteria of political correctness. Some might appear easier for the audience to identify with – for example the Kurdish women's movement – whereas others' causes might seem unacceptable, for example when it comes to nationalism, violence, patriarchy and hierarchies in many struggles for independence. The *New World Summit* welcomes very different organisations; there is no advice given on how to judge or relate to them. The only clarity comes in the critique of Western democracies which base their existence on undemocratic, secretive, and often – even by their own standards – illegal ways of excluding what doesn't fit in their own scheme.

Artist Organisations International (a project devised by Jonas Staal, Joanna Warsza and me in 2014 for the HAU theatre in Berlin) came from a similar approach but pushed farther the idea of a specific dramaturgy within a theatrical setting. *Artist Organisations International (AOI)* brought together twenty representatives of organisations founded by artists whose work confronts today's crises in politics, economy, education, immigration and ecology. It explored the current shift from artists working in the form of temporary projects to building long-term organisational structures: 'What specific artistic value and political potential do such organisations have? How do they perform? What could their concrete impact on various sociopolitical agendas and possible internationalist collaborations be?'[5]

Just as the invited artist organisations inherently question the form of the organisation itself by connecting the field of ethics with aesthetics, *Artist Organisations International* also aimed at making its own conditions visible – and enhancing communications and discussions. While the purpose of the congress was to discuss the possibility of creating a common *meta* artist organisation in the tradition of the historic Internationals, the event's set reversed the logical order of things by proposing an already existing structure with clear visual identity and ceremony. AOI was set up as a *preenactment* – a proactive artistic anticipation of a possible future development.[6] This (by us, the organisers, not announced or commented)

---

5 | "Artist Organisations International – About", January 2014, http://www.artistorganisationsinternational.org (last accessed May 25, 2019).

6 | Cf. Oliver Marchart, "Public Movement: The Art of Preenactment" in Florian Malzacher (Ed.), *Not Just a Mirror; Looking for the Political Theatre of Today* (Berlin: Alexander Verlag 2014), 146-50.

change in procedural order created from the very beginning tense discussions that ranged from the feeling of being trapped in an artistic or political vision of others to the accusation that using theatre as a curatorial means devalues all political urgency – 'making theatre out of something' as a synonym for making it fake. Only on the third day, the end of the congress, was the set finally changed to mark the beginning: in an improvised circle, without any banners and visual reminders of the *AOI*, a discussion was held that would normally open such an event.

AOI did not aim to avoid conflicts but rather to make them visible – albeit with the hope of overcoming at least some of them. It postponed the moment of real participation until the end in order to create substantial discussions and by this also made visible that participation is not necessarily a matter of consensus: it can also aim at direct confrontation and can experiment with miscommunication or even abuse. Artist and theorist Pablo Helguera differentiates between *nonvoluntary* (with no negotiation or agreement involved), *voluntary* (with a clear agreement or even contract) and *involuntary* participation – the negotiations in the latter being rather subtle, not direct, a play of hidden agendas in which 'deceit and seduction play a central role'.[7] These categories of participation can shift and mix, of course, and maintaining a lack of clarity around them can be a useful artistic tool. *AOI* used the image of a possible International founded by artists not to create consensus but to open up an agonistic field.

As much as theatre can be a space of collective or collaborative imagination, it has also always been a medium for showing conflicts and oppositions between ideas, powers, nations, generations, couples, or even within the psyche of a single character. Different forms of realism have sharpened this aspect of theatre by focusing on the internal contradictions of society. Brecht's dialectical theatre looked at the different aspects of concrete struggles to enable the audience to understand how they were created by the system they lived in instead of simply identifying with one position. Following Marx, this kind of theatre was driven by the belief that when the class struggle would finally be won, a harmonious communist society would be created. Later philosophers like Jürgen Habermas and John Rawls tried – in very different ways – to save the ideal of a consensus society, believing that rationality would encourage humankind to overcome its individual interests. But we are not only rational beings; emotion will always play a role, as Chantal Mouffe stresses: 'While we desire an end to conflict, if we want people to be free we must always allow for the possibility that conflict

7 | Pablo Helguera, *Education for Socially Engaged Art; A Materials and Techniques Handbook* (New York: Jorge Pinto Books 2011), 62.

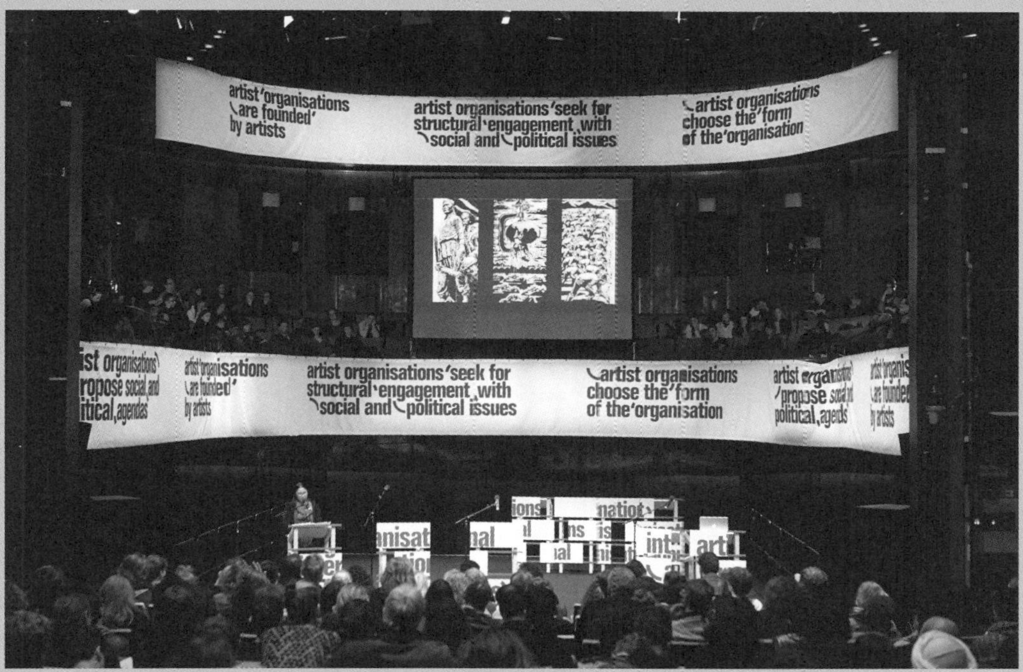

Figure 10.3.2 Artist Organisations International, Berlin, 2015. Photo: © Lidia Rossner

may appear and to provide an arena where differences can be confronted'.[8] Mouffe's concept of 'agonistic pluralism' therefore aims for democracy to be an arena in which we can act out our differences as adversaries without having to reconcile them. At a time in which the once frowned upon dictum 'You're either with us or against us' is having a renaissance on all sides of the political spectrum, we need playful (but serious) agonism where contradictions can not only be kept alive, but above all be freely articulated. Only through this can we prevent an antagonism that ends all negotiation. It is not by chance that Mouffe's concept draws its name from theatre, from *agon*, the game, the competition of arguments in Greek tragedy.

Before Milo Rau's *General Assembly* stand a line of predecessors in his own oeuvre, a series of stagings of political trials that seem almost textbook examples of an agonistic theatre. While most of the more conventional theatre works by Rau rely instead on a very well crafted realism *The Moscow Trials* (2013), for instance, presented a theatrical setup in which three traumatic legal cases against Russian artists and curators were brought again in front of a judge, but this time in the realm of art. Protagonists of the actual trials as well as other closely linked people were confronted with each other in an artificial but simultaneously highly realistic situation in

8 | Chantal Mouffe, "Hearts, Minds and Radical Democracy", *Red Pepper*, June 1, 1998, https://www.redpepper.org.uk/hearts-minds-and-radical-democracy/ (last accessed May 25, 2019).

which curators, artists and critics fought for artistic freedom on one side, conservative TV moderators, orthodox activists and priests for the primacy of religion and nation on the other. For three days the Sakharov Centre in Moscow became an agonistic space in which radically different opinions were exchanged in a way that was not possible anymore outside of the theatrical set. In front of an audience that was just as involved in the piece as the performers, the independent jury in the end decided – by the smallest possible margin – that art was innocent.

As Mouffe suggests, public space is 'the battleground'[9] for the agonistic struggle between opposing hegemonic projects. On a small scale, theatre can create such spheres of open exchange, even in societies where free speech is scarce or in western democracies where the space between consensus and antagonism is becoming increasingly narrow. Art – using a differentiation by art theorist Miwon Kwon – not *in* but *as* public space might be one of the most important things theatre can offer.[10] This public space is not limited to the physical and material space of the performance. As much as the trials initiated by Milo Rau were one-time events with a quite limited audience, they extended their stage far into the realm of news and other media, where discussions about politics and art continued. This use of media goes behind the usual PR work for an artistic project, it is part of the artistic work itself – and a political strategy of a 'leftist populism' as Chantal Mouffe propagates.

IMMERSION AS PARTICIPATION WITHOUT POLITICAL AWARENESS

Such a theatre of assembly, a theatre as public space, might be an intensive experience – but it clearly stands in opposition to recent concepts of immersive art as, for example, brought forward as the leitmotif of the Berliner Festspiele's current program.[11] While such concepts are often also based on forms of participation (the Berliner Festspiele talk rather vaguely about 'artistic positions [...] that recalibrate our relationship between activity and passivity'),[12] this participation is evidently not meant to be emancipatory.

9 | Ibid.
10 | Miwon Kwon, *One Place After Another: Site Specific Art and Locational Identity* (Cambridge: MIT Press 2002).
11 | Under the title 'Immersion', Berliner Festspiele started a programme in autumn 2016 that takes the motto from Allan Kaprow 'Go in instead of looking at' and often presents works between exhibition and performance. The list of artists includes Mona el Gammal, Lundahl & Seitl, Omer Fast, Rimini Protokoll, Chris Salter, Vegard Vinge & Ida Müller, Ed Atkinds and Jonathan Meese – a list of works that shows that the field of Immersion is instead defined in a very wide way.
12 | "Immersion", Berliner Festspiele, 2016, https://blog.berlinerfestspiele.de/theater-und-immersion/ (last accessed May 24, 2019).

The term immersive theatre seems to span over a wide field: from an ecstatic theatre of intoxication referring, for instance, to Dionysus or Artaud via the pre-cinematic forms of the sophisticated illusion machines of the Baroque to the fourth wall of Diderot and his successors – the trick being of course that now this wall is supposed to keep the audience members *in* the same room as the performance.[13] By this, at least Diderot's paradox of a wall that is only created to be ignored can be considered solved. But even though Berliner Festspiele prominently argue with Allan Kaprow's desire to be inside the artwork rather than looking at it from the outside, a closer look at their program as well as the contextualising texts on their website clearly show that rather than following the path of happenings, immersive art is strongly related to the very illusionist forms of theatre Kaprow et al. were fighting against. The aesthetical dilemma of such an approach is rather obvious when reading e.g. Doris Kolesch's short history of immersive theatre on the Berliner Festspiele's blog where she connects the phenomenon of the popular virtual reality game *Pokémon Go* to theatre:[14] as the invention of film and the victory of cinema brought illusionist theatre to its limits in the beginning of the 20th century, latest developments of VR-techniques have made immersive theatre (or is it actually still just realistic or illusionist theatre with a new name?) look outdated before it even had a chance to mature. A real immersive theatre does not give room for critical thinking; it does not allow any construction of at least a temporary distance. It claims an endless world – but only for those who don't want to explore it thoroughly. The doors of the expanded stage should not be opened, the rules not questioned.

This leads to the political implication of immersive theatre. Here the manipulative totality clearly becomes a problem that goes much further: immersion demands surrender and submission to an artistic vision or ideology. It aims at the affect created by a shock-and-awe realism Stanislavski could only have dreamt of. In such a world no emancipated spectator can exist, since any emancipation would just happen within the given artistic limits. Immersion is participation without reflection and without any political awareness. Theatre critic Esther Slevogt polemically but rightfully pointed out in a column on Berliner Festspiele's immersion project: 'Bert Brecht demanded after Germany had sunk in the immersion project of national socialism that a staging should always be recognisable as a staging. Perhaps one should read the *Short Organum* again'.[15] Real

13 | Cf. Doris Kolesch, Berliner Festspiele Website, September 22, 2016, https://blog.berlinerfestspiele.de/theater-und- immersion/ (last accessed May 24, 2019).
14 | Ibid.
15 | Esther Slevogt, "Das große Eintauchen", nachtkritik.ce, May 24, 2016, trans. FM, https://www.nachtkritik.de/index.php?option=com_content&view=article&id=12602:kclumne-aus-dem-buergerlichen-heldenleben-esther-slevogt-ueber-das-neue-zauberwort-immersion&catid=1506&Itemid=100389 (last accessed May 25, 2019).

participation implies giving up responsibility and power. Brecht's *Lehrstücke* ('learning plays') were to be performed by the audience itself, the working class. Brazilian theatre maker Augusto Boal not only followed this idea in his Theatre of the Oppressed but even handed over the responsibility for how the performance developed to the 'spect-actors' (spectators that during the performance turned into actors). Kaprow, by the way, was very clear that being inside an artwork should not mean forgetting about reality: 'The situations for a happening should come from what you see in the real world, from real places and people rather than from the head. If you stick to imagination too much you'll end up with old art again, since art was always supposed to be made from imagination'.[16]

REPRESENTATION AND THE POSSIBILITIES OF PREENACTMENT

The question of participation is necessarily linked to the question of representation. Everyone who comes to the theatre – whether as actor, performer, spect-actor or audience – is always part of a larger community, marked by colour, gender, class, body, profession... The questions that currently beset all democracies – who is represented how, by whom, in what way and by what right – are reflected in the theatre. Can a middle-class actor represent a refugee? Can the West represent the global South? Can a man represent a woman? Does the representation of stereotypes (gender, race and so on) unmask them, or does it only repeat degrading insults? The roots of recent discussions such as the so-called black-face debate go deeper than merely questioning the right and competency of white actors to play black characters. The challenges are complex – politically and artistically. They will outlast current debates about political correctness and occupy the theatre for a time to come.

That even a theatre aiming to be critical often can't avoid the dilemma that in the end its representations are just another repetition of the very miseries it wants to fight, was called by Brecht 'Menschenfresserdramatik'[17] ('cannibal's dramatic art'): 'The physical exploitation of the poor is followed by a psychological one'[18] when the pitied character is supposed to produce feelings of sadness, guilt or even anger in a spectator, who most likely – at least structurally – is part of keeping the very system of exploitation alive. The thin line between presence and representation is always at stake in

16 | Allan Kaprow, *How to Make a Happening*, Primary information, 2019, http://primaryinformation.org/files/allan-kaprow-how-to-make-a-happening.pdf (last accessed May 24, 2019).
17 | Bertolt Brecht, "Die dialektische Dramatik", in *Werke. Band 21* (Frankfurt/Main: Suhrkamp Verlag 1992), 435.
18 | Ibid, 433, trans. FM.

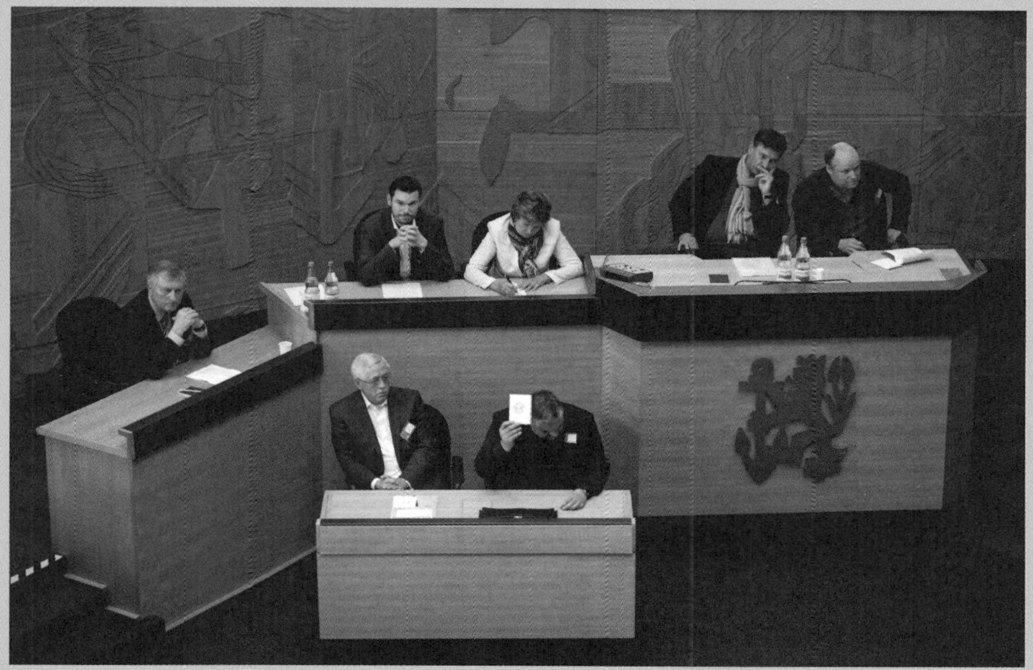

theatre – so it is not by chance that Jonas Staal often chooses theatres as venues for his projects. Here things can be shown and said that don't find a form elsewhere, and where radical imagination is, in rare moments, still possible.

Figure 10.2.1
Public Movement,
Macht Kunst Politik,
Düsseldorf, 2016.
Photo: © Robin
Junicke

While Staal's *New World Summit* gives representation to those who are excluded from democratic representation, *Make Art Policy* by the Israeli 'artistic research body' Public Movement, directed by choreographer Dana Yahalomi, put elected or incumbent representatives into the spotlight. For over ten years Public Movement has investigated political actions and studied and created public choreographies, forms of social organisation, overt and covert rituals which they describe as 'preenactments' of possible rituals of the future. As political theorist Oliver Marchart points out, one of their choreographic rituals actually became part of the social protests in Israel 2011 and could be described as a preenactment in form of 'the artistic anticipation of a political event to come'.

'The pre-enactment presents itself as something like the pre-formance of a future political event. I would thus propose to use pre-enactment as a term for the artistic anticipation of a political event to come. But this event cannot be anticipated through simple extrapolation from well-known contemporary tendencies (as in the sense of role playing science fiction scenarios). In the realm of politics, nobody can see what the future brings: it is unclear where and when social

conflicts will break out. The artistic pre-enactment could, in this sense, be subsumed under the category of the rehearsal – the rehearsal of a future political event. To the extent that this event is unknown, however, the pre-enactment – with its entirely open outcome – cannot be a rehearsal of a determinate event; at best, it could be the rehearsal of an entirely indeterminate event, the event of the political. For this reason, it is perhaps preferable to think of pre-enactments not so much as rehearsals in the strict sense (as if the definite script of the future political event were available), than as training sessions. These sessions are there to produce the skills necessary to engage in the 'actual thing', should it occur. In the latter sense, the pre-enactment is what in the world of classical ballet would be the exercise, the training of basic movements at the barre. It would be the warming up for something that may or may not occur. If it occurs, an artistic intervention at a crossroads may turn into a collective protest format of a social movement'.[19]

In this vein, *Make Art Policy* aimed at creating a new way of talking about cultural policy. After a first realisation at the 2014 Baltic Circle Festival in Helsinki shortly before the national elections in Finland, a second version under the German title *Macht Kunst Politik* took place at the initiative of Impulse Theater Festival and FFT theatre in Düsseldorf in 2016, before the state elections in North Rhine-Westphalia. Politicians from all relevant parties were invited to present their party's cultural policy. The assembly took place in the city hall of Düsseldorf, a typical postwar parliamentary setting, following a strict set of rules and with music steering the course of discussion. *Macht Kunst Politik* set up a political debate in front of an audience and changed only slightly the rules of procedure, aiming at two things: making cultural policy a topic at all – and sharpening the differences between the political parties. Especially the latter turned out to be difficult in Germany: Rather than finding points of disagreements with the other parties, most cultural politicians saw their colleagues as allies in the common fight against other ministries, mainly the financial department. As understandable as this might be – it also means that cultural policy is removed from the arena of political argument and becomes merely a matter of lobbying. While we – the artists, dramaturges and curators – tried in several meetings and lengthy email exchanges to encourage the politicians to sharpen their differences, they kept aiming for consensus. With one exception: their clear opposition towards the newly rising right-wing party AfD (Alternative für Deutschland), which was also invited to participate.

When the event itself finally happened, it soon became clear: all attempts to create an agonistic, enthusiastic fight for different, clear-cut approaches towards cultural agendas failed. As did our plea not to recreate the situation of almost all political TV talk shows in Germany at that time: to spend most of the time talking about the AfD and disagreeing with their politics

19 | Oliver Marchart, "Public Movement: The Art of Preenactment", in Florian Malzacher (Ed.), *Not Just a Mirror; Looking fort he Political Theatre of Today* (Berlin: Alexander Verlag 2014), 149-50.

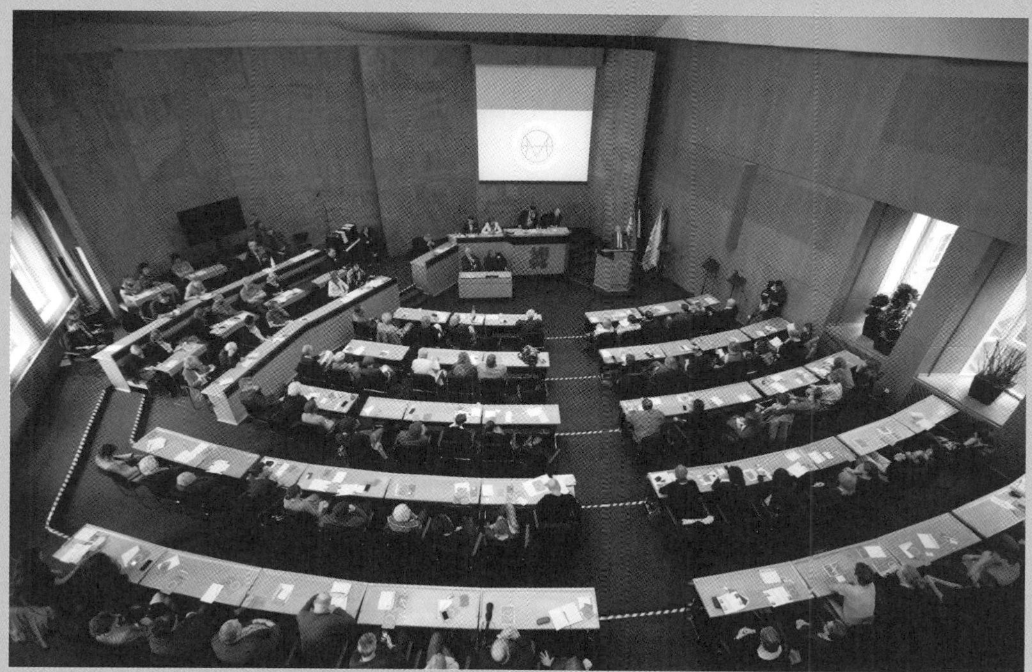

Figure 10.2.2
Public Movement,
Macht Kunst Politik,
Düsseldorf, 2016.
Photo: © Robin
Junicke

(especially since here it was clear that the audience was anyway largely disinclined to vote right wing). Instead of trying to win votes with strong contrasting visions, it became a show of blurry consensus – wasting most of the time on bashing the right wingers and avoiding one's own ideas. With the exception of the AfD representative, who was doing exactly this: trying to win the audience over for his conservative and sometimes reactionary ideas of culture. *Macht Kunst Politik* was an exciting and important endeavour that created insights that were not necessarily pleasant. In its aim to change, at least for a short while, the very narrow field of cultural policy of the state of North Rhine-Westphalia, and by this at least offering a glimpse of what might be possible, it clearly failed. But as a more conventional political theatre, it succeeded perfectly: it mirrored the situation of cultural policy and made it, through its framing, visible. In other words: while the Helsinki assembly of Make Art Policy actually managed to trigger important conversations also amongst the local art scene, *Macht Kunst Politik* became a reenactment of the existing situation rather than a preenactment of something that could be instead.

Equally quasi-parliamentarian settings were taken by two projects dealing with the climate conference that took place in December 2015 in Paris: *World Climate Change Conference* by Rimini Protokoll and *Théâtre des Négociations*, created by philosopher Bruno Latour and theatre directors Frédérique Aït-Touati and Philippe Quesne.

Rimini Protokoll's *World Climate Change Conference* (2015/16) generally followed the concept and rules of the official Nations Framework Convention on Climate Change, 21st Conference of the Parties (COP 21): 670 audience members represented the 670 members representing the 196 participating nations. Trying to understand and respect the concrete situations, the forces, restrictions, fears and hopes of 'their' respective countries as well as the limited time of the performance, which lasted about three hours, lead to pragmatic rather than utopian results not too far away from the results of the real climate conference – even if once in a while in Rimini's version the USA did actually say '"ok, listen, let's go balls to the wall, we're just going to pay" – and simply replenish the Green Climate Fund'.[20] For Daniel Wetzel, part of Rimini Protokoll and co-director of *World Climate Change Conference*, 'the point is to inhabit one of the different positions, not so much the actual modus operandi of the UN. You leave the piece having shared the space with 195 different perspectives'. In this sense, the performance has aspects of Brecht's famous concept of the learning play where one is simultaneous spectator and actor learning how to understand different positions better – though it lacks its political and pedagogical bias.

A much more critical stance towards the system behind the world climate conference was taken by Latour's, Aït-Touati's and Quesne's *Théâtre des Négociations*[21] with its belief that the failure of these conferences is in the end 'a consequence of representational issues: representations of the problems at stake and representations of the different communities and beings that coexist on earth'. Inviting some 200 students from all over the world and many more spectators, this simulation of the international conference was mainly aimed at creating visibility, as the co-director Frédérique Aït-Touati describes: 'It was a question of making theatre a place where transparency and visibility prevailed, the opposite of negotiations behind closed doors'. And it was about 'including in climate negotiations those entities directly impacted by global warming (indigenous peoples, young people, forests, oceans, endangered species, imperilled territories), but who have no possible way of having "their" voices heard'.

Different from Rimini Protokoll, the emancipation of the spectators was central: not only did different scientists propose explanations and solutions whilst artists explored alternative forms of representation. Students were also involved – partly based on the Model United Nations (MUN), a pedagogical device invented at Harvard that simulates UN-like

20 | "Almost Like a Learning Play; Daniel Wetzel of Rimini Protokoll in a conversation with Florian Malzacher", in Katia Arfara, Aneta Mancewicz and Ralf Remshardt (Eds.), *Intermedial Performance and Politics in the Public Sphere* (Houndmills and New York: Palgrave Macmillan 2018), 191–208.
21 | "Théâtre des Négociations", live performance at the Théâtre Nanterre-Amandiers, May 9–31, 2015.

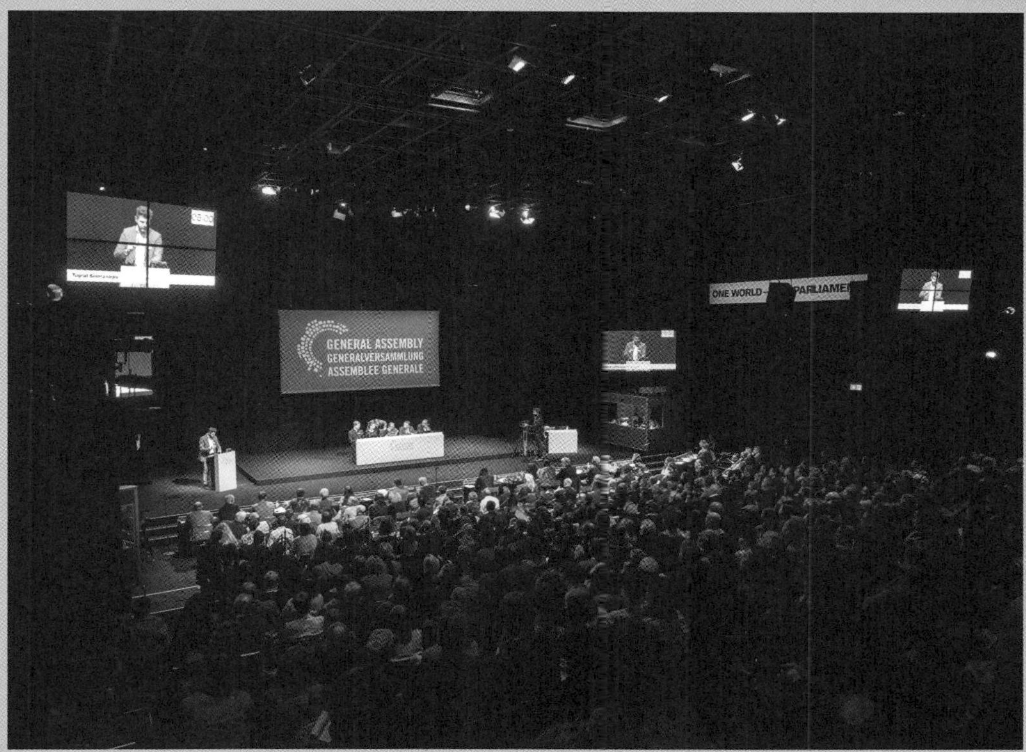

international negotiations in order to train students. It was about concrete solutions for stopping climate change as well as finding different models of representation.

Figure 10.1. Milo Rau, *General Assembly*, Berlin, 2018. Photo: © Daniel Seiffert

While Rimini Protokoll's project aimed at making the climate negotiations' functioning transparent and giving, in a way, a realistic view on what is possible within this system, *Théâtre des Négociations* gave freedom to renegotiate the rules and create new alliances – whilst at the same time not distancing itself too far from the original rules of the game: 'Should our attempt be too close to existing negotiations, the experience would have resembled a classic reenactment exercise. If too distant, it risked having no heuristic impact and being only an imaginary version of utopian negotiations'.[22]

> 'Happening half a year before the real COP21 took place in the French capital, "we proposed that the students **not** play out their future roles, but instead a future possible for international climate negotiations"'.[23]

22 | Frédérique Aït-Touati, "For a Speculative Policy. Bruno Latour & Nanterre-Amendier's Le Théâtre des négociations / Make It Work (2015)", in Florian Malzacher & Joanna Warsza (Eds.), *Empty Staged, Crowded Flats; Performativity as Curatorial Strategy* (Berlin: Alexander Verlag 2017), 156.
23 | Ibid.

> '*On the evening of May 31, a "treaty" was signed by all parties involved. Needless to say, it had no political ramifications, its impact occurring on another level. Bruno Latour saw it having a major constituent role: the entrance into the political arena of oceans, soils, forests, and endangered species. As I see it, this was, from the theatrical perspective, above all a fruitful experience. Thoroughly performative, in every sense of the word, it conveyed the slightly mad hopes of bringing about a new form of political representation by activating theatre's place through a new kind of political community, one not exclusively human, by including others actors from our common world*'.[24]

Like *Make Art Policy*, *Théâtre des Négociations* also drew its strength from the concept of preenactment:[25] both events did not create completely new settings, they used existing forms of political assemblies and tried do shift their procedures, contents and ethics. They were – as most assemblies referred to in this essay – utopian in a pragmatic way, envisioning change within existing institutions or imagining new institutions that are pushing existing models further.

WHEN REALISM IS TURNED INTO REALITY

Also Milo Rau's *General Assembly* aimed at opening a perspective towards the future by proposing a new take on existing parliamentarian models:

> '*While Europe and the US are debating the modernization, losers and underdogs, the proletariat and the shift to the right in their own countries, the General Assembly goes one step further with regard to the global reality of politics and economy, giving a voice to those who are underrepresented, who are not heard, the global Third Estate: labour immigrants, children and future generations, war victims, textile workers, miners, farmers, economic and climate refugees, the victims of the dawning ecocide, the oceans, the atmosphere, animals and plants*'.[26]

What makes the *General Assembly* a preenactment different from the other examples is Rau's artistic departure point as a theatre director with a deep belief in aesthetic realism used as a means to create highly affective moments of catharsis: cleansing through emotional identification – as for example in the acclaimed *Hate Radio* (2011), which convincingly reconstructed the original studio of the Hutu propaganda station RTLM, a driving force in the Tutsi genocide of 1994.

Rau's realism is effective, complex and not easy to dismiss, since as much as he believes in the artistic legitimation of representation, he is – different

---

24 | Ibid, 157.
25 | Frédérique Aït-Touati herself uses the term: Ibid, 154.
26 | "General Assembly", http://www.general-assembly.net/en/ (last accessed May 24, 2019).

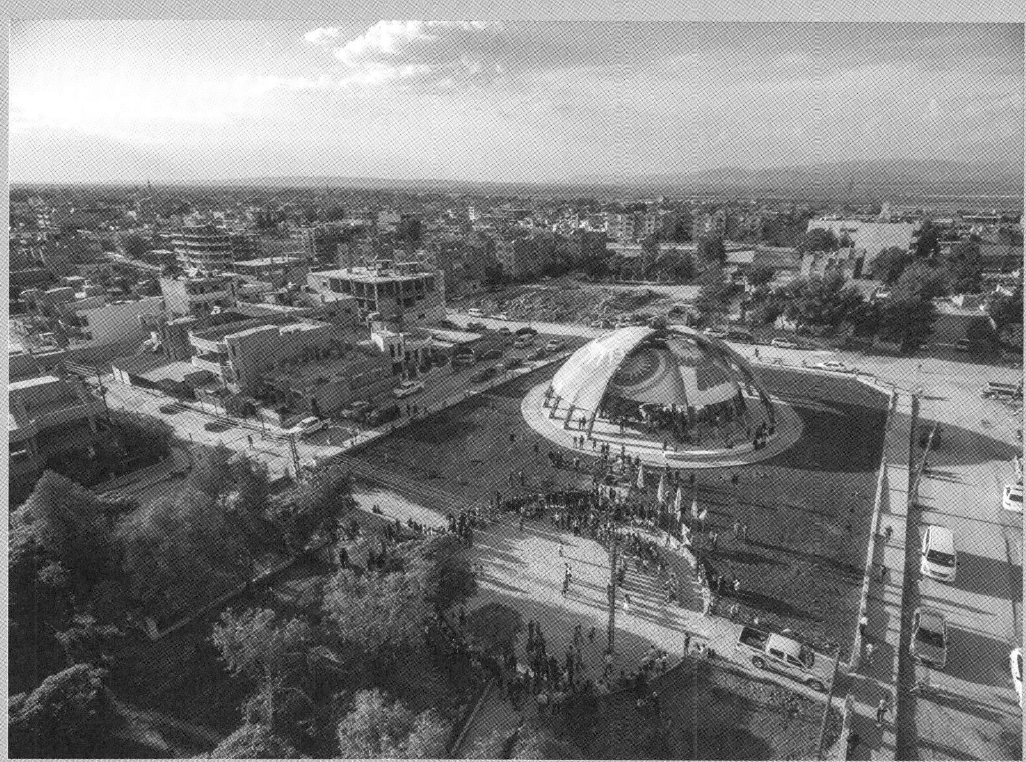

Figure 10.4.d.1
Democratic Federation
of North–Syria &
Studio Jonas Staal,
New World Summit,
Rojava, 2015-18.
Photo: © Ruben
Hamelink

from many other protagonists of representational theatre[27] – well aware of its ethical limitations: Not only are all the actors Tutsi survivors of the war, the piece was conceived collaboratively in a – as Rau stresses – quite difficult process, since the actors indeed had to face their very own traumas:[28] The actress Nancy Nkusi returned for the first time to her home country in order to impersonate the murderer of her own family. Devising as well as performing this work clearly shows Rau's artistic aim 'to traverse a trauma together with the involved in order to give them – of course only symbolically [...] an active, representational role'.[29] The ethical belief in the impossibility of, for instance, German actors assuming these roles coincides with the artistic belief that an authentic personal involvement of the performers creates a more realistic performance. Milo Rau speaks of the 'simultaneity of biographical and, accordingly, political and actorly presence' that are at the core of most of his works.[30]

When Rau explains, 'working realistically simply means dragging the real

27 | Cf. Bernd Stegemann, "Wie frei ist das Theater noch?", *Frankfurter Allgemeine Zeitung*, May 4, 2018.
28 | Milo Rau in an email to F.M., February 23, 2018, trans. F.M.
29 | Ibid.
30 | Ibid.

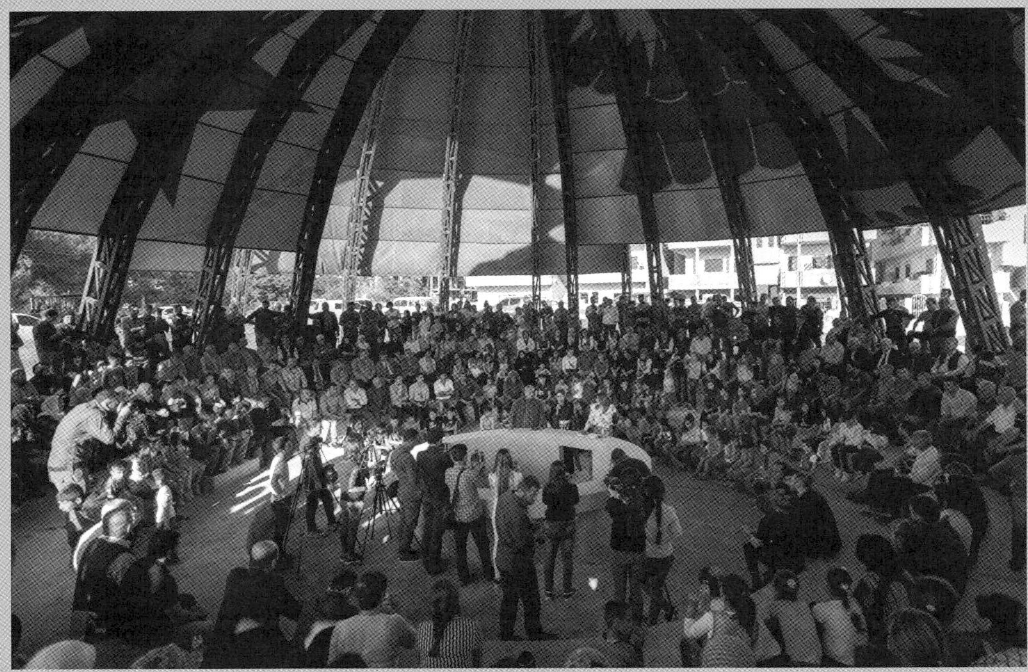

Figure 10.4.d.2
Democratic Federation
of North-Syria &
Studio Jonas Staal,
New World Summit,
Rojava, 2015-18.
Photo: © Ruben
Hamelink

out of the shadow of the documents, the so called "actuality" into the light of truth and presence',[31] this very concept of 'truth and presence' points directly at the core problem: *Hate Radio* is in the end neither a documentary nor a documentation. It condenses piles of original material into two hours of theatre – and by this becomes fiction just as much as truth. Rau's belief, that in order to show reality on stage one needs to transform the material, rightfully dismisses the naïve idea of an exact reenactment as a possible shortcut to historic truth. But at the same time, it replaces this concept with the no less problematic claim that an artistic creation could be capable of exactly this: showing how it was. The performance does not come as a version of a historical reality. It comes with the force of a truth to which one must surrender. However collectively conceived, in the end the struggle, dramaturgy, montage, filling of gaps etc. stay invisible just as Milo Rau himself as a theatre director and at least *primus inter pares* does during the performance.

While Rau contributes an important body of discourse in his essays, interviews, books etc. – in the performances themselves he often seems to aim, rather, at the affect than the intellect. In more recent works like *Five Easy Pieces*, where kids present the case of the paedophile murderer Marc Dutroux, he even moved on to refine this method by virtuously using

<hr>

31 | Milo Rau, 'Buchenwald, Bukavu, Bochum. Was ist globaler Realismus? Milo Rau im Gespräch mit Rolf Bossart", *Theater der Zeit*, Oktober 2015, trans. F.M.

Brechtian estrangement effects to create fake havens of rationality just to stab the stranded, off-guard audience in the back with an even more forceful emotional manipulation: As much as Rau might indeed offer the protagonists of his works a moment of empowerment and participation, for the spectator there is not much space for emancipation.

Politically Rau might be closer to Brecht, but aesthetically he is closer to Stanislavsky. In direct opposition to Brecht's dictum that representation of the oppressed's agony basically just repeats the very injustice with aesthetical means, Rau follows Aristotle in the belief that representation of suffering enables emancipation – and uses a well crafted shock and awe realism in Stanislavsky's tradition to create cathartic affects in the audience.

One has to keep this context of Rau's repertory work in mind when looking at the very different strand in his work consisting of trials, tribunals and assemblies, which offer within a strict procedural dramaturgy a lot of space for the protagonists and sometimes for the audience.[32] They can be seen as an attempt to bridge the two poles of Rau's work and artistic/ intellectual personality. Here the directing aspect is drastically reduced, the emancipatory moment enhanced. These works propose a reality that does not exist, but that in Rau's view should exist. In this regard they are quite close to works like those by Jonas Staal. But, again, the difference lies in the approach: While both aim at creating situations that could or should become real (very much in the sense of a preenactment), Rau still relies on the tools and the belief system of aesthetical realism. He not only marks or frames symbolically a possible reality (like Staal in form of procedures and set), his staging goes deep into the dramaturgical tissue, creates narratives through the selection of protagonists, the order of topics, speakers etc. In order for a situation to have the potential of becoming real, for Rau it has to *look* as realistic as possible. But this 'realism', as Rau himself states, 'is something completely artificial',[33] a composition that in the end lies much more in Milo Rau's hands than in those of the participants. The 'acting' in these preen*act*ments has its emphasis just as much on its denotation in drama than on its political meaning. While the concept of 'emancipation through submission'[34] might be considered as a merely aesthetic question in Rau's repertory work, in the context of politics it crosses a crucial line.

---

32 | In *The Moscow Trials* (2013) three traumatic legal cases against Russian artists and curators were brought again in front of a judge, but this time in the realm of art. *The Zurich Trials* (2013) brought the right wing Swiss newspaper *Die Weltwoche* to court, and – most ambitious and most discussed – *The Congo Tribunal* (2015– ongoing) investigates the ongoing war around the great lakes.

33 | Ibid.

34 | Milo Rau in an email to F.M., February 23, 2018, trans. F.M.

This dilemma also becomes visible in the 'Ghent Manifesto', published by Rau and his colleagues to mark the beginning of his directorship at the Belgium NT Ghent municipal theatre: 'It's not just about portraying the world anymore. It's about changing it. The aim is not to depict the real, but to make the representation itself real'.[35] While the first part of this paragraph is a variation of many political artists' credo, the second half, in a remarkable twist, points right at the core of the problem: Who created this representation, with what right, in whose name? The second paragraph of the manifesto states: 'Theatre is not a product, it is a production process. Research, castings, rehearsals and related debates must be publicly accessible'. But why then is this very process (including aspects of hierarchies, authorship, legitimation of representation etc.) not made visible – 'accessible' – within the performance itself? This obviously would obstruct the aim for realism, for affective catharsis, for emotional identification, but it would allow for a very different degree of emancipation and empowerment.

It is this very contradiction that brought *General Assembly*, in the discussions about AKP supporter Tuğrul Semanoğlu's genocide denial, to a turning point at which not only the case itself but also the artistic setup became the centre of attention. The problem of 'the first world parliament in the history of mankind'[36] was not the hubris of this endeavour, which actually gave the work its utopian quality, but the belief that this could be contained within a preconceived director's dramaturgy. While the agonistic (and sometimes antagonistic) spheres that Rau creates indeed reflect his belief in an urgent democratic need for more open confrontation, the way they are created follows a dramaturgical logic that – like in Greek tragedies – is based on tension and competition as a driving force.

As much as in *General Assembly* a meta-discourse about theatre and parliamentarian politics was very present, the degree and means of staging were at the same time obscured: What was staged, what anticipated? To what degree could the course of events be influenced? What reality will come out of a representation in which the director finally is the one pulling the strings?

This dilemma of theatre mirrors – as so often – a dilemma of current politics: The manipulative aspect of Rau's work is a main reason for it's impressive success. Of all mentioned examples his assemblies and trials clearly create the widest media coverage and attract the largest audiences

---

35 | NT Gent-team, "The city theatre of the future – Ghent Manifesto", May 1, 2018, http://international-institute.de/en/news/ (last accessed May 24, 2019).
36 | "General Assembly".

(the most diverse, though, might be found in Jonas Staal's work).[37] But as much as there is a need for affect in politics, as Chantal Mouffe advocates, as much as there indeed might be a need for a leftist populism in current crises – emancipation through manipulation is a profound contradiction to the very concept of assemblies. The hierarchy of knowledge between director and audience becomes unbearable.

An agonistic space obviously needs agonism. But it also needs sincere participation. Indeed, such participation in art needs not be a friendly or pleasant experience.[38] As Claire Bishop points out: participation in art should create a sense of 'unease and discomfort rather than belonging'. But at the same time, it requires treating all involved as 'subject[s] of independent thought' – this is the 'essential prerequisite for political action'.[39] The éclat at the end of *General Assembly* did turn the participants into 'subjects of independent thought'. And a theatre work into a political situation, into a real assembly.

Theatre can reenact, enact, preenact assemblies. It can create a space of analysis, of reflection or imagination and invention – but the moment it becomes a real assembly, realism ends and reality begins. With all its theatricality.

---

37 | And even more: Rau's work also shows success in political reality: *The Congo Tribunal*, for example, led to a campaign to establish further tribunals in the country, with support from the Congolese lawyers association, the tribunal in Den Haag, et al.
38 | For further reflection on participation in theatre cf. Florian Malzacher, "No Organum to Follow", in Florian Malzacher (Ed.), *Not Just a Mirror. Looking for the Political Theatre of Today* (Berlin: Alexander Verlag 2015), 16–30.
39 | Claire Bishop, "Antagonism and Relational Aesthetics", *October* 110 (fall 2004): 70.

 GORAN SERGEJ PRISTAŠ

GORAN SERGEJ PRISTAŠ

1. BLACK BOX DARKNESS

The experience of darkness and the black box in the cinema is significantly different from the equivalent experience in the theatre, because the cinema radicalises darkness, from which one watches the film, whereas the theatre primarily emerges from darkness, peered into by the spectator. Unlike in the theatre, the cinema experience is hypnotic, healing. The assumptions of going to the cinema are idleness, free time, lethargic states, states that give rise to daydreaming. It was such pre-spectatorial states that likewise led Roland Barthes to the cinema, where he was 'finally burying himself in a dim, anonymous, indifferent cube'.[1]

The spectator, buried in that 'indifferent cube', is presented with the 'festival of affects known as a film'; the spectator's gaze travels, choreographed by the camera (or image) and the darkness of the cinema engulfs her like a silkworm's cocoon, as the very substance of daydreaming and the colour of a 'diffuse eroticism'. Unlike the theatre – still an inheritor of the bourgeois pose of watching, 'cultural appearance', wherein the very act of watching theatre is still a gesture – the cinema draws the spectator into dreaming. In the cinema, the 'body's freedom is generated', eroticism arises not from exposing bodies but from their inoccupation and accessibility – the

1 | Roland Barthes, *The Rustle of Language* (New York: Hill and Wang 1986), 346–49.

darkness of the movie theatre condenses human presence, empties the space of all worldliness and relaxes bodily postures and attitudes. For Barthes, the cinema is only a retrofitted infrastructure of darkness, an upgraded theatrical black box. For him, however, the polar opposite of the cinematic experience is not the theatre, but watching television at home. In watching a film at home (I'm trying not to say 'home cinema'), 'darkness is erased, anonymity repressed; space is familiar, articulated (by known objects), tamed'. The de-eroticised space of watching television is familiar, it takes us to the family, not to dreaming.

The eroticised space of the cinema is a place of hypnosis, Barthes argues, the cinematic image is a perfect bate: 'coalescent (its signified and its signifier melted together), analogical, total, pregnant'. However far the spectator might be sitting from the screen, she is 'coalescent with representation' and it is the image that melts them together, an image consisting of all the ingredients of technique and functioning entirely according to the principles of the *ideological*. This text by Barthes, as well as his abandoning of the movie theatre, becomes even more exciting now, because Barthes asks how one might unglue from the mirror of the repertory of images offered by the cinema and ideology. How to separate from the experience of coalescence, the safety of similitude, the naturalness generated by the 'truth' of the image, both in the cinema and in the cinema of society?

Barthes uses here a term that has a double meaning: *décollant* (taking off), both as in taking off in aeronautics and coming off of drugs. Of course in these matters one can always resort to the methods of epic theatre, where the spectator watches critically; however, apart from resorting to counter-ideology, Barthes proposes the method of being fascinated twice over: by the image and by the *situation of the cinema*. For Barthes, the situation of the cinema comprises the image and all that surrounds it, its environment: 'The texture of the sound, the hall, the darkness, the obscure mass of the other bodies, the rays of light, entering the theater, leaving the hall'. In order to 'come off', Barthes complicates the 'relationship' of the spectator with the 'situation' of watching. For Barthes, that distance, created by situating watching in the qualities of the circumstances of watching is 'discretionary' and not critical, if we read discretion according to its etymological profile, but it is worth thinking discretion in terms of its dictionary definition as well, as 'the freedom to decide what should be done in a particular situation'.[2]

2 | "Deiscretion", *Oxford English Dictionary Online*, June 2017, http://www.oed.com/ viewdictionaryentry/ Entry/11125 (last accessed October 11, 2017).

This experience of watching is quite similar to the one Tomislav Gotovac described in his short pamphlet titled 'Whilst Watching a Movie': 'a structure comes to life, pulsating, seeking and finding its own rhythm, freeing, in midflight, its tensions, and carrying the mass that accompanies all of that. The screen and the eye as part of the same organism. The image and movement. That is film. The only genuine and the only possible definition of film is already contained in its name: motion picture'.[3]

2. A FLAME AND A FLASH

A night in 2017, a small, improvised stage in a gallery,[4] the lights are off. The artist, standing on the podium, lights up a lighter, which he is holding in his hand pressed against his heart, gazing at the flame, as though he were trying hard to keep it from going out or trying to set his own shirt on fire. At first, the flame illuminates the artist's chest and face, framing it as a portrait. As time passes, the flame subsides and illuminates only the hand holding it. The spectator's attention is imperceptibly narrowed down to the location of the heart, where the hand becomes the stage of the flame, but that hand is at the same time framing the place of the heart. By narrowing down the source of light, the portrait scene slowly becomes an icon of care, a scene that resonates with Christian representations of the heart of Jesus. As the lighter is running out of fuel, the flame is reduced to a flicker, which can no longer illuminate anything but simply goes on for a while as a speck of light whose final flame of life, before it goes out, sheds light on the personal history of the artist – Slaven Tolj, performing now for the first time following a recent life-threatening stroke. The duration of the performance was only a few minutes, shorter than Tolj had anticipated, which means that it was seen only by the few people who managed to get into the room on time, but those who came in late remained in the room for a while longer, hoping that due to the brevity of the act something may yet transpire, something that only a premature cut may promise.

The same space, eighteen years earlier, a few hundred people sitting in the dark, endlessly waiting for the beginning of Oleg Kulik's performance *White Man, Black Dog*. Finally, several photographers start taking pictures in the dark, with flashes – the only source of light during the performance. A naked Kulik and a dog (wearing its own fur) enter the space. Kulik kisses

3 | Bojana Cvejić and Goran Sergej Pristaš (Eds.), *Parallel Slalom: A Lexicon of Non-Aligned Poetics* (Belgrade and Zagreb: Walking Theory – TkH & CDU 2013), 133–34.

4 | Galerija HDLU (Gallery of the Croatian Association of Artists), performance by Slaven Tolj, *Bez naziva* (Untitled), as part of the opening of the final exhibition in the cycle "Janje moje malo…" (My Little Lamb…), organised by the curatorial collective *Što, kako i za koga* (What, How, and for Whom)/WHW, in collaboration with Kathrin Rhomberg, 2017.

and pets the dog and after a while the dog walks over to the spectators, who are sitting on the floor. Kulik follows the dog, walking across the people, their bodies, faces, the dog is licking them, jumping all over them. The spectators, although for the most part 'experienced' professionals and aficionados of radical art, are in a state of shock and some are running away from the dog; some are running away from the artist or the performance space, but remain outside, discussing, not dispersing. According to Kulik, the performance did not follow its regular course because there were too many people in the space and there was panic, so the dog did not behave the way it and Kulik had 'agreed' either. Kulik spent most of the time chasing the animal, fearing an unpredictable reaction both from the dog and the spectators.

Both of these performances made the most of darkness – the density of its structure, the power to immerse ourselves in it into the background, to immerse ourselves into the depth of a black box (even though both performances took place in a white box). A white box separates, it interpolates interstices and gap zones between objects, allows objects to generate exemplary worlds or fragments thereof, seeds or ruins of worlds. A black box or at least a dark box renders the world indifferent; the image emerging from the dark is only a membrane of meaning separating individual layers of enframing (*Gestell*).[5] By itself, the manifesting of enframing does not guarantee meaning – Slaven Tolj holding a lighter and burning with it lighter fluid; a dog and a naked man chasing each other amongst the audience.

Different techniques of (literal) illumination reveal different levels of the enframing, which are in both instances linked to the specific time of visibility that frames them. What was constituted in Tolj's performance by the long time the lighter took to burn its fuel is equivalent to the millisecond of a photographic flash in Kulik's performance. They both extract, out of the indifference of darkness, an image into the excess of temporal intensity, and that excess feeds directly on the virtuosity of the performing apparatus.

3. THE BLACK BOX

Although the body has been displayed and dissected in galleries for decades, in all of its performative capacities, including being brought to the brink of death, the gallery is still a diurnal place, a place of attentiveness, before

---

5 | Martin Heidegger, *The Question Concerning Technology, and Other Essays* (New York: Harper Perennial Modern Classics 2013).

which the performer is always obliged to demonstrate the objectness of the body, to expose it to tools and procedures, to bring it to the light of day. I already pointed out that Barthes viewed the movie theatre only as a retrofitted invariant of the theatrical black box; however, the black box comes to the theatre with a spectator whose gaze was trained in the cinema, a spectator whose gaze no longer seeks the portal architectonics of a frame but always-already includes an integrated frame. Amidst the darkness of a black box, the theatre invariably also includes the spectators and their gazing, even in the rehearsals, when their gaze is only assumed, when theatre is occurring in front of a spectator who has yet to be born. The taking place of theatre, unlike its showing, has a refractory rather than reflexive character. And that refraction occurs precisely at the membrane that separates its two different local manifestations: the theatre as the institutional relationship of the audience (the public) and the artist (the producer), and the theatre as the poetic aggregate of the spectators and actors of a performance (animate and inanimate alike). Here, however, I am not talking about refraction as the effect produced by an idea passing through two media or two ideologies. Rather, this is about a deflection in the style of existence of those participating in theatre (spectators and artists), which occurs as a consequence of the encounter at the membrane between the institution and poetics. In that duality, the theatre realises its refractory power, is materially factual and puts the world on display not only *in* theatre but also *through* theatre, which makes theatre a training ground *par excellence* for reflecting social objects, its simultaneous integration in social processes as well as ways of separating from them. Theatre is always similar to, but also different from other social processes, but this double status of theatre is increasingly difficult to preserve, given the transformations in its mode of production.[6]

4. INNERVATION

With a certain dose of generalisation, one may argue that the following are the two dominant poles to which gravitates the organisation of representation (and watching) in theatre: one pole is closer to processes of subjectification and the other to the reification of relations. The former seeks expression in the subject of representation or viewing, in the procedures of shaping a character, performing presence, working on critical awareness, or, rather, the spectator's subjectification. Whether comprising individuals or a collective subject, performers or a spectator, the subject and her perception perform a constitutive function in the performance.

<hr>

6 | For more on the monetisation of artistic labour and the growth of so-called anti-production, see "Anti-production of Art", *TkH* 23 (2016).

The latter pole rests on processes of objectification, spanning a wide range of procedures, from turning persons into things to the panpsychism of objects, whether processes of forming images,[7] 'expanded' choreography,[8] or contingency performances.[9] However, these two processes occur on two sides of a thin membrane, a membrane whereon, in one direction, material relations are reshaped into subjects and, in the other direction, life conditions are reified. This membrane is that of the performance apparatus, the form of the enslaving conditions of production as well as the aggregate of the potentialities of previously unexplored models of production. The processes whereby the characters, performers and spectators are subjectified are a side effect of the apparatus, and when that apparatus disappears, the distribution of roles disappears as well. Some authors have sought to bridge the problem of the apparatus by alloying those two tendencies. On the one hand, the apparatus begets subjects and Artaud attempts to transcend it by means of a rebirth, giving birth without a father, without resemblance to the creator, whereas after him, Beckett attempts to implant the being of the as-yet unborn into the very infrastructure of theatre. If we accept Artaud's need for a rebirth of man, this time not in the image of his father, as an aspiration to avoid the closure of representation, how should one understand the unborn status of Beckett's characters? His synthetic play *Breath* is an attempt to encompass the gaze (by means of an increase and decrease in the intensity of the light) and the world of objects (rubbish as pure presence of de-functionalised objects) in a single integrated, operative and machinic unit – the composite and aggregate unity of the objects of gazing, the apparatus of gazing, the spectators and attention as connective material. Similarly, buried in the ground, living in rubbish, deferred to waiting, insecurely visible in semidarkness, Beckett's characters are not integral subjects but are instead integrated in matter, subjects who are manifested in matter but have not yet physically taken place. Their gaze, if they have one at all, is short-sighted; it does not collide with, attract, or refract the spectator's gaze. What extends the spectator's gaze is precisely the breath, the rhythm of the expansion of matter, the rhythm of activity, the rhythm of the caesurae indicated by two or three dots, the rhythm of exhausting movement in a square, leaves falling from the tree... Beckett's stage features no discontinuity between the body and matter, it is a scene of total integration synchronised with the spectator's immobilisation in her seat in the auditorium, the spectator's immersion

---

7 | From the extreme of predominantly visual forms of representation (Schlemmer, Wilson, Dehlholm, Vinge...) via ideological spectacles and constructivist theatre (Eisenstein, Piscator, Meierhold...) to the theatre of cruel integration (Artaud, Beckett, Stelarc...).

8 | I borrowed the concept from the conference *Choreography as Expanded Practice* (2012), I attended in Barcelona, https://choreographyasexpandedpractice.wordpress.com/.

9 | Some examples would be totalizing performances like Stano Filko's *HAPPSOC* (1965), Tomislav Gotovac's *A Total Portrait of City Zagreb* (1979) or the whole *U.F.O.* series by Julius Koller.

in the darkness of the hall. Beckett's theatre comes close to a realisation of the images from Benjamin's innervation machine, the prayer wheel from the fragment of the same name in *One-way Street*.[10] The notion of innervation is a wandering concept in Benjamin, a notion that emerged in earlier and disappeared again in later versions of his essay on the work of art in the age of mechanical reproduction.[11] With the enigmatic argument that 'there is no imagination without innervation', Benjamin argues for his thesis that only a visual image (not verbal) can generate a healthy will. We may divine the riddle of innervation if we return once more to the aforementioned description of the work of film by Tomislav Gotovac, as a living, pulsating structure encompassing into a single whole (composite) the screen and the spectator's eye as parts of one and the same organism. Benjamin invokes the mimetic function of innervation that would transfer to the viewer the impulse of the moving image and thus make room for a more direct operation of the apparatus, for the sake of the possibility of intervening in the social space of viewing. In his more mature materialist phase, Benjamin probably got scared that innervation might also harbour the danger of numbing the will of the spectator faced with the impact of moving images, so he retreated from further consideration of its mimetic function. For us, however, it is interesting that in Benjamin's description of his 'prayer wheel' in *One-way Street*, what performs the regulative function in innervation is breath. Breath, Benjamin argues, operates in the canon of formula sounds, the 'sacred syllables' of the image, like in yoga exercises, a prayer wheel regulated by breathing. We are faced again with a metaphor of an organism, of breathing, of an image, the body, the stretching of matter and so on. The composite image of a body that stretches and regulates the operation of matter in a yoga exercise is another metaphorical image of the apparatus that Benjamin uses to conjure up for understanding the work of creating tensions and articulations. Innervation justifiably generates fear from an anaesthetic effect of the image, but in theatre, in the encounter of mutual gazes upon the image and from the image, innervation creates a potential for the utopian moment of watching – the view from matter.

Dragan Živadinov offered an ingenious example of this in a performance that was (probably) named after Benjamin's fragment: *Noordung Prayer Machine*. The spectators were led to the performance in two groups: one group was led into a regular theatre auditorium, while the other was taken to a grid of frames made of wooden beams. In that grid, the spectators were sitting de facto underneath the stage, their heads peering from those frames

10 | Walter Benjamin, *One Way Street and Other Writings* (London: NLB 1979), 75.

11 | 'Related to the notion of an optical unconscious familiar from the artwork essay, innervation refers, broadly, to a neurophysiological process that mediates between internal and external, psychic and motoric, human and mechanical registers.' in Miriam B. Hansen, "Benjamin and Cinema, Not a One-way Street", *Critical Inquiry* 25 (1999): 312.

with their backs facing the regular auditorium and their gazes directed at the shallow stage, the almost two-dimensional performance space. The performance was for the most part coordinated by the breathing of the ballerinas, who performed segments of a visually elaborate choreography both on the shallow stage and the beams, amongst the spectators embedded in them. Another break of continuity happened amongst the spectators 'pinched' by the stage and those in the auditorium – the director himself was 'directing' the reactions of the audience in the regular auditorium by giving signals for applauding, whistling and the like, without any regard for what was happening on the stage. In this rather intense structure of performing, breathing, watching and surveying, Živadinov opened quite disparate registers in the innervation of the machine – distraction was generated by the spectators' directed 'emotive' reactions, thus the view from the matter of an image was becoming a view into the matter of a performance.

What am I referring to here when I write 'the matter of an image'? Every image or tableau is viewed from somewhere, from a specific point of view. This is a practical law of the geometric grounding of representation, says Barthes: 'a fetishist subject is required to cut out the tableau'.[12] A point of view is also a point of meaning and in different constellations, it is determined by the 'law of society, law of struggle, law of meaning'.[13] For Brecht and Eisenstein, this is the place of the social struggle or party, while for Diderot it was the place of the gaze with bourgeois values, the gestic differentiation [*gestička diferencijacija*] of the citizen. The gestic character of a specifically theatrical image or tableau rests on the law that regulates the scene, not on the choice of subject. That is why from every tableau, from its perspective, one may also determine the depth of the opposing triangle. That triangle is where the gaze is preserved, its impetus, its momentum. The intensity of the saved *momentum* will also determine the power of the militancy of that view, that is, the advocating force of the image and the law of representation that grounds it. By the same token there is validity to Barthes's claim that 'all militant art cannot but be representational, legal'.[14] By framing the spectator, Živadinov almost literally preserves the gaze, as in a can or a jar, and displays it to the spectators sitting behind in the regular auditorium. However, their gaze too is framed by the director's mediation, again by a literal staging of an instance of directing, of the director himself in a point of meaning, directing the reactions of the spectators in the audience. The moment the first of the 'shackled' spectators turns her gaze backwards, towards the darkness of the auditorium, her

12 | Roland Barthes, *Image, Music, Text* (New York: Hill and Wang 1977), 76.
13 | Ibid, 77.
14 | Ibid.

gaze explodes, there occurs a sort of liberation of the saved gaze and the gaze starts travelling through the darkness of the black box, the darkness of the auditorium, forming new relations between the laws of watching, of the image, of affective reaction and so forth. From that moment on, the spectator is no longer confined to the function of watching, of occupying a point of view, but instead, becomes an 'attender',[15] one whose interest is dislocated from the field of the image, ex-centred; whose gaze becomes a side gaze – and the spectator's position and relation regarding the image, theatre and the world is no longer just reflexive. The apparatus of theatre becomes a place of the density of the gaze (of the matter of an image), wherein (all) people and things crossing from the world into theatre undergo refraction, a deflection in the ray of vision.

That view from the apparatus and through its cuts, the leap from the matter of an image into the complex matter of performance, the explosion of the gaze that occurs at the membrane, at the cut between an image and performance, opens a new regime of interests, already by the very encounter in the disproportionate experience of watching, within a one-off assembly of a heterogeneous population of spectators. I wonder: if the coalescence of the factory machine, the apparatus of cinematic representation and the performer's body once gave birth to the eccentric actor,[16] may we also speak of an eccentric spectator in the friction between the theatrical apparatus of encountering, technologies of mediation and the spectator's body?

5. THE GAZE OF THE UNDEAD

The price that one must pay in order to have a representation without an origin, without a law, is death, Barthes concludes,[17] offering the example of a vampire's gaze, a gaze through the closed eyes of an un-dead deceased person who is taken, in Dreyer's film *Vampyr*, from his house to the graveyard while the camera transmits his subjective view. Barthes claims that representation is thereby fooled, because the spectator cannot occupy the vampire's point of view, which leaves the image without the support of the law. But is there a form of complicating one's point of view more sublime than the one in Joseph Beuys' performance *Wie man dem toten Hasen die Bilder erklärt*? While the performer takes an explanatory position in a gallery, the audience is attending the performance from outside through the (fourth) glass wall and TV screen. The gaze of the inhuman,

15 | Bojana Cvejić, *Choreographing Problems* (London: Palgrave Macmillan 2014), 62–72.
16 | Factory of the Eccentric Actor (FEKS), *Eccentric Manifesto*, trans. and introduction Marek Pytel (London: Eccentric Press 1992), 22.
17 | Barthes, *Image, Music, Text*, 77.

the gaze of the dead hare carried by Beuys renders vectors of watching visible, because here the gaze of the one watching from a side, and not frontally, is channelled through the gaze of the disinterested object, a gaze that is not constitutive of an image but of rationalisation of the triadic object of making-performing-attending.

'The dead hare is a dead external organ of humanity'.[18] From today's perspective, one might conclude that Beuys was a precursor of some kind of 'object-oriented art', but contrary to that, in a series of interviews and texts Beuys asserted his anthropocentric beliefs, whereas he regarded animals, trees and other materials that served as media for accessing the substance as external organs of humanity. Therefore, the hare is above all a representative of a ruined environment as well as a deactivated prosthetic extension of humanity. In a way, the dead hare embodies the gaze without momentum, the gaze of the environment, indifferent, but not for that reason any less important or consequential. However, there is but one step from the environment to the apparatus, only a single step from a dead hare's indifferent gaze without momentum to the preserved gaze of an 'un-dead' camera, or, to put it more accurately, to the 'disembodied gaze', as Judith Butler calls it in her description of the camera's masculine privilege to be a gaze that produces bodies without itself being a body.[19] However, there is always an in-between.

6. THE VIEW FROM MATTER

There are no clean apparatuses. Institutional apparatuses are ticking time bombs. Institutions are the perseverance of certain forms composed in rhythms and compile different temporal dynamics, patterns and periods. Every theatre is a conglomerate of time patterns that have acquired their formal organisation – elements of institutions often link material with immaterial forms of architecture, management, repertoire calendars and schedules, working hours, modes of presentation, technology, organisation of watching, design, style periods etc. that have accumulated in epistemologically and productively different historical periods. Institutions therefore repeat time patterns that make them recognisable, as well as juxtapose incommensurable rhythms in the social whole, which is precisely the cause of their problematic relationship with the present; their iterability rests in performances of routines and norms through practices of

18 | Cf. Gene Ray and Joseph Beuys, *Mapping the Legacy: Papers from a Symposium* (Sarasota: 1998, New York: Distributed Art Publishers 2001), 110.
19 | Judith Butler, *Bodies that Matter: On the Discursive Limits of "Sex"* (London and New York: Routledge 1993), 136.

work, communication, moving and phenomenality that are not necessarily or are seldom synchronous with the rhythms of more mobile economic, social and cultural actors.[20]

However, it is an ideological tendency of every apparatus, every institution, to sanitise its perspective, to lubricate and programme its own operations in order to reproduce a certain image of reality (and the order of things) as clearly as possible and thereby also ways of producing that reality. If we want to bring about an explosion of the automatised gaze, to vaporise its perspectives and points of view, we need to bring its momentums to a juncture, to a collision, to crack open the cans of the gaze and fold over, rearrange their apparatuses. We already learned that lesson from Dziga Vertov, whose *Kino Eye* is not the gaze of a man who penetrates, cuts a *tableau* into matter; nor is it a gaze from the environment, the gaze of a bird or a frog. It is the gaze of matter, the gaze that issues from the collision of the camera and montage, wherein the gaze as well as the interval cut and leap to encounter each other.[21]

A similar lesson comes from Ion Grigorescu as well, in his diary entry on analogue photography, renouncing mastery in the quest for the right angle and position.[22] Grigorescu finds the real excitement of discovery in playing with light by combining different kinds of lenses, or in darkness, developing photographs. Thus he surrenders the genius of articulation to the camera, because 'nobody has seen things standing still so far'. The photographic darkroom is a place of deceleration, the place where the process of image creation is naturalised, whilst developing an image is an art only for the artist. The artist, says Grigorescu, is the only one who looks behind the image that does not resemble reality and sees the month-long process of choosing the right lens for transforming the gaze and converting it into the eyes of matter. However, let us push that speculation a little further still. If the apparatus (of performance, for instance) is a sort of machine, a machine made of a different kind of metal and if, as we know from Brecht's and Benjamin's criticism, it emerges from a crystallisation of social relations, conditions of production and conditions of life, then that apparatus too is dead labour, a vampire sucking living labour from the work of art and

20 | Caroline Levine, *Forms: Whole, Rhythm, Hierarchy, Network* (Princeton: Princeton University Press 2015), 57–65.

21 | 'Vertov realizes the materialist program of the first chapter of *Matter and Memory* through the cinema, the in-itself of the image. Vertov's non-human eye, the kino-eye, is not the eye of a fly or of an eagle, the eye of another animal. Neither is it – in an Epsteinian way – the eye of the spirit endowed with a temporal perspective, which might apprehend the spiritual whole. On the contrary, it is the eye in matter, not subject to time, which has "conquered" time, which reaches the "negative of time" and which knows no other whole than the material universe and its extension'. Gilles Deleuze, *Cinema 1: The Movement-Image* (London: Athlone 2000), 83–84.

22 | Ion Grigorescu, Andreiana Mihail and Georg Schöllhammer, *Ion Grigorescu: Diaries 1970–1975* (Berlin: Sternberg Press 2014), 208–11.

reproducing the dominant patterns of the division of labour, specialisation and insight gained through reception. If we wish to change those patterns, we need to occupy the gaze precisely from the viewpoint of that vampire, the viewpoint of a diagram wherein the relations of subjectification and knowledge are physicalised, a point of view that is neither the viewpoint of the subject (because the subject is blind) nor the object (because the object is conditioned by its relation to the subject), but a third-person point of view, a point of view 'from the side', one that sees the theatre simultaneously as a place where things are shown and seen, as well as a local manifestation of the encounter in watching.

We already saw above, in the respective performances of Slaven Tolj and Oleg Kulik, how the temporality of black-box darkness produces friction in a white box, but there are countless modes whereby the apparatuses may be permeated, encased and alloyed – let us cover a black box with a photographic darkroom, or an algorithmically led TV studio, or a prison TV room, or a sitcom TV sofa; let us rock the gaze of a theatre spectator back and forth[23] or dislocate it following the logic of Bacon's triptychs; let us stage a play on a film set; let us pay film extras to perform as spectators; let us impose on a repertoire institution the apparatus of an observatory or biosphere, a tourist camp on an abandoned factory, a painter's studio on a theatre auditorium, an x-ray room or infrared laboratory, or ... . In order to open a portal into the gaze of matter, perhaps even to invoke it as the materialist gaze, we need to collide different apparatuses, to cause friction between their drives and temporal accumulations. Those repositories of time and technique will open the possibility for a view from the noise of matter, the possibility that *poïesis* might reach its highest state, to become *physis*, that theatre might become something in itself, a meeting site where meeting itself might transcend the individual functions of authorship, exposing and watching and become a 'flower' of performance/production, to use a poetic metaphor that was equally important to Martin Heidegger when he was paving the road for the un-concealment of truth and to Zeami, who was looking for paths to reach an ultimate harmony between performing and watching.[24]

23 | Like in Michael Snow's film *Back and Forth.*
24 | Cf. Martin Heidegger, *The Question Concerning Technology, and Other Essays* (North Richmond: Harper Torchbooks 1977), and Shelley Fenno Quinn, *Developing Zeami: The Noh Actor's Attunement in Practice* (Honolulu: University of Hawaii Press 2005).

 SILVIA BOTTIROLI

It's July 22, 2012, and we are in the main square of Santarcangelo di Romagna, a small Italian city that since 1971 hosts a famous festival of contemporary performing arts. It's Sunday, and it's the last night of the festival. Rain has been looming for hours and there's lightning and thunder in the distance. There is a stage in the square: it's tall, as the stages often used for local festivals or popular shows in this area are, and it leans against the wall of the primary school, dominated by the big 'Scuole Comunali' sign. The stage is filled with lights and decorations; two men and a woman sit on one of the two short sides. The rest of the stage is busy with colourful couples spinning around in various folk dances (waltz, polka, mazurka...), wearing sparkling and often scanty outfits. They are engaged in a competition, one type of dance quickly following the other, and some couples are looking tired, while every once in a while a member of the jury stands up and guides off the stage a couple that has been standing still for too long or that made a mistake with a step. However, it's not the music they're dancing to that fills the electric atmosphere of the square, but a cloud made of repeated, processed and digitally altered snaps, creating a density that literally fills the void whilst leaving intact a surrealistic sensation of silence. The dancers, as one can see by getting closer to them, all wear earphones. Sometimes during particularly quick or whirling moves, some earphones fall and hang loose, their thin chord messily dancing with the dancers.

The square is packed, the audience stands very close to the stage and there's a feeling of emotional involvement and suspense in the air. Many people are friends or relatives of the dancers. They are here to support and root for them during the course of this 'marathon', and they are not going to walk away from the stage until the very end, after spending more than four hours with bated breath. Others are festival goers (some of them are involved in the organisation, some are artists on the billboard): many of them know Zapruder filmmakersgroup, the independent collective of filmmakers behind this performance, which is the last one in this edition of the festival that brought the theatre back to the square and that is now filling the space with sound and progressively emptying it of dancers, playing with the void. In the audience some people are more focussed on the live sound work done by Francesco 'Fuzz' Brasini: they are listening to a concert of concrete sounds and electronic manipulations, and the dance marathon is mainly a background image. Others live in Santarcangelo and, like they are used to doing in the Summer months, they are just having a walk in the square after dinner, knowing they will find something to see or listen to – after all, this is a typical feature of the festival, which has always been known as the 'festival internazionale del teatro in piazza' (literally, the 'international festival of theatre in the squares'). Amongst these spectators are either many elderly or children: the former immediately recognise the event as a dance marathon, as they have likely seen one before in one of the many dance halls scattered throughout the countryside; the latter stare at the colours and the movements until something more interesting catches their attention. There are also two invisible spectators – maybe they can be seen by looking closely at the windows on the school building, but no one seems to raise their eyes up to that level: it's Monaldo Moretti and David Zamagni, Zapruder's camera operators. They are filming the marathon from a 'sharpshooter's perspective', as they will write, that is to say, from a point of view where they can film the audience by looking literally through the performance, recording ambient sounds and mixing them with the dancers' steps, recorded through contact microphones placed under the stage.

On the other side of the square, the festival centre – some tables spread under the portico of the city hall and on the street, where the artists and the public can have dinner together – is still open, as well as the ticket office and the info point. Here, people can find the last catalogues of this edition of the festival, where the performance we are attending is titled *I topi lasciano la nave (Yes Sir, I Can Boogie)* and is presented with a text that aims to be evocative and evasive at the same time without being very specific about the nature of the event: 'For centuries folk wisdom has attributed to rats the providential power of foretelling the imminence of catastrophic events about to occur in that part of the world they inhabit. Nobody has ever demonstrated the existence of these presumed and unknown paranormal faculties, but we do know that rats benefit from a particularly acute auditory apparatus, a formidable sensitivity to the noises surrounding them, the sounds of creaking, hissing, high and low frequencies. The 'teatro in piazza' programme at Santarcangelo •12 says goodbye with this image which, in its fulfilment, cancels itself out: at once an invitation to listen and a bow to the beauty of removal and the void'.[1] What is it, then, this object taking shape in front of us, dissolving and disappearing while it becomes real? What kind of promises, expectations, betrayals and memories does it contain? What forms of spectatorship does it trigger and involve, or reject and drop? What are the hundreds of spectators in this square looking at? What will the visitors of art galleries and film festivals, where the recorded version of this work will be shown, be looking at? What are we looking at *now* as we recall the event in our memory and try to bring it back to life through writing?

It's impossible to give a unique answer to all these questions: different spectators would give different answers, and they would all be right. No compromise between their visions is necessary, nor would it be possible, as all the perspectives that have been activated in this square do not meet in a single point of observation. Not even the artists' perspective is able to embrace them all, as they choose not to be able to anticipate them. The performance is, indeed, the trigger of an event imagined for a long time and patiently prepared in the subtle weaving of relationships with all the involved actors: dancer's associations, musicians, technicians and producers of the festival, judges of the competition. However, this action triggers an uncontrollable mechanism, not devoid of unpredictability, whose evolution will be determined by the interaction of many elements, including weather and fate. This is why there is not and there cannot be a unique point of view, a single interpretation of the event we are looking at, which is consequently *undecidable*. I have spent the last five years wondering about the mystery of this feature, feeling both proud and inappropriate for having curated and coproduced this project during my first year of artistic direction in Santarcangelo[2] without understanding it completely. What did we witness during that night in July? What kind of space did we share in that square? What kind of reality and time? Who was the author? How was the event produced, and what different kinds of spectatorship did it generate? Finally, what kind of public, social gathering and society did it

1 | Zapruder filmmakersgroup, "I topi lasciano la nave. Yes Sir, I Can Boogie!" in *Catalogue of Santarcangelo •12 Festival Internazionale del Teatro in Piazza* (Santarcangelo: Maggioli Editore 2012), 47. The work was later presented as a film installation with the title *Yes Sir, I Can Boogie*, that I will use from now when referring to it.
2 | This edition was co-directed with Rodolfo Sacchettini and Cristina Ventrucci.

create? The mystery of *Yes Sir, I Can Boogie* also highlights a feature shared with other art projects that can be very different from one another but still share the intention to challenge the concepts of visibility and readability and in this way create a space that I can only describe as *political*.

THE EVENT OF UNDECIDABILITY

The word *undecidable* appears in *Six Memos for the Next Millennium*, written by Italo Calvino in 1985 for his Charles Eliot Norton poetry lectures at Harvard University. Calvino's fourth memo,[3] 'Visibility', revolves around the capacity of literature to generate images and create a kind of 'mental cinema' where fantasies can flow continuously. The main concern that he brings forth lies within the relation between contemporary culture and imagination: the risk to definitely lose, in the overproduction of images, the power of bringing visions into focus with our eyes shut and in fact of '*thinking* in terms of images'.[4] In the last pages of the lecture, he proposes a shift from understanding the fantastic world of the artist not as indefinable, but as *undecidable*. With this word Calvino means to define the coexistence and the relation, within any literary work, between three different dimensions. The first dimension is the artist's imagination – a world of potentialities that no work will succeed in realising. The second is the reality as we experience it by living. Finally, the third is the world of the actual work, made by the layers of signs that accumulate in it; compared to the first two worlds it is 'also infinite, but more easily controlled, less refractory to formulation'.[5] Calvino calls the link between these three worlds 'the undecidable, the paradox of an infinite whole that contains other infinite wholes'.[6] For him, all artistic operations involve – by means of the infinity of linguistic possibilities – the infinity of the artist's imagination and the infinity of contingencies. Therefore, 'attempts to escape the vortex of multiplicity are useless'.[7] In his fifth memo, he subsequently focuses on *multiplicity* as a way for literature to comprehend the complex nature of the world that for the author is a whole of wholes, where the acts of watching and knowing also intervene in observed reality and alter it.

In *Yes Sir, I Can Boogie*, we also witness the staging of a multiplicity, a whole of wholes, that works by superimposition, thus creating a specific condition of experience and visibility. It's as if something has been placed

---

3 | Out of five, the sixth lecture was never written, as the author died suddenly and the series remained unfinished, yet published with its original and now misleading title.

4 | Italo Calvino, "Visibility", in *Six Memos for the Next Millennium* (Harvard: Harvard University Press 1988), 92.

5 | Ibid, 97.

6 | Ibid.

7 | Ibid, 98.

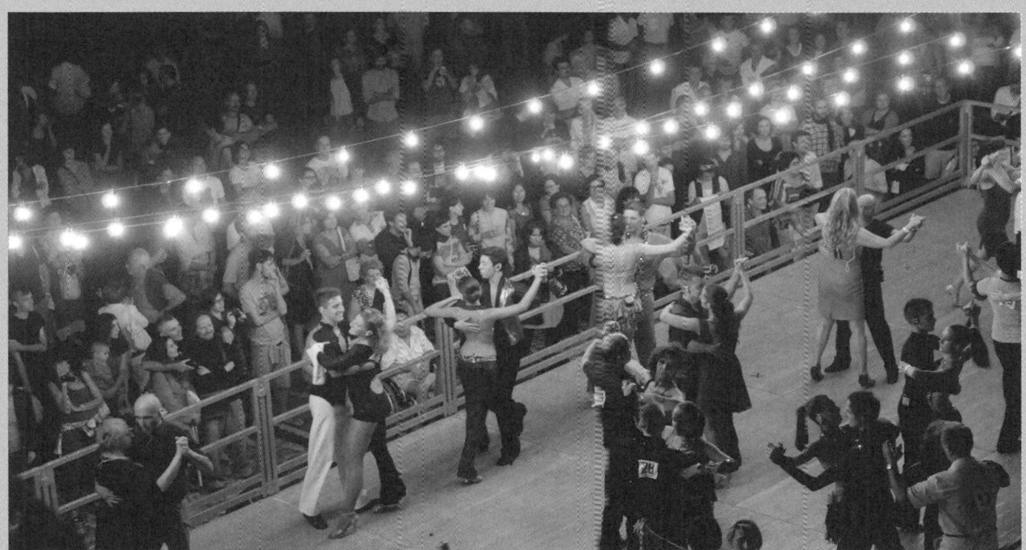

Figure 12. Zapruder filmmakersgroup, *I topi lasciano la nave (Yes Sir, I Can Boogie)*, Santarcangelo di Romagna, 2012. Photo: Mariano Marini. Courtesy of the author.

between the spectator and the image: a different density is stuck to our vision and the conditions of visibility have been modified. The objects we have in front of us remain unchanged, but their superimposition makes it impossible to define their nature unanimously and without any doubt. Because of this specific form of visibility, different eyes can look at the same object and see different realities. Each one of them is right, yet no one can define completely what he or she sees they only understand one side, which is real, somewhat autonomous and independent from the others, although it does not complete the object that is seen. Specifically, this performance includes a dance competition, a contemporary music concert, a live performance, the closing event of a festival, a celebration in a city in Romagna, an artistic work in a public space, the location for an artist's film. Each element also carries different forms of experience and the production of reality: elements from the real world are transposed on the stage using the same coordinates we normally experience them with; or slightly shifted. At the same time, a context dimension that we may call *curatorial* comes into play, a dimension which constitutes a framework for understanding the work and contextually provides the necessary conditions for supporting it. Above all, however, it's the strictly artistic dimension that loads the work with creative and fictional elements, stories and arguments, languages, codes and forms. Therefore different natures, precisely defined and definable, coexist in *Yes Sir I Can Boogie* and, by sharing the same space in the work and overlapping simultaneously, they generate an irresolvable complexity in which everything is what it is, though at the same time it is more, and something else.

In turn, the different natures that constitute the performance also imply an equal amount of forms of spectatorship that, during that same night and in that same square, coexisted one next to the other, sharing the same context and putting themselves in front of the same event, even though they were witnessing totally different *objects*. And there's more: when looking at *Yes Sir, I Can Boogie*, we are both spectators and witnesses, but also creators of an event that develops in front of us and takes a different shape depending on the spectator's perspective. Therefore, the spectators take on a generative function, since without their look some aspects of the work would simply not exist. The most clear example for this is the presence of cameras that transform the stage in a movie set, but the same mechanism also operates in the coexistence of different angles amongst the views of spectators, generated by a superimposition of three different levels in the work: reality (the town square, the couples dancing and the dance marathon); the contextual and curatorial dimension (the dramaturgical design of a festival questioning public space and the expectations generated by the contemporary presence of different audiences, gathered for its final event after ten days); and finally the strictly artistic dimension, made more complex by the coexistence of three dimensions: live performance, film and music.

The complexity in the fruition of *Yes Sir, I Can Boogie* expands and deepens some traits of its aesthetic *undecidability*, that is, by the way, inherent to any work of art, and something that Calvino relates to *visibility*. Performance is already connected, in our imagery, to the production of images rather than just words or concepts; in the present context, it also faces the infinite production of images that surrounds us. Under these circumstances one could argue that performance, and art in general, should rather operate by means of opacity, creating a space free from the obligation to be clearly visible and communicable. A lot has been written in the art field about the need for darkness, which sometimes ends up being an adoration of invisibility and disappearance.[8] What is maybe more productive is to consider darkness as a specific condition of sight, one that demands other means and attitudes, other capacities and desires. This is the case with Georges Didi-Huberman's metaphor of fireflies, which remains as a (literally) bright image for what art can do for us and what we can and must do for art.[9] Giorgio Agamben also uses a similar figure when he defines the contemporary as 'he who firmly holds his gaze on his own time so as to perceive not its light, but rather its darkness', since 'to perceive this darkness is not a form of inertia or of passivity, but rather implies an activity

---

8 | Cf. Byung-Chul Han, *The Transparency Society* (Stanford: Stanford University Press 2015), and Jonathan Crary, *24/7: Late Capitalism and the Ends of Sleep* (London: Verso 2014).
9 | Georges Didi-Huberman, *Survival of the Fireflies* (Minneapolis: University of Minnesota Press 2018).

and a singular ability. In our case, this ability amounts to a neutralisation of the lights that come from the epoch in order to discover its obscurity, its special darkness, which is not, however, separable from those lights'.[10] From a different perspective, Rebecca Solnit, following Virginia Woolf's line of thought in *To the Lighthouse*, focusses on the connection between darkness and being, or more precisely 'being oneself, a wedge-shaped core of darkness' where this self, 'having shed its attachments [is] free for the strangest adventures' and thus the 'horizon [seems] limitless'.[11] In *Hope in the Dark*, Solnit goes even further, using the metaphor of the theatre: 'Imagine the world as a theatre. The acts of the powerful and the official occupy center stage. The traditional versions of history, the conventional sources of news encourage us to fix our gaze on that stage. The limelights there are so bright that they blind you to the shadowy spaces around you, make it hard to meet the gaze of the other people in the seats, to see the way out of the audience, into the aisles, backstage, outside, in the dark, where other powers are at work. A lot of the fate of the world is decided onstage, in the limelight, and the actors there will tell you that all of it is, that there is no other place'.[12]

Thinking of undecidability, the metaphor or image that seems more appropriate to me is rather that of *opacity*, meaning a specific form of visibility that operates through overlapping or sticking one material on the other (like, for example, steam on glass): a form of *density* that art can produce and that curatorial contexts can support and maintain, or even enlarge and intensify. Therefore, the work we are looking at resists the temptation of darkness and invisibility, and challenges reality on its very level, that of complexity (or multiplicity) and visibility. In other words, *Yes Sir, I Can Boogie* seems to aim at preserving a space in which the way things come to visibility makes it impossible to decide about their nature: it is the logical connection, the law of necessity that normally binds visibility and readability, that is broken by means of a surrender a deviation, a different logic. In this way, the work creates an empty space, an inclination that is not directed at meanings (which are by nature determinable) but at a sense, or better, at multiple senses. This creates the chance of an event: a moment in which meanings are suspended, and everything that we know does not help us understanding what's happening. Two features define the experience of the event: the perception that something unexpected is possible and the act of returning space and time to a concept of singularity rather than homogeneity. This means that the event creates possibilities

10 | Giorgio Agamben, "What Is the Contemporary?", in *What Is an Apparatus? and Other Essays* (Stanford: Stanford University Press 2009), 45.

11 | Rebecca Solnit, *A Field Guide to Getting Lost* (London: Penguin 2005), 15–16.

12 | Rebecca Solnit, *Hope in the Dark: Untold Histories, Wild Possibilities* (Edinburgh and London: Canongate Books 2016), 25.

and beginnings that are open and unpredictable but also real: in the event, *this* is the space, *this* is the time when something can really happen, and this space and time are also 'anywhere out of the world'[13] at all times. In this sense, the event exposes us to something that is not decided; for *Yes Sir, I Can Boogie*, it is the art work that exposes itself to the event of its own happening, by radically putting at stake its own performative statute and, above all, with the rejection of control and direction carried out by its own authors.

A crucial element in the apparatus of this work, and of the possibilities it opens up, is its time, its duration. The work lasts enough to create in the spectator a sense of coexistence with it, and a chance to pass through different states of perception and emotion. Moreover, the duration of this time is not predetermined, thus it is unknowable and oriented towards an infinite continuation: the fundamental meaning of every marathon is to go on in time and ideally – hyperbolically – to be endless. Lastly, the time of work is unknown to the authors themselves, since they choose to trigger an apparatus that is independent of their will and potentially uncontrollable. A further crucial element of the work is the presence of different actual worlds living next to each other yet not sharing a common horizon: the worlds arranged by the artists, and the worlds brought by the audience members. The coexistence of these real and fictional worlds generates a potential world that would not actualise itself into one actual form and whose potentiality is grounded in a logic of addition and contradiction; a logic of 'and... and... and...' as opposite to the logic of 'either... or...' that seems to rule reality. In fact, undecidability is produced by the coexistence, within the work of art, of contradictory realities that don't withdraw or cancel each other out, and images that let go of their representational nature and just exist as such. None of the images created by *Yes Sir, I Can Boogie* is more or less real than the others, no matter whether they come as pieces of reality or as products of individual or collective fantasies. It is the artwork as such that creates a ground where all the images share the same gradient of reality, no matter whether they harmoniously coexist or are radically conflicting. If every artwork creates systems, inviting spectators inside them, undecidability happens when a space is created where also the real world and all the spectators' fictional worlds are equally welcomed. The artwork may then be navigated either by choosing just one layer of reality, or by continuously stepping from one world to another: different dimensions are made available without any form of hierarchy or predicted relations. Thus, a form of emancipation is (being) offered to the public

---

13 | Cf. Baudelaire, Charles. "Anywhere out of this world (N'importe où hors du monde)", in *Le Spleen de Paris*, 112-14. Bibebook (1869). http://www.bibebook.com/files/ebook/libre/V2/baudelaire_ charles_-_le_ spleen_de_paris.pdf

of this work, which is given by the fact that *Yes Sir, I Can Boogie* opens up new possibilities for the understanding and practice of the live arts as a space for conversation between different layers and realities that constitute different forms and politics of spectatorship.

A MULTIPLICITY OF GAZES

A multiplicity of gazes is indeed gathered by *Yes Sir, I Can Boogie*, and by artworks that practice their undecidability, offering themselves as a space where different and even contradictory individual experiences unfold and coexist, with no hierarchical structure and no orchestration. It is a space where the gazes of spectators are not composed into a common horizon but are let free to wildly engage with all the realities involved, connecting or not connecting them, and in the end to experience part of the complex 'whole of wholes' that is the artwork.

The peculiar element in these kinds of artworks, the one that can produce an understanding of the place of art and its politics today, is that they generate multiple forms of spectatorship that coexist next to each other without mediating between their own positions and points of view. The multiplicity of gazes produced and gathered by undecidable artworks does not create a community, as there is no 'common' present. Rather, it generates a radical collectivity based on multiplicity and conflicting positions that are not called to any form of negotiation yet affect each other and together come to determine the ultimate nature of the work itself. They don't merge in one common thought and don't see or reflect one common image, yet they affect each other with their sheer presence and existence, operating as a prism that multiplies the reality it reflects. A space of communication is opened here that is not meant for unilateral or bilateral exchanges, but for a circulation of information and interpretations. A circulation over which no one – not even the artist – has full control. The position of the author is then challenged and responsibility is shared with the audience not as a participant, but rather as an unknowable and undecidable collective body that receives, reverberates and twists the artwork.

The collective dimension of fruition, the fact that it is a live gathering assembling a wide multiplicity and not trying to homogenise it but rather let it shine, is without any doubt a crucial aspect of *Yes Sir, I Can Boogie*: the dimension of undecidability and unknowability of the event is also clear thanks to this 'prismatic' reception that breaks up the image and divides it into segments rather than assembling it into one single reality.

Within this radical collectivity, spectatorship also enacts its own being as an act of testimony and thus, etymologically, of survival. In Latin, 'witness' is 'testis', and has the same root of the word that originates the term 'survivor': the witness is, literally, someone who survived an event, as some theatre and dance theorists have underlined in recent years.[14] The event that the collective body of the audience of *Yes Sir, I Can Boogie* survives is the event of becoming sensitive to the political through a theatrical scene that reclaims the public sphere and shows its network of representations, inclusions and exclusions, opening up to the possibility of experiencing multiplicity and plurality. Multiple forms of public spaces and collective subjectivities arise from this event and start inhabiting a productive dimension that extends far beyond the artwork itself and is still loaded with the specific geography of infinities that it has produced. The kind of collective body that undecidability produces could of course be seen as an image of a possible or future societal structure, but instead it is an enigmatic subject: it is not there to actualise itself but to keep being a glimmering potentiality. Indeed, as a practice of undecidability, art produces a collectivity, an elsewhere and a future time, but does not claim any agency over them: it does not tend towards a preexisting, visible image but proceeds in the darkness in order to produce different forms of visibility within it.

In sum, it could be said that *Yes Sir, I Can Boogie* creates an instant community which is composite and impossible, that in turn affects the artwork in a decisive and irrevocable way. The presence of a heterogeneous community made up of radical and incompatible diversities that witnesses the event without being able to decide its nature, creates a convergence of points of view and reality levels. This intensifies and amplifies the work, but also causes, due to intensification and multiplication, the loss of its quality of representation, which succumbs to the weight of its levels of existence. We can indeed imagine every performance as something that can be placed at some point in the spectrum from event to representation, that is, from the reality of something that happens to the fiction of something that can be represented because it already happened. Before an undecidable event, the two extremes merge like particles that have been excessively accelerated or heated, and on the stage there is a trace of this fire that went through the spectator as well. There is therefore a circularity of effects and affections between the undecidable work and its spectators, with a deeply transformative aspect that, because of its nature, is incalculable and difficult to observe. The aspect that seems more generative to me is

14 | See Freddie Rokem, *Performing History: Theatrical Representations of the Past in Contemporary Theatre* (Iowa: University of Iowa Press 2000), and Andre Lepecki in the closing pages of his work *Singularities: Dance in the Age of Performance* (London and New York: Routledge 2016).

the political dimension generated by an audience that is not only made up of incompatible diversities but also cohabitates in a complex and unstable matter that constantly sets up new networks of relationships, new placements, new 'distributions of the sensible', as Jacques Rancière would call them. Taking part in a redistribution of positions and meanings, a redefinition of relationships and hierarchies, a constant reconfiguration of the field of the sensible, is a suitable practice for art in every form, and it surely finds a specific application in theatre, which is by nature an art of dialogue, a space where two (or more) contrasting points of view coexist in the same stage and challenge one another, not to dilute or resolve the matter in a common agreement but to promote the persistence of a duality, therefore of a form of competitiveness or dialogical dynamics.[15]

Something more than a sheer persistence of duality is at stake here, thanks to the short-circuit between reality and representation produced by the negotiations in place between the performance and the audience, and amongst all the members of the audience. Both the possibility for the work of art to operate as a trigger of senses and significabilities, and the experience of spectatorship as an individual adventure within a collective subject are deeply transformed. In particular, the experience of undecidability radically challenges the conditions that normally characterise theatrical spectatorship: gazes, and behind them bodies that also embed imaginaries, narratives, ethics and political behaviours, become aware not only of the constellation of singularities that they compose but, more importantly, of the world that is among them. The world that is among *us*: a world that exists thanks to our commitment towards it and within it, a world we live with and that is constantly done and undone by negotiating our different positions. Hence a precarious world, not because it is in danger but because it is indeed alive, not permanently determined, open.

Within this world, the very nature of individual identity is at the same time reinforced and challenged, and the mutual agencies that individuals and collectivities operate on each other become the site of a political plasticity that redefines each subject as a transforming entity. Transformation does not mean liquidity or changeability, though, since plasticity is a quality intrinsically linked to persistance and consistency. In the end, the live gathering constituted by undecidable artworks challenges the paradigm of political subjectivation and its mechanisms. In this sense, the spectatorship generated by an undecidable object is a dimension of radical democracy, a democracy of bodies and gazes, presents and memories, expectations and promises that every element carries and triggers. This dimension is

---

15 | With these two terms, I refer respectively to the thought of Chantal Mouffe and Richard Sennett, both widely influential within contemporary practices and artistic theories.

even more important because it is not a representation of the community of citizens we belong to, nor it is an exercise, a test, a simulation or an attempt. On the contrary, a work that remains undecidable – or that, like here, hyperbolically magnifies its own undecidability – claims its own uselessness, intended not to have a specific purpose. Acknowledging undecidability as specific to art, and thus as a means without ends, seems to better protect the inner nature and intact potentiality of a quality that does not make itself available for any use and does not serve any agenda, but stays autonomous and operates by creating its own conditions all over again.

The possibility of experience offered by *Yes Sir, I Can Boogie* to its audience on that night, a possibility we all may have found in other encounters or aesthetic experiences, is a kinetic force, triggered by impact with a fast moving object that does not belong to itself and cannot therefore belong to us, but whose air we can breathe, whose temperature and atmosphere we can share. If all this has any consequence on reality, it concerns the fact that in this rarefied and temporary space, the spectators get to perceive themselves as co-authors of an event, explorers of a space that is given and, at the same time, created by the steps that go all over it; openers of doors and possibilities, multipliers of meanings. The game of experience, translation and writing that is the act of gazing unravels here in all its extent, but it's not just that: another space is created, another world or 'whole of wholes', that the artwork would not be able to generate autonomously, because it is also made up of the images, the worlds and representations that every spectator carries with himself or herself, and because this happens as a form of vibration between the voids thus created. Ultimately, a political dimension does spring from an art that practices its undecidability and from its encounter with a multiplicity of gazes. Its political feature lies in the ability to set the conditions for an intensity that can last in time and reverberate much wider and much longer than in the actual shared space and time of the performance. A condition of existence is hence produced that is intrinsically and utterly political as it is, as Samuel Beckett writes in *The Unnamable*, about being 'all these words, all these strangers, this dust of words, with no ground for their settling'.[16]

16 | Samuel Beckett, *Molloy, Malone Dies, The Unnamable* (London: Calder Publications 1994), 390.

TABLE OF FIGURES

Agamben, Giorgio. "Poiesis and Praxis." and "Privation Is Like a Face." In *The Man Without Content*, 68–94 and 59–68. Stanford, CA: Stanford University Press, 1999.
Agamben, Giorgio. "What Is the Contemporary?" In *What Is an Apparatus? and Other Essays*, 39–55. Stanford University Press, 2009.

Aït-Touati, Frédérique. "For a Speculative Policy. Bruno Latour & Nanterre-Amendier's Le Théâtredes négociations / Make It Work (2015)." In *Empty Staged, Crowded Flats; Performativity as Curatorial Strategy*, edited by Florian Malzacher and Joanna Warsza, 152-57. Berlin: Alexander Verlag, 2017.

Althusser, Louis. "On the Materialist Dialectic." In *For Marx*, 161-219. London: Verso, 1969.

L'Asilo, (Ex Asilo Filangieri). "Dichiarazione d'uso civico de l'Asilo." January 2, 2016. http://www. exasilofilangieri.it/regolamento-duso-civico.

Assmann, Aleida. "Shapes of Time. Transformations of the Modern Time Regime." In *Vol. 1 How to Build a Manifesto for the Future of a Festival. Build the Time*, 58-77. Santarcangelo Festival Teatro 2015.

Arendt, Hannah. "Freedom and Politics." In *Freedom and Serfdom*, edited by Albert Hunold, 191-217. Dordrecht: Springer Netherlands, 1961.
Arendt, Hannah. *The Human Condition*. Chicago: University of Chicago Press, (1961) 2013.

 BIBLIOGRAPHY

Arendt, Hannah. *Was ist Politik? Fragmente aus dem Nachlass*, edited by Ursula Ludz. Munich and Zurich: Piper, 2003.
Arendt, Hannah. "What is Freedom?". In *The Portable Hannah Arendt*, edited by Peter Baher, 438-62. London: Penguin, 2000.

Austin, J. L. *How to Do Things with Words*. Oxford: Clarendon Press, 1962.

Bank, Mark, and Justin O'Connor. "Inside the whale (and how to get out of there): Moving on from two decades of creative industries research." *European Journal of Cultural Studies* 20, no. 6 (2017): 637–54.

Baravalle, Marco. "Tra Governamentalità e Autonomia." *Opera Viva Magazine*, August 3, 2018. operavivamagazine.org/alteristituzioni-e-arte/.

Barthes, Roland. *Image, Music, Text*. New York: Hill and Wang, 1977.
Barthes, Roland. *Sade, Fourier, Loyola*. Translated by Richard Millet. Berkeley: University of California Press, 1989.
Barthes, Roland. *The Rustle of Language*. New York: Hill and Wang, 1986.

Bascetta, Marco, ed. *Economia politica della promessa*. Rome: manifestolibri, 2015.

Baudelaire, Charles. "Anywhere out of this world (N'importe où hors du monde)." In *Le Spleen de Paris*, 112-14. Bibebook (1869). http://www.bibebook.com/files/ebook/libre/V2/baudelaire_charles_-_le_spleen_de_paris.pdf.

Bayat, Asef. "Revolution in Bad Times." In *New Left Review* 80 (March/April 2013): 47-61.

Bengtsson, Arvid, ed. *Adventure Playgrounds*. London: Crosby Lockwood Staples, 1973.

Benjamin, Walter. *One Way Street and Other Writings*. London: NLB, 1979.

Bergson, Henri. *Time and Free Will: An essay on the immediate data of consciousness*. New York: Dover Publications, 2001.

Berlant, Lauren. *Cruel Optimism*. Durham: Duke University Press, 2018.

Berlant, Lauren. "The commons: Infrastructures for troubling times." *Environment and Planning D: Society and Space* 34, no. 3 (2016): 393-419.

Bishop, Claire. "Antagonism and Relational Aesthetics." *October* 110 (Fall 2004): 51–79.
Bishop, Claire. "Black Box, White Cube, Public Space." In *Out of Body*, (Spring 2016). Skulptur Projekte Muenster 2017. http://www.skulptur-projekte.de/skulptur-projekte-download/SP17-Out/Out_of_Body_EN.pdf.

Boggs, Carl. "Marxism, prefigurative communism and the problem of workers' control." *Radical America* 6 (Winter 1977): 99-122.

Bogost, Ian. *Persuasive Games: The Expressive Power of Videogames.* Cambridge: MIT Press, 2007.

Brecht, Bertolt. "Die dialektische Dramatik." In *Werke.* Band 21, 433-35, Frankfurt/Main: Suhrkamp, 1992.

Buden, Boris. *Cona Prehoda; O koncu postkomunizma.* Ljubljana: Krtina, 2014.
Buden, Boris. "The Post-Yugoslavian Condition of Institutional Critique. On Critique as Countercultural Translation." *European Institute for Progressive Cultural Policy, transversal* 11 (2007). https://transversal.at/transversal/0208.

Butler, Judith. "Bodies in Alliance and the Politics of the Street." *transversal "#Occupy and Assemble ∞"* (2011). http://transversal.at/transversal/1011/butler/en.
Butler, Judith. *Bodies that Matter: On the Discursive Limits of "Sex."* London and New York: Routledge, 1993.
Butler, Judith. *Notes Toward a Performative Theory of Assembly.* Cambridge: Harvard University Press, 2015.

Calvino, Italo. "Visibility." In *Six Memos for the Next Millennium*, 81-101. Cambridge: Harvard University Press, 1988.

Cedillo, Raúl Sánchez. "15M als Aufstand der Körper-Maschine." Translated by Dominic Widmer. In *Inventionen 2: Exodus. Reale Demokratie. Territorium. Immanenz. Maßlose Differenz. Biopolitik*, edited by Isabell Lorey, Roberto Nigro, and Gerald Raunig, 43–61. Zürich: Diaphanes, 2012.

Cedillo, Raúl Sánchez. "15M: Something Constituent This Way Comes." *South Atlantic Quarterly* 111, no. 3 (2012): 573-84.

Celakoski, Teodor. "Interview to Teodor Celakoski from Right to the City Zagreb." An interview with Teodor Celakoski by Zemos98. Video. https://archive.org/details/TeodorCelakoski.

de Certeau, Michel. *The Practice of Everyday Life.* Berkeley: University of California Press, 1984.

Chilton, Stephen. "The Problem of Agreement in Republicanism, Proceduralism, and the Mature Dewey: A 'Two Moments of Discourse Ethics' Analysis." *Steve Chilton's Home Page.* Last modified November 5, 2001. http://www.d.umn.edu/~schilton/Articles/Tilburg.html.

de Coninck-Smith, Ning. *Natural Play in Natural Surroundings; Urban Childhood and Playground Planning in Denmark, c. 1930 – 1950*, Working Paper 6. Odense: Odense University Printing Office, 1999.

 # BIBLIOGRAPHY

Cooper, Melinda. *Family values: Between neoliberalism and the new social conservatism.* Cambridge: MIT Press, 2017.

Crary, Jonathan. *24/7: Late Capitalism and the End of Sleep.* London and New York: Verso, 2013.

Cvejić, Bojana. *Choreographing Problems.* London: Palgrave Macmillan, 2014.

Cvejić, Bojana, and Ana Vujanović. "Exhausting Immaterial Labour in Performance." *TkH* 19 and *Journal des Laboratoires* (August 2010): 4-6.

Cvejić, Bojana. "In the Making of the Making of: The Practice of Rendering Performance Virtual." *TkH*, no. 15 (January 2008): 27-38.

Cvejić, Bojana, and Goran Sergej Pristaš, eds. *Parallel Slalom: A Lexicon of Non-Aligned Poetics.* Belgrade: Walking Theory [TkH] & Zagreb: CDU, 2013.

Dalla Costa, Mariarosa, and Selma James. *The Power of Women and the Subversion of the Community.* Bristol: Falling Wall Press, 1973.

Dardot, Pierre, and Christian Laval. *Del Comune, O Della Rivoluzione Nel 21. Secolo.* Rome: DeriveApprodi, 2015.

Debord, Guy. *The Society of Spectacle.* New York: Zone Books, 1995.

Degl'Innocenti, Maurizio. *Le Case Del Popolo in Europa: dalle Origini alla Seconda Guerra Mondiale.* Florence: Sansoni, 1984.

Deleuze, Gilles. *Cinema 1: The Movement Image.* London: Athlone, 2000.
Deleuze, Gilles. *Cinema 2: The Time-Image.* Minneapolis: University of Minnesota Press, 1989.
Deleuze, Gilles, and Félix Guattari. *A Thousand Plateaus: Capitalism and Schizophrenia.* Minneapolis: University of Minnesota Press, 1987.

Derrida, Jacques. *Of Grammatology.* Corrected Edition. Translated by Gayatri Chakravorty Spivak. Baltimore and London: Johns Hopkins, 1997.

Didi-Huberman, Georges. *Survival of the Fireflies.* Minneapolis: University of Minnesota Press, 2018.

Dighton, Robert. "The History of Adventure Play." *Adventure Play,* last accessed May 1, 2017. http://www.adventureplay.org.uk/history2.htm.

Döşemeci, Mehmet. "Don't move, Occupy! Social movement vs social arrest." *Roar Magazine.* November 5, 2013. https://roarmag.org/essays/occupy-revolution-mehmet-dosemeci/.

Dowling, William C. *Jameson, Althusser, Marx: An introduction to the political unconscious*. Ithaca: Cornell University Press, 1984.

EZNL. "Que retiemble en sus centros la tierra." October 14, 2016. http://enlacezapatista.ezln.org. mx/2016/10/14/que-retiemble-en-sus-centros-a-tierra/.

Factory of the Eccentric Actor (FEKS). *Eccentric Manifesto*. Translated by Marek Pytel. London: Eccentric Press, 1992.

Fisher, Tony, and Eve Katsouraki, eds. *Performing Antagonism: Theatre, Performance & Radical Democracy*. Basingstoke: Palgrave, 2017.

Fourier, Charles. *The Theory of the Four Movements*, edited by Gareth Stedman Jones and Ian Patterson. Cambridge: Cambridge University Press, 1996.

Fragnito, Maddalena. "Key Concepts for a New Cultural Institution." In *Competition and Cooperation*, edited by Open Humanities Press, 15-26. Coventry: Post Office Press, Rope Press and Open Humanities Press, 2018.

Gadd, Stephen. "The Junk Playground – Denmark's Eco-Contribution to Outdoor School Education." *The Copenhagen Post*, March 19, 2017. http://cphpost.dk/history/the-junk-playground-denmarks-eco-contribution-to-outdoor-school-education.html.

Gareth, Morgan. *Images of Organization*. London: Sage, 1986.

Garnham, Nicholas. "From cultural to creative industries: An analysis of the implications of the 'creative industries' approach to arts and media policy making in the United Kingdom." *International Journal of Cultural Policy* 11 (2005): 15–29.

Graeber, David. "A Movement of Movements: The New Anarchists." *New Left Review* 13 (2002): 61-73.

Graziano, Valeria. "Prefigurative practices. Raw materials for a political positioning of art, leaving the avant-garde." In *Turn Turtle Turn. Performing Urgency #2*, edited by Elke van Campenhout and Lilia Mestre, 158-74. Berlin: Alexander Verlag, 2016.

Graziano, Valeria. "Towards a Grammar of the Recreative Industries." In *Competition and Cooperation*, edited by Open Humanities Press, 26-34. London: Open Humanities Press, 2018.

Greece Solidarity Campaign, last accessed February 22, 2019. http://greecesolidarity.org/.

Grigorescu, Ion, Andreiana Mihail, and Georg Schöllhammer. *Ion Grigorescu: Diaries 1970–1975*. Berlin: Sternberg Press, 2014.

 # BIBLIOGRAPHY

Habermas, Jürgen. *The Structural Transformation of the Public Sphere: An Inquiry into a Category of Bourgeois Society.* Cambridge: MIT Press 1991.

Hallward, Peter. "From Prescription to Volition." In *The Politics of Alain Badiou. Politics and Culture* (special issue September 2014): 1–16. http://politicsandculture.org/2014/09/01/from-prescription-to-volition-by-peter-hallward/.
Hallward, Peter. "The will of the people: Notes towards a dialectical voluntarism." *Radical Philosophy* 155 (May/June 2009): 17-29.
Hallward, Peter. "The Politics of Prescription." *The South Atlantic Quarterly* 104, no. 4 (Fall 2005): 769-89.
Hallward, Peter. "Concentration or Representation: The Struggle for Popular Sovereignty." *Cogent Arts & Humanities* 4, no. 1 (2017). https://doi.org/10.1080/23311983.2017.1390916.

Han, Byung-Chul. *The Transparency Society.* Stanford: Stanford University Press, 2015.

Hansen, Miriam B. "Benjamin and Cinema, Not a One-way Street." *Critical Inquiry* 25, no. 2: "Angelus Novus": Perspectives on Walter Benjamin (Winter 1999): 306-43.

Hardt, Michael, and Antonio Negri. *Assembly.* Oxford: Oxford University Press, 2017.
Hardt, Michael, and Antonio Negri. *Empire.* Cambridge: Harvard University Press, 2000.

Harney, Stefano. "Unfinished business: Labour, management, and the creative industries." *Cultural Studies* 24, no. 3 (May 2010): 431-44.

Harvey, David. *The Condition of Postmodernity.* Oxford: Blackwell Press, 1989.

Hegel, G.W.F. *Phänomenologie des Geistes, Werke in zwanzig Bänden*, Bd. 3. Frankfurt/M.: Suhrkamp, 1970.

Heidegger, Martin. *The Question Concerning Technology, and Other Essays.* New York: Harper Perennial Modern Classics, 2013.

Helguera, Pablo. *Education for Socially Engaged Art; A Materials and Techniques Handbook.* New York: Jorge Pinto Books, 2011.

Holmes, Brian. "Disconnecting the dots of the research triangle: Corporatisation, Flexibilisation and Militarisation in the Creative Industries." In *My Creativity Reader: A Critique of the Creative Industries*, edited by Geert Lovink and Ned Rossiter, 177-91. Amsterdam: Institute of Network Cultures, 2007.

Jackson, Steven J. "Rethinking Repair." *Media Technologies: Essays on Communication, Materiality, and Society* (2014): 221-39.

Jameson, Fredric. *The Political Unconscious: Narrative as a Socially Symbolic Act*. Ithaca: Cornell University Press, 1981.

Jesi, Furio, and Andrea Cavalletti. *The Suspension of Historical Time*; *The Book of Books, 100 Notes – 100 Thoughts* dOCUMENTA(13). Berlin: Hatje Cantz, 2012.

Keil, Marta. "The Institutional Practices of a Festival." *Polish Theatre Journal (PTJ)* 1-2 (2017). http://polishtheatrejournal.com/index.php/ptj/article/view/98/495.

Kelleher, Joe. *Theatre and Politics*. Basingstoke: Palgrave, 2013.

Kershaw, Baz. *The politics of performance: Radical theatre as cultural intervention*. London: Routledge, 1992.

Knittler, Käthe. "Wissensarbeit und militante Untersuchung: Zwischen Produktion und Rebellion. Über Möglichkeiten widerständiger Wissensproduktion." *Kurswechsel. Zeitschrift für gesellschafts-, wirtschafts- und umweltpolitische Alternativen,* no. 1 (2014): 74-83.

Koloktronis, Alexander. "Building Alternative Institutions in Greece." An Interview with Christos Giovanopoulos. *Counterpunch*, March 11, 2016. http://www.counterpunch.org/2016/03/11/building-alternative-institutions-in-greece-an-interview-with-christos-giovanopoulos/.

Kozlovsky, Roy. "Adventure Playgrounds and Postwar Reconstruction." In *Designing Modern Childhoods: History, Space, and the Material Culture of Children; An International Reader*, edited by Marta Gutman and Ning de Coninck-Smith, 171-90. New Brunswick: Rutgers University Press, 2008.

Krasny, Elke. "The Domestic is Political: The Feminization of Domestic Labor and Its Critique in Feminist Art Practice." In *Critical Cartography of Art and Visuality in the Global Age*, edited by Anna Maria Guasch et al., 161-76. Newcastle: Cambridge Scholars Publishing, 2014.

Kunst, Bojana. *Artist at Work: Proximity of Art and Capitalism*. London: Zero Books, 2015.
Kunst, Bojana. "The Project Horizon: On the Temporality of Making." *Manifesta Journal* 16 (2012): 112-15.

Kwon, Miwon. *One Place After Another: Site Specific Art and Locational Identity*. Cambridge: MIT Press, 2002.

Lazzarato, Maurizio. "Immaterial Labour." 1996. http://www.generation-online.org/c/fcimmateriallabour3.htm.

Lee, Pamela. *Chronophobia: On Time in the Art of the 1960s*. Cambridge: MIT Press, 2004.

 # BIBLIOGRAPHY

Lefebvre, Henri. *The Production of Space.* Translated by Donald Nicholson-Smith. Oxford: Basil Blackwell, (1974) 1991.

Latouche, Serge. *Farewell to Growth.* Cambridge: Polity Press, 2009.

Lepecki, Andre. *Singularities: Dance in the Age of Performance.* London and New York: Routledge, 2016.

Levine, Caroline. *Forms: Whole, Rhythm, Hierarchy, Network.* Princeton: Princeton University Press, 2015.

Lorde, Audre. *The Collected Poems of Audre Lorde.* New York: W.W. Norton and Company, 1997.
Lorde, Audre. "The Master's Tools Will Never Dismantle the Master's House." In *Sister Outsider: Essays and Speeches*, 110-14. Berkeley: Crossing Press, 2007.

Lorey, Isabell. "Autonomy and Precarization. (Neo)Liberal Entanglements of Labour and Care in the Former West." Translated by Aileen Derieg and Kelly Mulvaney. In *FORMER WEST: Art and the Contemporary after 1989,* edited by Maria Hlavajova and Simon Sheikh, 427–39. Cambridge and London: MIT-Press, 2016.
Lorey, Isabell. "Constituent Immunisation. Paths Towards the Common." *Open! Platform for Art, Culture and the Public Domain,* January 24, 2015, series "Communist Aesthetics". http://www. onlineopen.org/essays/constituent-immunisation-paths-towards-the-common/.
Lorey, Isabell. *Figuren des Immunen. Elemente einer politischen Theorie.* Zürich: diaphanes, 2011.
Lorey, Isabell. "On Democracy and Occupation. Horizontality and the Need for New Forms of Verticality." Translated by Aileen Derieg. In *Institutional Attitudes. Instituting Art in a Flat World,* edited by Pascal Gielen, 77-99. Amsterdam: Valiz, 2013.
Lorey, Isabell. "Presentist Democracy. Reconceptualizing the Present." Translated by Aileen Derieg. In *documenta 14 – Reader,* edited by Quinn Latimer and Adam Szymczyk, 169-202. München: Prestel, 2017.
Lorey, Isabell. "Presentist Democracy. The Now-Time of Struggles." In *Subjectivation in Political Theory and Contemporary Practices,* edited by Andreas Oberprantacher and Andrei Siclodi, 149-63. London, South Yarra and Sydney: Palgrave Macmillan, 2016.
Lorey, Isabell. "The 2011 Occupy Movements: Rancière and the Crisis of Democracy." Translated by Aileen Derieg. *Theory, Culture & Society* 31, special issue on Jacques Rancière, no. 7-8 (2014): 43-65.
Lorey, Isabell. *State of Insecurity. Government of the Precarious.* Translated by Aileen Derieg. Brooklyn: Verso, 2015.

Lutticken, Sven. "On the occupation of the Volksbühne in Berlin." *Texte zur Kunst*, October 3, 2017. https://www.textezurkunst.de/articles/sven-lutticken-volksbuhne-occupation/.

MACAO. "Desire Week." *Macao website*, last accessed May 1, 2018. http://www.macaomilano. org/spip.php?rubrique146

Maeckelberg, Marianne. "Doing is Believing: Prefiguration as Strategic Practice in the Alterglobalization Movement." *Social Movement Studies* 10, no. 1 (2011): 1-20.

Malzacher, Florian. "No Organum to Follow." In *Not Just a Mirror; Looking for the Political Theatre of Today*, edited by Florian Malzacher, 16-31. Berlin: Alexander Verlag, 2014.

Marchart, Oliver. "Public Movement; The Art of Pre-enactment." In *Not Just a Mirror; Looking for the Political Theatre of Today*, edited by Florian Malzacher, 146–50. Berlin and London: Alexander Verlag, 2014.

Marx, Karl. *Capital, Volume One* (1867). *Marxist.org.* http://www.marxists.org/archive/marx/works/1867-c1/index.htm.

Massey, Doreen. "Vocabulary of the economy." In *After Neoliberalism: The Kilburn Manifesto*, edited by Doreen Massey, Stuart Hall and Michael Rustin, 8-22. London: Lawrence & Wishart Ltd, 2013.

McKenzie, Jon. *Perform or Else: From Discipline to Performance.* London and New York: Routledge, 2001.

Milohnić, Aldo. "Artivism." *republicart: real public spaces*, 2005, last accessed February 22, 2019. http://republicart.net/disc/realpublicspaces/milohnic01_en.htm.

Moretti, Franco. *The Bourgeois: Between History and Literature.* London and New York: Verso, 2013.

Morgan, Margot. *Politics and Theatre in Twentieth-Century Europe.* New York: Palgrave Macmillan, 2013.

Moroni, Piero, ed. *Centri Sociali: Geografie del Desiderio.* Milan: ShaKe Underground, 1996.

Mouffe, Chantal. "Hearts, Minds and Radical Democracy." *Red Papper,* June 1, 1998. https://www.redpepper.org.uk/hearts-minds-and-radical-democracy/.

Murray, Daniel. "Prefiguration or Actualization? Radical Democracy and Counter-Institution in the Occupy Movement." *Berkeley Journal of Sociology*, November 3, 2014. http://berkeleyjournal.org/author/daniel-murray.

Naukkarinen, Ossi, and Yuriko Saito, eds. "Artification." *Contemporary Aesthetics*: "Artification", Special Volume 4 (2012). https://digitalcommons.risd.edu/liberalarts_contempaesthetics/vol0/iss4/1/.

 # BIBLIOGRAPHY

Oxford English Dictionalry Online Online. "Discretion." last accessed October 2017. http://www.oed.com/viewdictionaryentry/Entry/11125.

Palladini, Giulia. "Il disagio della performance: per una tecnica poietica del lavoro vivo." *Operaviva Magazine,* April 25, 2017. https://operaviva.info/il-disagio-della-performance/.

Peter, Fabienne. "Political Legitimacy." *Stanford Encyclopedia of Philosophy,* April 29, 2010. http://plato.stanford.edu/entries/legitimacy/.

P2P Foundation. "A Synthetic Overview of the Collaborative Economy." 2012. https://p2pfoundation.net/wp.../Synthetic-overview-of-the-collaborative-economy.pdf.

Phelan, Peggy. *Unmarked: The Politics of Performance.* London and New York: Routledge, (1993) 2005.

Pristaš, Goran Sergej. "Anti-production of Art." *TkH*, no. 23 (2016): 29-32.

Puig de la Bellacasa, Maria. "Nothing comes without its world': thinking with care." *The Sociological Review* 60, no. 2 (2012): 197-216.

Quinn, Shelley Fenno. *Developing Zeami: The Noh Actor's Attunement in Practice.* Honolulu: University of Hawaii Press, 2005.

Rancière, Jacques. *Disagreement: Politics and Philosophy.* Minneapolis: University of Minnesota Press, 1999.
Rancière, Jacques. "Political Impurity." Translated by Mary Foster. In *Moments politiques: Interventions 1977-2009*, 216-33. New York: Seven Stories, 2014.
Rancière, Jacques. *The Emancipated Spectator.* Translated by Gregory Elliot. London and Brooklyn: Verso, 2009.
Rancière, Jacques. *The Ignorant Schoolmaster.* Translated by K. Ross. Stanford: Stanford University Press, 1991.
Rancière, Jacques. *The Politics of Aesthetics: The Distribution of the Sensible.* London: Continuum, 2004.

Rau, Milo. "Buchenwald, Bukavu, Bochum. Was ist globaler Realismus?" Milo Rau im Gespräch mit Rolf Bossart. *Theater der Zeit* (Oktober 2015).

Raunig, Gerald. *Dividuum. Machinic Capitalism and Molecular Revolution.* New York: Semiotext(e), 2016.

Ray, Gene. *Joseph Beuys: Mapping the Legacy. Papers from a Symposium, Sarasota, Florida, USA 1998.* New York: Distributed Art Publishers, 2001.

Reinelt, Janelle, and Shirin Rai. *The Grammar of Politics and Performance.* London and New York: Routledge, 2015.

Rokem, Freddie. *Performing History: Theatrical Representations of the Past in Contemporary Theatre.* Iowa: University of Iowa Press, 2000.

Rolnik, Suely. "Anthropophagic Subjectivity." In *Arte Contemporânea Brasileira: Um e/entre Outro/s,* edited by Paulo Herkenhoff and Adriano Pedrosa, 137-45. São Paulo: Fundação Bienal de São Paulo, 1998.

Rousseau, Jean-Jacques. *On the Social Contract.* Translated and ed. Donald A. Cress. Indianapolis: Hackett, (1762) 1988.

Rubio-Pueyo, Vicente. *Municipalism in Spain from Barcelona to Madrid, and Beyond.* New York: Rosa Luxemburg Stiftung, 2017.

Schechner, Richard. *Environmental Theatre.* New York: Applause Books, (1973) 1994.
Schechner, Richard. *Performance Studies: An Introduction.* London: Routledge, 2006.

Schneider, Rebecca. *Performing Remains; Art and War in Times of Theatrical Reenactment.* London and New York: Routledge, 2011.

Schumpeter, Joseph A. *The Theory of Economic Development: an Inquiry into Profits, Capital, Credit, Interest, and the Business Cycle.* New Brunswick: Transaction Publishers, (1934) 1983.

Sennett, Richard. *The Fall of Public Man.* New York and London: W. W. Norton, 1976.

Shaviro, Steven. "Processes and Powers." *The Pinocchio Theory,* August 18, 2011. http://www.shaviro.com/Blog/?p=995

Slevogt, Esther. "Das große Eintauchen." Translated by Florian Malzacher *Nachtkritik,* July 14, 2019. https://www.nachtkritik.de/index.php?option=com_content&view=article&id=12602:ko lumne-aus-dem-buergerlichen-heldenleben-esther-slevogt-ueber-das-neue-zauberwort-immersion&catid=1506&Itemid=100389.

Smith, Mark K. "Friedrich Froebel (Fröbel)." *Informal Education Encyclopaedia* (YMCA George Williams College, 1997). http://infed.org/mobi/fredrich-froebel-frobel/.

Solnit, Rebecca. *A Field Guide to Getting Lost.* London: Penguin 2005.

Solnit, Rebecca. *Hope in the Dark: Untold Histories, Wild Possibilities.* Edinburgh and London: Canongate Books, 2016.

 # BIBLIOGRAPHY

Stegemann, Bernd. "Wie frei ist das Theater noch?" *Frankfurter Allgemeine Zeitung*, May 4, 2018.

Támás, Gáspár Miklós. "The rule of the market in East-Central Europe is absolute." Interview by Jaroslav Fiala. *Political Critique*, July 28, 2016. http://politicalcritique.org/cee/hungary/2016/the-rule-of-the-market-in-east-central-europe-is-absolute-interview/.

Teatro Valle Occupato. "Lo Statuto della Fondazione Teatro Valle Bene Comune." *Teatro Valle website*, June 14, 2014. http://www.teatrovalleoccupato.it/statuto-fondazione-teatro-valle-bene-comune.

Tsing, Anna Lowenhaupt, Nils Bubandt, Elaine Gan, and Anne Swanson Heather, eds. *Arts of Living on a Damaged Planet: Ghosts and Monsters of the Anthropocene*. Minneapolis: University of Minnesota Press, 2017.

Van Campenhout, Elke. "Curating as environmentalism (2011)." *N.O.W.*, November 16, 2013. http://www.nowperformingarts.eu.

Virno, Paolo. *A Grammar of the Multitude*. New York: Semiotext(e), 2004.
Virno, Paolo. "Angels and the General Intellect: Individuation in Duns Scotus and Gilbert Simondon." *Parrhesia*, no. 7 (2009): 58-67.
Virno, Paolo. *Déjà Vu and the End of History*. London: Verso, 2015.
Virno, Paolo. *L'idea di Mondo: Intelletto Pubblico e Uso della Vita*. Rome: Quodlibet, 2015.

Vujanović, Ana. "What do we actually do when… we make art." *Amfiteatar,* no. 2 and *Maska*, no. 127-130 (2010): 47–86.

Wetzel, Daniel. "Almost Like a Learning Play; Daniel Wetzel of Rimini Protokoll in a conversation with Florian Malzacher." In *Intermedial Performance and Politics in the Public Sphere*, edited by Katia Arfara, Aneta Mancewicz and Ralf Remshardt, 191-208. Houndmills and New York: Palgrave Macmillan, 2019.

Willett, John, ed. *Brecht on Theatre; The Development of an Aesthetic*. London: Penguin, 1964.

Williams, Raymond. *Keywords; A Vocabulary of Culture and Society*. Oxford: Oxford University Press, 2014.

Wochen Klausur. "From the Object to the Concrete Intervention." *Wochenklausur website*, last accessed October 19, 2017. http://www.wochenklausur.at/kunst.php?lang=en.

Yates, Luke. "Rethinking Prefiguration: Alternatives, Micropolitics and Goals in Social Movements." *Academia.edu website*, last accessed in October 2017. https://www.academia.edu/5696621/Rethinking_Prefiguration_Alternatives_Micropolitics_and_Goals_in_Social_Movements?auto=download.

BIBLIOGRAPHY

Zelik, Raul. *Mit PODEMOS zur demokratischen Revolution? Krise und Aufstand in Spanien*. Berlin: Bertz+Fischer, 2015.

Zerilli, Linda. "The Arendtian Body." In *Feminist Perspectives on Hannah Arendt*, edited by Bonnie Honig, 167-94. University Park: Pennsylvania State University Press, 1995.

Žižek, Slavoj. *Living in the End Times*. London: Verso, 2010.
Žižek, Slavoj. "The Jacobin Spirit." *Jacobin*, no. 3–4, May 26, 2011. http://jacobinmag.com/summer-2011/the-jacobin-spirit/.

INDEX

IMPRESSUM

A LIVE GATHERING: PERFORMANCE AND POLITICS IN CONTEMPORARY EUROPE

PUBLISHED BY:
b_books
Luebbener str. 14
10997 Berlin
x@bbooks.de, verlag@bbooksz.de
www.bbooks.de
On behalf of b_books:
Stephan Geene

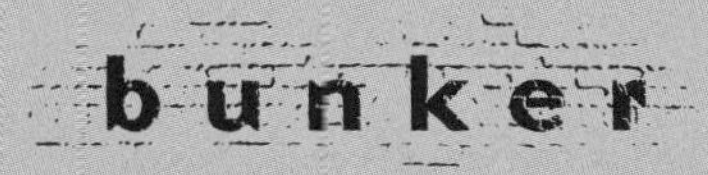

PRODUCED BY:
BUNKER, Ljubljana
www.bunker.si
On behalf of Bunker:
Nevenka Koprivšek

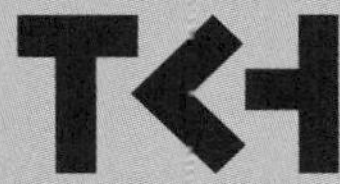

IN COLLABORATION WITH:
TKH (WALKING THEORY), Belgrade
www.tkh-generator.net
On behalf of TkH:
Ana Vujanović

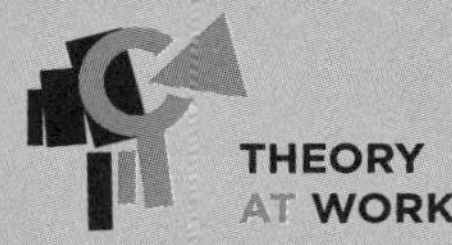

THEORY AT WORK, Belgrade
On behalf of Theory at Work:
Marta Popivoda

EAST EUROPEAN PERFORMING ARTS
PLATFORM, Lublin
www.eepap.culture.pl
On behalf of EEPAP
Marta Keil

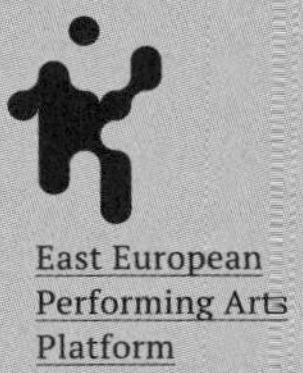

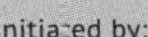

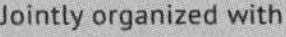

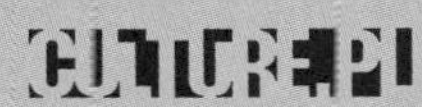

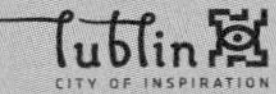

IMPRESSUM

THIS VOLUME IS REALISED
as part of Create to Connect project
(www.createtoconnect.eu).
Thanks to the support of Alma R.
Selimović and Maja Vžin from Bunker,
leaders of the Create to Connect network.
and
In frames of the „And what if?
Imaginary School for the future of the
(art) institution" project, lead by East
European Performing Arts Platform,
with thanks to the support of Allianz
Kulturstiftung.

FINANCIAL SUPPORT:
Culture, Programme of the European
Union, Ministry of Culture and
Information of Republic of Serbia

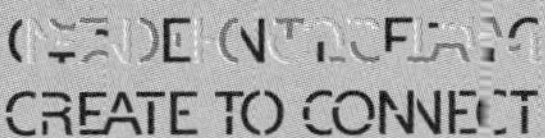

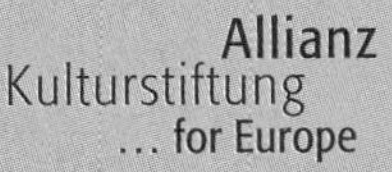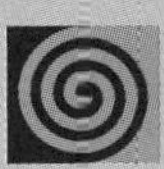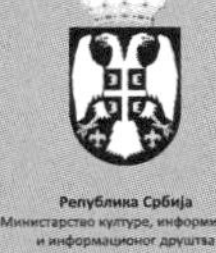

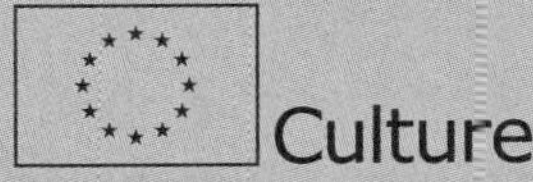

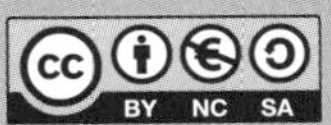

The book is published under the Creative Commons License:
Attribution – Non-Commercial – Share Alike. For individual
contributions, please contact the authors.

This project has been funded with support from the European
Commission. This publication reflects the views only of the
author, and the Commission cannot be responsible for any use
which may be made of the information contained therein.

EDITED BY
Ana Vujanović
with Livia Andrea Piazza

AUTHORS:
Ana Vujanović, Bojana Cvejić, Bojana
Kunst, Florian Malzacher, Giulia
Palladini, Goran Sergej Pristaš, Isabell
Lorey, Livia Andrea Piazza, Silvia
Bottiroli, Stina Nyberg, Valeria Graziano

TRANSLATORS:
Kelly Mulvaney, Matteo Camporesi,
Žarko Cvejić

COPYEDITING AND PROOFREADING:
William Wheeler, Livia Andrea Piazza,
Stephan Geene, Ana Vujanović and Chris
Prickett

EXECUTIVE PRODUCER AND COORDINATOR:
Jelena Knežević

GRAPHIC DESIGN AND LAYOUT:
Katarina Popović

COVER:
Democratic Federation of North-Syria &
Studio Jonas Staal, *New World Summit*,
Rojava, 2015-18. Photo: © Ruben
Hamelink

PRINTED BY
Dardedze Holografija, Riga

PRINT RUN:
1,000

Berlin, 2019

ISBN:
978 3 942214 29 2